CLARENCE DARROW

Photograph of Clarence Darrow courtesy of International Museum of Photography at George Eastman House.

CLARENCE DARROW

The Creation of an American Myth

Richard J. Jensen
Foreword by Halford R. Ryan

Great American Orators, Number 12

Bernard K. Duffy and
Halford R. Ryan, Series Advisers

Greenwood Press
New York • Westport, Connecticut • London

Library of Congress Cataloging-in-Publication Data

Jensen, Richard J.
    Clarence Darrow : the creation of an American myth / Richard J.
Jensen ; foreword by Halford R. Ryan.
       p. cm.—(Great American orators, ISSN 0898-8277 ; no. 12)
    Includes bibliographical references and index.
    ISBN 0-313-25990-9 (alk. paper)
    1. Darrow, Clarence, 1857-1938—Oratory. 2. Lawyers—United
States—Biography. 3. Oral pleading—United States—History—20th
century. 4. Forensic orations. I. Darrow, Clarence, 1857-1938.
II. Title. III. Series.
KF373.D35J46 1992
340'.092—dc20   90-20675
[B]

British Library Cataloguing in Publication Data is available.

Library of Congress Catalog Card Number: 90-20675
ISBN: 0-313-25990-9
ISSN: 0898-8277

First published in 1992

Greenwood Press, 88 Post Road West, Westport, CT 06881
An imprint of Greenwood Publishing Group, Inc.

Printed in the United States of America

The paper used in this book complies with the
Permanent Paper Standard issued by the National
Information Standards Organization (Z39.48-1984).

10 9 8 7 6 5 4 3 2 1

This book is lovingly dedicated to
Carol Jensen in appreciation for her
patience and support during the
lengthy period of time required for
its completion.

Contents

Series Foreword

The idea for a series of books on great American orators grew out of the recognition that there is a paucity of book-length studies on individual orators and their speeches. Apart from a few notable exceptions, the study of American public address has been pursued in scores of articles published in professional journals. As helpful as these studies have been, none has or can provide a complete analysis of a speaker's rhetoric. Book-length studies, such as those in this series, will help fill the void that has existed in the study of American public address and its related disciplines of politics and history, theology and sociology, communication and law. In books, the critic can explicate a broader range of a speaker's persuasive discourse than reasonably could be treated in articles. The comprehensive research and sustained reflection that books require will undoubtedly yield many original and enduring insights concerning the nation's most important voices.

Public address has been a fertile ground for scholarly investigation. No matter how insightful their intellectual forebears, each generation of scholars must reexamine its universe of discourse, while expanding the compass of its researches and redefining its

purpose and methods.   To avoid intellectual
torpor, new scholars cannot be content simply
to see through the eyes of those who have come
before them. We hope that this series of books
will stimulate important new understandings of
the nature of persuasive discourse and provide
additional opportunities for scholarship in the
history and criticism of American public
address.

This series examines the role of rhetoric
in the United States. American speakers shaped
the destiny of the colonies, the young republic, and the mature nation. During each stage
of the intellectual, political, and religious
development of the United States, great orators, standing at the rostrum, on the stump,
and in the pulpit, used words and gestures to
influence their audiences. Usually striving
for the noble, sometimes achieving the base,
they urged their fellow citizens toward a more
perfect Union. The books in this series chron-
icle and explain the accomplishments of representative American leaders as orators.

A series of book-length studies of American persuaders honors the role men and women
have played in U.S. history. Previously, if
one desired to assess the impact of a speaker
or speech upon history, the past was, at best,
not well marked and, at worst, littered with
obstacles.   To be sure, one might turn to
biographies and general histories to learn
about an orator, but for the public address
scholar these sources often prove unhelpful.
Rhetorical topics, such as speech invention,
style, delivery, organizational strategies, and
persuasive effect, are often treated in passing, if mentioned at all. Authoritative speech
texts are often difficult to locate, and the
problem of textual authenticity is frequently
encountered. This is especially true for those
figures who spoke one or two hundred years ago,
or for those whose persuasive role, though significant, was secondary to other leading lights

of the age.

Each book in this series is organized to meet the needs of scholars and students of the history and criticism of American public address. Part I is a critical analysis of the orator and his or her speeches. Within the format of a case study, one may expect considerable latitude. For instance, in a given chapter an author might explicate a single speech or a group of related speeches, or examine orations that comprise a genre of rhetoric such as forensic speaking. But the critic's focus remains on the rhetorical considerations of speaker, speech, occasion, and effect. Part II contains the texts of the important addresses that are discussed in the critical analysis that precedes it. To the extent possible, each author has endeavored to collect authoritative speech texts, which have often been found through original research in collections of primary source material. In a few instances, because of the extreme length of a speech, texts have been edited, but the authors have been careful to delete material that is least important to the speech, and these deletions have been held to a minimum.

In each book there is a chronology of major speeches that serves more purposes than may be apparent at first. Pragmatically, it lists all of the orator's known speeches and addresses. Places and dates are also listed, although this is information that is sometimes difficult to determine precisely. But in a wider sense, the chronology attests to the scope of rhetoric in the United States. Certainly in quantity, if not always in quality, Americans are historically talkers and listeners.

Because of the disparate nature of the speakers examined in the series, there is some latitude in the nature of the bibliographical materials that have been included in each book. But in every instance, authors have carefully described original historical materials and collections, and have gathered critical studies, biographies and autobiographies, and a variety of secondary sources that bear on the speaker and the oratory. By combining in each book bibliographical materials, speech texts, and critical chapters, this series notes that text and research sources are interwoven in the act of rhetorical criticism.

May the books in this series serve to memorialize the nation's greatest orators.

Bernard K. Duffy

Halford R. Ryan

Foreword

He reviled the rich for their cupidity, and
they found his rhetoric repulsive. Plebians
believed him their champion, and patricians
knew he was their bete noire. The dispossessed
had in him an eloquent spokesman for their
interests at the bar, and the captains of
industry and their lawyers felt his verbal
barbs against their selfishness in the courts
of law and of public opinion. No less a per-
sonage than William Jennings Bryan, the "Great
Commoner," verbally dueled with this uncommon
advocate at Dayton, Tennessee, with no more
success than Bryan's conservative counterparts
in commerce had. Clarence Darrow accomplished
all of this with rhetoric.

Although many famous oral advocates in the
twentieth century come to mind, none of them is
known as much for his/her speeches in the
courtroom as for some celebritylike quality
that is distinctly non-rhetorical. One could
name lawyers who made their fame and fortune
defending movie stars, but one does not read
their speeches; so, too, with those who prosecute or defend the rich and famous, not to
mention the infamous, but their courtroom
rhetoric has not been anthologized. Not so

with Clarence Darrow, for his speeches were to
be digested by a populace that hungered for
equity at a time in U.S. history when justice
seemed to be in the establishment's vest pockets.   Subsequent generations have read his
speeches as political statements and as models
of persuasive pleading and pathos.

Darrow was a preeminent forensic persuader
who often used the courtroom as a deliberative
forum to sway not only the immediate jurors,
but also the entire country to his definition
of justice.   He achieved mythical stature
during his lifetime, although he was demeaned
by those over whose interests he prevailed, and
he was at pains during his career to nurture
the carefully cultivated image of the underdog's lawyer, although he could defend equally
well those with substantial wealth. Darrow was
something less than the myth that he, the
media, and his enemies created, and his successes in some cases often hinged more on the
prosecutor's self-inflicted wounds or inability
to present a compelling case than on Darrow's
summary speeches.   Yet, those caveats do not
detract from the necessity of understanding
rhetorically a man who played himself--for
Clarence Darrow succeeded better than anyone
else in the twentieth century in his ability to
enact the role of a Darrow.

Professor Richard Jensen undertakes in
this book the burden of proof to explain those
forensic issues needing explication, to delineate new rhetorical findings needing discovery,
and to demythologize certain received tenets
needing debunking.   It will fall to others to
offer a burden of rebuttal, but one imagines
that onus will not be shouldered in the fore-
seeable future.

First, Jensen has made rhetorical sense of
Darrow's legal career. As Jensen demonstrates,
Darrow developed several _koinoi topoi_, to bor-
row Aristotle's terminology for common topics
that orators might use in their addresses, that

he applied with slight modification in his appeals to juries throughout his career.   Although the defendants and the nature of the charges varied over time, Jensen documents the common threads that informed Darrow's successes with twelve jurors good and true.

Second, without stealing his thunder, Jensen revises not so much how Darrow's rhetoric operated as how his argumentation, aided and abetted by an eager print medium bent on selling newspapers, lent itself to exploitation and to myth making.   In all fairness, though, it should be mentioned that Darrow was equally adept at using the newspapers to reach a national audience.   Aside from his critical treatment of Darrow's forensic argumentation in the <u>Scopes</u> trial and the <u>Leopold-Loeb</u> case, which is compelling in its own right, Jensen delivers a graceful coup de grace, which metaphor Darrow would have found repulsive, to received opinions concerning what did and did not happen in those famous trials.   Moreover, Jensen examines some of the lesser known trials, of which a few were failures, in order to balance Darrow's successes.

Last, Jensen has selected with care those forensic orations that belong in the canon of Darrow's great speeches.   Everyone probably has his or her favorite, but his short speech to the inmates of the Cook County Jail has always reinforced the truth of the aphorism "There but for the grace of God go I," which seems to delineate in Darrow's conception one's position relative to iron bars.

A man of the twentieth century who helped to birth legally the twentieth century at a time when the country was ruled more by plutocrats than democrats, Darrow's crusades may seem today dated, his concerns timeworn, and his enemies--capitalists and intolerant conservatives--the heroes of contemporary society. Yet his theme was and is the eternal struggle between those who have and those who have not.

Whether one identifies with Darrow's clients is
not the point.   As Jensen sensitively chronicles in this book, the vested interests spawned Darrow,   they   enacted   the   very   role   he
charged they played, and consequently they lost
their   selfish   cases   at   a   bar   that   usually
valued men   over   money.   Darrow   deserves   our
attention,   not   so   much   for   his   mythical
stature, as rich as it is, as for the role that
humane rhetoric, of which his was an exemplar,
can play in the conscience and the courtroom of
a democratic nation.

        Halford R. Ryan

I

CLARENCE DARROW

Introduction

In his book <u>Great American Speeches, 1898-1963</u>, John Graham described the oratorical career of Clarence Darrow: "Clarence Darrow is undoubtedly the best-known trial lawyer in American history. It is estimated that he was active in over two thousand trials, many of which dramatically reflected major social and philosophical issues in a changing America. A brilliant impromptu courtroom pleader he varied his speeches by massive evidence, by portraying the lives and plights of the accused, and, most important, by arguing broad issues of labor and management, science and religion, determinism and free will."[1] Although Darrow is remembered mainly as a defense attorney, he was also a famous public lecturer and debater as well as a prolific writer. Several books including his autobiography, <u>The Story of My Life</u>, an autobiographical novel, <u>Farmington</u>, and dozens of articles and pamphlets of his speeches presented his ideas and beliefs to the American public in written form. This combination of oral and written discourse provided Darrow with two powerful channels of communication to get his message before the public.

Because of the controversial nature of many of his trials, lectures, and writings, Darrow was constantly in the public's view during his lifetime. Even after his death, interest in this controversial figure has continued. For example, in the 1950s a collection of Darrow's speeches entitled Attorney for the Damned became a nationwide best seller. Many of his lectures, debates, and writings have been collected in Verdicts Out of Court, and his speeches have been included in numerous collections as models of eloquence. His courtroom battles have also been portrayed in popular dramas such as "Inherit the Wind," a dramatization of the Scopes trial of 1925, and in best-selling books such as Meyer Levin's novel Compulsion, a fictional account of the Leopold-Loeb trial.

In his writings and speeches Darrow focused on many of the major issues affecting American life during the last half of the nineteenth and first half of the twentieth centuries. Often he took an unpopular stance on controversial subjects in order to make sure all sides of an issue received public airing. Thus, a study of his speeches and writings will provide insight into the period of time in which he lived as well as insight into his public discourse.

Although there have been several biographies of Darrow, no one book has focused specifically on Darrow as a speaker. This study will attempt to fill that void by focusing on the events in his life that helped shape the form of Darrow's rhetoric, his training as an orator, his speech preparation, and the arguments used in his speeches and writings. The book will detail Darrow's major themes and arguments, how those themes and arguments were used in legal and public settings, and how these themes and arguments evolved or remained constant over his lengthy career.

In his superb study of Darrow, Martin Maloney argued that at the time of his death Darrow had become a "living myth," a status

achieved by few individuals in their lifetime.
Maloney proclaimed that the myth portrayed
Darrow "as a defender of the underdog, a
devil's advocate, a man who stood perpetually
opposed to the great and powerful of the
earth." Maloney then stated that the legend in
Darrow's lifetime "had significance because so
many people in the United States recognized
themselves as underdogs, as outcasts, either
real or potential."[2]

Maloney did not explore the implications
of Darrow's myth building in detail, but
proposed that later studies should focus on
that area. This study will attempt to build on
Maloney's ideas by describing how Darrow
created and then enlarged his personal myth
through his speeches, writings, and actions.
It will also discover how others either
accepted or enlarged Darrow's myth through
their writings about him. Each chapter of the
study will focus on particular segments of the
Darrow myth.

Chapter 1, "The Making of a Nonconformist," will provide a brief biography of
Darrow, an overview of his rhetoric, and some
initial comments on the elements that make up
the myth. It will focus on forces that
affected Darrow's ideas and therefore his
rhetoric, his training as an orator, and
significant events in his life. Much of the
Darrow myth seems to be based on his growing up
in a nonconformist family in a small town.
Both of his parents were well-read freethinkers
who raised their children to question society's
norms and values. That questioning continued
throughout Darrow's life. He spent much of his
life trying to teach others about unpopular
views and hoping that they would then begin to
question many assumptions and beliefs held by
members of society.

Chapter 2, "Schoolmaster of the
Courtroom," chronicles Darrow's image as

defender of the downtrodden, which was first created in his early trials in defense of labor unions and their leaders. During those early trials Darrow attempted to educate people about the rights of and need for labor unions. He argued that men had a right to form such organizations, that conspiracy laws were unfair, that labor leaders deserved to be defended because they were helping the downtrodden, and that great movements like labor unions could not be destroyed by eliminating their leaders. Those labor trials made Darrow a national figure at the same time they gave him a national platform from which to discuss what he believed were the major social issues of the day. In those early trials he also developed tactics that he used in later courtroom pleas:

> . . . the attempt to present the facts in a case as a broad backdrop of history, and so to alter their significance; the suggestion that the prosecution is the tool of some blackly evil force . . . the use of invective especially against agencies associated with the prosecution, the insistence upon the honesty, kindliness, and in general the ordinary qualities of the client.[3]

Chapter 2 will also focus on Darrow's self-defense in two trials. His need to defend himself grew out of charges that he bribed a jury during the McNamara trial, his last major labor case. Those trials also focused on labor issues, so Darrow's self-defense will fit into this category.

Chapter 3, "The Old Lion: Defending Leopold and Loeb," examines one of his most famous defenses. After the two trials in self-defense, Darrow began his career as a defense attorney in criminal trials. In 1924 his defense of Richard Loeb and Nathan Leopold captured the attention of the American public and made Darrow a national figure. His stirring speech at the conclusion of that trial is considered to be one of the most famous speeches in American legal history. Although his critics questioned his motives in defending two wealthy clients, Darrow ably used the national publicity as a means of arguing against the death penalty. This chapter will analyze Darrow's reasons for accepting the case and his arguments in defense of his clients. The effect of the trial on the myth will also be analyzed.

Perhaps the most famous trial in recent American history, the Scopes trial in Dayton, Tennessee, in 1925, will be analyzed in Chapter 4, "Educating the Masses: Darrow in Tennessee." In that trial Darrow defended John Thomas Scopes for teaching evolution in the public schools, an act that violated the laws of Tennessee. The trial is also famous because of the dramatic confrontation between Darrow and William Jennings Bryan, a three-time candidate for president of the United States and a leader of the fight against the teaching of evolution in public schools. The speech given by Darrow during that trial is a ringing defense of free thought and academic freedom. It has often been quoted as a model for defending the First Amendment rights of Americans.[4]

Chapter 5, "Speaking for the Poor and Weak," details another part of Darrow's ethos. Darrow's myth as defender of the weak was created in defense of labor and expanded through his defense of other less fortunate members of society, particularly the poor, radicals, and blacks. This chapter will explain the arguments Darrow used to defend those individuals, with particular attention being paid to the Sweet trial and those involving radicals (Gitlow, Persons, and communists). The chapter will also discuss

Darrow's last trial, the Massie case in Honolulu in 1932.

Darrow was an extremely active speaker and debater on the lecture circuit, and Chapter 6, "Verdicts Out of Court: Darrow as Lecturer and Writer," delineates that part of his rhetoric. Some biographers have argued that Darrow was more comfortable as a performer before large audiences than in the courtroom. This chapter will detail both Darrow's career as a lecturer and his themes and arguments. A comparison will be drawn between Darrow's legal and public presentations.

Throughout his life Darrow wrote numerous significant essays and works of fiction. Chapter 6 will analyze Darrow's writings in an attempt to compare the ideas in those writings with those in his speeches. It will also focus on how Darrow helped to sustain and enlarge his myth through his writings.

As an aid to the researcher of Darrow's rhetoric, authoritative texts of several of Darrow's most famous speeches have been included. The following speeches, keyed to the critical chapters, represent the core of Darrow's legal and public rhetoric: Speech in Self-Defense, 1912; Speech in Defense of Leopold and Loeb, 1924; Speech at Scopes Trial, 1925; Speech at Sweet Trial, 1926; Speech at Massie Trial, 1932; Eulogy of John P. Altgeld, 1902; and the Address to Prisoners in the Cook County Jail, 1902.

The back matter contains a chronological list of Darrow's speeches and addresses, a bibliography subdivided into appropriate categories, and a thorough index.

NOTES

1. John Graham, <u>Great American Speeches, 1898-1963</u> (New York: Appleton-Century-Crofts, 1970), p. 31.
2. Martin Maloney, "Clarence Darrow," in <u>A History and Criticism of American Public</u>

Address, vol. 3, ed. Marie Kathryn Hochmuth (New York: Longmans, Green, 1955), p. 267.

3. Maloney, "Clarence Darrow," p. 286.

4. For a discussion of the Scopes trial, see Thomas M. Lessl, "The Scopes Trial: "Darrow vs. Bryan" vs. "Bryan vs. Darrow," in Oratorical Encounters, ed. Halford Ross Ryan (Westport, Conn.: Greenwood Press, 1988), pp. 17-28.

1
The Making of a Nonconformist

In <u>A History and Criticism of American Public Address</u>, Martin Maloney categorized Clarence Darrow as one of those rare individuals in American history who achieve "a special status in public life; they are possessed by an indescribable charm which seems to lend their least action a disproportionate significance. They may be 'heroes' or 'villains' by label, but their fascination for great numbers of people is undeniable." According to Maloney, such individuals often achieve the status of "myths during their own times."[1]

To Maloney, much of the Darrow legend was based on the image that he "was a defender of the underdog, a devil's advocate, a man who stood perpetually opposed to the great and powerful of the earth." Maloney believed that such a myth may have been possible in Darrow's lifetime "because so many people in the United States recognized themselves as underdogs, as outcasts, either real or potential."[2]

Lore about Darrow has grown and evolved since his death. In attempting to explain how legends grow and change, Waldo W. Braden declared that a myth "draws upon memory and imagination, that it results from a collective effort over a considerable period of time, that it represents an oversimplification of events, persons, and relationships, that its substance is more emotional than logical, and that it combines both reality and fiction."[3]   The Darrow myth meets this description.

Much of the Darrow myth since his death has been either expanded or attacked in writings and speeches about his life.   In Clarence Darrow for the Defense, Irving Stone spent a considerable amount of effort building Darrow's image for his readers: "He had become a myth during his own time.   Few people in America did not know his name and his face.   No one of his day was more discussed, more loved and more hated; nor was he unaware of this split in the public affection for him."   In his later biography of Darrow, Kevin Tierney expanded on Stone's ideas: "Darrow was unique. Neither before nor since has any man arisen with his particular greatness.   He carved his own niche in history, a voice for the inarticulate, the oppressed, the poor, and besides a figure of genuine intellectual importance and an artist with words who in America has never been surpassed."[4]

Much of Darrow's persona was based on his physical appearance and his unconventional world view.   Over "six feet tall, broad-shouldered, slightly stooped, he gave the impression of being even larger than he was. And his face--a craggy island reflecting the pain and suffering of the damned.   He preached love and mercy, and in a deep clear voice, not above using seduction, he fought always for what he believed was justice."[5]

Darrow was further described as "a bundle of inconsistencies."   In an often repeated line, Stone portrayed him as "a sentimental cynic.   He was a gullible skeptic.   He was an organized anarchist.   He was a happy pessimist. He was a modest egocentric.   He was a hopeful

defeatist.   And was perhaps aware of the
various contradictions he was housing under one
dome."   Yet this bundle of contradictions has
continued to intrigue people to this day.
Melvin Belli, one of the most famous contemporary trial lawyers in the United States,
described Darrow as "not only a hell of a great
lawyer, cross-examiner and arguer, but lecturer
and idealist as well."[6]

ROOTS OF THE MYTH

Clarence   Seward   Darrow   was   born   in
Kinsman, Ohio, on April 18, 1857, the son of
Arimus and Emily Darrow.   He attended local
schools in Kinsman where he also participated
in debates and gave speeches before the local
literary   society.   Darrow   was   a   mediocre
student who was more interested in baseball
than his studies.   Although he was a poor
student in formal educational settings, he was
an avid reader throughout his life.

His upbringing was not conventional by
local standards.   Although Arimus Darrow made
his living as a woodworker and casket maker, he
was a self-educated individual who was constantly reading.   He was also considered the
village infidel. Emily Darrow was also a well-
read,   free-thinking   individual.   Darrow's
unique homelife had a significant effect on his
thinking and self-image.   His defense of
unpopular causes can be traced to that
upbringing.

Although he admits that people do not
always set out to consciously create myths
about themselves, Maloney described Darrow as a
myth-maker in his own career. Darrow did seem
to help create, sustain, and build legends
about his life. Darrow's speaking and writing
supported his image as a heretic and an
outsider.   For example, in his autobiography
Darrow described his parents as free thinkers
without any "orthodox religious views."   He
portrayed his father in particular as the

village infidel and rebel, the descendant of
"rebels and traitors who took up arms against
Great Britain in the War of the Revolution. It
is easy for me to believe that my father came
of rebel stock; at least he was always in
rebellion against religion and political creeds
of the narrow and smug community in which we
dwelt." Darrow's spent his life attempting to
live up to the rebellious and heretical image
of his father. That unorthodox image was
constantly reinforced by Darrow in his
speeches, writings, and actions.[7]

His father was an abolitionist who had
spoken kindly of blacks: "as a child, I heard
my father tell of Frederick Douglass, Parker
Pillsbury, Sojourner Truth, Wendell Phillips,
and the rest of that advance army of reformers,
black and white, who went up and down the land
arousing the dulled conscience of the people to
a sense of justice to the slave. They used to
make my father's home their stopping place, and
any sort of vacant room was the forum where
they told of the black man's wrongs."[8]

Arimus Darrow's abolitionist sentiments
and support of John Brown have led to the often
repeated story that John Brown came to the
Darrow home and, laying his hand on the head of
the five-year-old Clarence, stated: "The Negro
has too few friends; you and I must never
desert him." Stone exclaimed that "Darrow had
followed this command, not out of a sense of
duty, but of love." Although the event was
historically impossible, it makes an intriguing
story that explains Darrow's lifetime of work
in support of blacks. His famous lecture on
John Brown would also seem to be a natural
outgrowth of that legendary meeting.[9]

The reality is quite different from the
myth. Brown was hanged when Darrow was only
two years old so the events in the story could
not have occurred. Such a story fits into what
Maloney calls a "spontaneous distortion of

history or biography" by individuals who seek to discover stories that explain beliefs and attitudes. This simplistic story, though false, provides an easy explanation of one facet of Darrow's support for the downtrodden.[10]

Darrow attended Allegheny College for one year and then taught in a county school for three years. While a teacher, he began to read law books. With family encouragement he entered the University of Michigan Law School, but left after one year. Darrow completed his legal training by reading at a law office in Youngstown, Ohio, and then was admitted to the bar in 1878. He practiced in Andover and Ashtabula, Ohio, until he moved to Chicago in 1888.

The legend of how Darrow went from a country lawyer in Ashtabula, Ohio, to a world-renowned attorney in Chicago also forms a part of the myth. Late in life Darrow described his early career in Ohio as providing the roots of his image as defender of the downtrodden: "my feelings were always so strong that fees were a secondary matter." That lack of money led to a semifamous battle over the ownership of a harness. Apparently a wealthy local individual had ordered a harness that cost $25, but then refused to pay for it. Darrow was frustrated that the person would not pay, so he took the case to recover the money for his client. Darrow fought the case twice and finally prevailed in the Ohio Supreme Court, all the time paying all expenses himself. In his autobiography Darrow discussed the significance of the case: "outside of the immediate jurisdiction it was not a famous case, but there are still living in Trumbull County, Ohio, a number of people who remember the case of 'Jewell versus Brockway'--which involved the title of a harness."[11] This was not the last time that Darrow paid the expenses of a trial without reimbursement.

Such victories make it clear that Darrow could have remained in Ohio and had a successful career there. An event occurred, however, that Darrow claimed jarred him out of his small town practice. Darrow had agreed to purchase a house for thirty-four hundred dollars. He paid five hundred dollars down, but the deal was never finalized because one of the owners of the house felt that Darrow would not be able to pay off the note. "I had made up my mind to buy this home. I was peeved, to put it mildly, but managed to control my temper and answered bluntly, 'all right, I don't believe I want your house because--because--I'm going to move away from here.'" This supposedly spontaneous action is described as dramatically changing his life. Not all of Darrow's biographers accept this story, arguing that he had already decided to move and that this event only hastened the inevitable--the myth, however, makes the move more interesting and dramatic.[12]

Once he moved to Chicago, Darrow "foresook rural life with only momentary hesitation and never showed any desire to return except for brief visits to bask in the glory of a hometown boy made good which he kindled periodically by sending back accounts of his triumphs in the city." For example, in 1893 he sent the following notice to the local paper: "Clarence Darrow is now a leading lawyer in Chicago, who recently came to notice by winning a long contested land case involving $455,000."[13]

Once in Chicago, Darrow set out to make a name for himself. He joined clubs and spoke as often as he could, hoping to attract attention: "I had long wanted the newspapers to notice my existence but the reporters refused to even look at me." He finally achieved his goal at a meeting in Central Music Hall. The main speaker of the evening was Henry George--Darrow was scheduled to speak immediately after

George.   After the main speech the audience
began to leave.   Darrow quickly had the
chairman introduce him: "I had discovered
enough about public speaking to sense that
unless a speaker can interest his audience at
once, his effort will be a failure."   He began
with "the most striking phrases that I could
conjure from my harried, worried brain."   The
audience began to sit and listen: "I have
talked from platforms countless times since
then, but never again have I felt that
exquisite thrill of triumph after a speech.
This was forty years ago, and even now I
occasionally meet some one who tells me that he
heard my speech that night."[14]

The next day Darrow's effort was reported
in detail by the Chicago newspapers.   He had
achieved his desired goal.   The speech and the
resulting attention helped Darrow obtain a
position in the legal department of the city of
Chicago where he eventually rose to the
position of corporate counsel.

Although Darrow held several political
appointments, Maloney stated that "Darrow was
not a politician."   His supposed unwillingness
to become involved in politics is an enduring
part of the Darrow myth.   Again, reality is
different from the myth: his office in City
Hall "became one of the most flourishing
political centers Chicago had ever seen."   His
later election to the Illinois legislature and
unsuccessful campaign for Congress also call
the legend into question.   Although Darrow
stated, "I do not want to be in political
life," much of his career was spent in the
political arena in one form or another.[15]

After leaving the job as corporate counsel
for the city of Chicago, Darrow served as an
attorney for the Chicago and Northwestern
Railway.   His dramatic change from railroad
attorney to defender of railway workers is also
an enduring part of the Darrow myth.

In 1894 Darrow faced the difficult decision of whether to defend Eugene V. Debs and his union in their battle against the railroads. Stone began his biography of Darrow with a dramatic description of Darrow's agonizing decision to leave the railroad and defend the radical Debs:

His decision made, he stretched out his fingers before him on the mahogany desk, pushed upward and rose. It was only a short distance down the hall from the legal department, with the roar of the elevated trains pouring in on a level keel from the open third story windows, and up two flights of stairs to the office of the president, but if he traveled those few steps they might prove the longest journey he had taken in his thirty-seven years. He could cite few sustaining precedents in the casebook of lawyers: he knew he was not the stuff of which martyrs were made; he was not even the possessor of a cause to lend his courage to fanaticism. Yet his father had served as the Kinsman, Ohio, link of the Underground Railroad, and many a midnight the boy had been awakened to ride to the next village on top of a load of hay that concealed an escaping Negro slave.[16]

Darrow's decision to defend Debs proved to be a dramatic turning point in his career. In his autobiography Darrow described the results of that decision: "I had never had anything to do with criminal cases, and like most other lawyers, did not want to take them. But Mr. Debs insisted that I should defend him, so I undertook the case. Naturally the trial attracted a great deal of attention throughout the country, and, as it resulted in victory for the accused, I was asked to enter other labor cases, and criminal cases as well."[17]

The Debs case began the first era of Darrow's career as a trial lawyer. From 1894 to the McNamara case and his eventual indictment for bribery in 1911, Darrow was known as a labor lawyer, a defender of the rights of labor in an era of industrial warfare in this country. After his indictment, Darrow ceased defending labor leaders and became a champion of the downtrodden (especially blacks) and eventually achieved worldwide fame as a criminal lawyer. The myth of defender of the downtrodden was called into question by his defense of rich and prominent clients in the Leopold and Loeb and Massie cases, but even those trials did little to dim the luster of his image.

Darrow's defense of labor first brought his name before the nation. Beginning with his defense of Debs in 1894 and of Thomas Kidd in 1898, the anthracite hearings in 1903, the defense of Haywood, Moyer, and Pettibone in 1907, and the McNamara case in 1911, a "major labor case without Darrow" was unthinkable. Darrow fought for labor at the precise time that workers and management were thrown into violent industrial conflict in the United States. Darrow's defense of workers obviously made him unpopular with certain elements of American society. Stone stated that during the anthracite hearings, for example, "the name of Clarence Darrow was being blazoned in headlines across the continent, and America had set up a new idol to worship--and at whom to fling offal."[18]

Public exposure continued during the Haywood trial in Boise, Idaho, in 1907. That trial has been described as "one of the most famous cases in labor history"; "the most significant incident between the have-nots and haves in the first decade of the twentieth century"; and "one of the most interesting and dramatic chapters in the annals of the labor movement."   Such dramatic trials obviously would receive a great deal of media attention: "not only did the newspaper writers turn out thousands of words each day, but an enterprising pioneer motion picture producer filmed parts of the trial for showing in 'Hale's Touring Car. . . Admission 10 cents.'"   On top of all the reporting, Darrow wrote letters to the New York Times giving his impressions of the trial. For example, he wrote that "the little city of Boise seems to be entirely unaware of its prominence in the world.   The outsider who dropped into this city after crossing the prairies and plains might imagine that he was in a New England Congregational town on a Sunday morning.   No one seems excited."[19]   His letters to the newspaper put Darrow's name before the public, and particularly his views on the trial.   Such self-advertising obviously helped in building his national fame and myth.

Each of the labor trials attracted considerable attention.   For example, his own trial for bribery elicited the following response: "most newspapers across the country reported his trial in detail.   Since the Debs trial . . . Darrow's image had been as an honest defender of the poor, the weak, and the unpopular.   The unexpected charges against him shocked the nation, which eagerly devoured accounts of the trial."[20]

His two trials for bribery ended Darrow's career as a labor lawyer and forced him to accept whatever cases he could in order to survive financially.   On his return to Chicago he entered the phase of his life where he became the most famous criminal lawyer in the United States.   At first he defended many disreputable clients: "he was not proud of it, and rather shrank from the reputation he built

up as a good crook's mouthpiece, a miracle
worker, who could and regularly did snatch the
guilty from the clutches of justice." But
Darrow was to become a national celebrity
because of his defense in the Leopold and Loeb
trial. Before that trial he was "modestly
famous," but then he acquired fame that would
make him a household name; "he would be in a
class of his own, with no living lawyer to
compare him to. Indeed no other lawyer since
has achieved the fame that came to Darrow."[21]

The Leopold and Loeb case captured the
public's imagination as few crimes ever have:
"much has been written about the case:
newspaper features, magazine articles, books
both fiction and nonfiction, as well as theatre
and film productions." The trial became famous
because he skillfully saved his clients from
hanging and because for the first time psychiatric evidence was used as a major basis in
determining the sentence for a crime. Much of
Darrow's fame, and thus his myth, was built on
the fact that Darrow cheated the public out of
hanging Leopold and Leob, that he somehow
managed to get them out of a mandatory sentence
of death. He pleaded for mercy for his
clients, but ultimately a judge made the
decision against hanging: "that made no
difference in the minds of many--he was the one
who had pleaded for mercy, which was tantamount
to condonation, even approval, of what the boys
had done. As always myth-making depends on the
will to believe."[22]

Only the Scopes trial attracted as much
attention as was paid to the Leopold and Loeb
case. The trial has been portrayed in both
movie and play form of Inherit the Wind, and
much of Darrow's public image is based on his
portrayal in those films. The court transcript
of the trial has been digested into a book, and
several books have been written about the
trial. Darrow himself described the trial's

impact: "outside the huge rail were ranged over
one hundred magazine and newspaper representa-
tives from the four winds and beyond . . . each
sat with poised pencil and eagle eye . . .
ready to record the feature story of his
life."[23]

Most of Darrow's other famous cases during
this period, particularly his defense of black
clients, aided in expanding the myth.   The
legend was called into question during his his
final case, the defense of Navy Lieutenant
Thomas H. Massie for murder in Hawaii in 1932.
Darrow's "acceptance of the Massie defense . .
. puzzled those who knew him.   Everything about
the case was at variance with what he believed.
It was not a defense of the poor, a political
dissident, or labor.   It was neither a cause
nor a crusade."   Although Darrow argued that he
needed the money, he "had to deal with an
avalanche of reproachful mail from his friends
and strangers alike, who were scandalized that
he had apparently sold out to the forces of
reaction."[24]   The acceptance of Massie's defense
may not have fit the myth, but it did little to
tarnish it.

The myth held in spite of his own devi-
ations from it.   Records indicate that from a
third to a half of his legal efforts were in
behalf of clients who could pay nothing.   A
friend once stated that "he devoted more of his
time to widows and orphans than all the other
lawyers in Chicago put together."   Even if he
could not help people, "the most singular
testimony to his altruistic side was that
through fifty years of law practice, he always
found time to listen."   Darrow himself outlined
his view: "I have defended weak and poor, have
done it without pay, will do it again."[25]

His defense of the unpopular side of
issues extended into his public lectures as
well as legal settings: "In all his speaking
Darrow was dissenter, champion of the underdog,

and critic of the social order." On the lecture circuit he always took "the unpopular side of a subject, the side with which almost everyone in the audience disagreed and knew in advance he would be wrong about." He loved to stand alone against the infidels, "fighting for a hopeless cause." He "delighted in shocking or awing a crowd." He "took special pains to cultivate a platform image as a tortured intellectual in an imperfect world. How pleased he might have been to be billed as 'the intellectual and fearless' Clarence Darrow. . . . That was how he wanted the public to think of him, and he went to great pains to ensure that they did."[26]

Much of the Darrow myth is based on his courtroom appearance and actions. Although "he was modest and plain as an old shoe, he had a vigorous ego and all the innocent vanity necessary to men who do important work." In a trial he liked to close the case, not wanting others to follow him: "He liked to be standing under the spotlight when the final curtain fell. . . . he loved the limelight--perhaps because he did his best work under its white heat."[27]

Much of the attention in the courtroom was based on his appearance and actions. Stone described the Darrow so familiar to many Americans: "a man in short sleeves and suspenders, pacing the courtroom, his thumbs holding the suspenders under his armpits, his big round shoulders hunched forward, a now thinning wisp of hair hanging down over his eyes, his face lined and seamed, his eyes dark and brooding and hurt." David Grover agreed that the "casual, almost sloppy appearance of Darrow in courtrooms became in time almost a legend." Grover believed that the appearance was part of his ability to "look and act more like a juror than an attorney. This appearance was, perhaps, a part of the studied theatri-

cality in Darrow's courtroom technique."
Darrow played on the "jury and courtroom
spectators as a concert pianist sensitively
touches the keys of his instrument, and the
audience responded."[28]

But Darrow was interested not only in the
audience in the courtroom. He wanted to reach
as broad an audience as possible, and because
of the controversial nature of his trials and
the resulting broad press coverage, he was
successful. Early in his career, during the
Kidd trial, he bargained for the publication of
his speeches to the jury. The publication
"ensured that they would be quoted long after
the occasion of their initial delivery had been
forgotten" and was a potent force in spreading
his fame.[29]

In some of his "most famous cases he was
speaking to the press, not to the jury, and
making a plea to posterity, not for the
present." His speeches were often published
alone; therefore, the readers were not able to
compare the words of other lawyers to his.
Tierney goes so far as to say that Darrow's
reputation as an orator is based more on people
who read edited versions of his speeches than
those who saw him in action. Tierney added
that many of Darrow's published speeches were
edited and that the "published version of what
was said differed in substance from what was
said in court."[30]

Maloney made the interesting observation
that society's reactions to a person's death
measures whether that individual has become a
myth in his or her lifetime. He points to
Ghandi, Franklin D. Roosevelt, and Will Rogers
as examples of people whose passing brought
forth a response similar to that observed after
Darrow's death. Maloney described how throngs
of people came to pay their last respects, how
newspapers throughout the nation published
extensive obituaries, how numerous people paid

public tribute to Darrow in a variety of situations, and how many sermons were delivered in his honor. He also interviewed and corresponded with persons who knew Darrow or heard Darrow speak and concluded that "they had lost something meaningful and even necessary in their lives." From those reactions, Maloney concluded that Darrow "had become a myth by the time of his death."[31]

In the conclusion to his article, Maloney described the Darrow myth as being developed and dramatized by eight factors:

1. Because of his intimate relationship with his father, he learned that most organized groups are the enemy and are to be opposed.

2. Darrow lived during a time of turmoil in the country. The closing of the frontier, the development of rail transportation, the rise of industry, the massive waves of immigrants, and the psychological effects of the Civil War caused groups in power to protect themselves against other groups attempting to gain power. The conflicts in Darrow's life were similar to the conflicts in the larger society.

3. Darrow's speaking in courtrooms, writing, and debating were attempts to resolve the basic conflicts in his personal life.

4. Darrow was able to generalize moral, ethical, and other problems. Because of that ability, "a speaker like Clarence Darrow who expresses, dramatizes, or otherwise deals with conflicts common to many members of his audience may achieve a special sort of popular success and public status." He then tended to create myths and "become identified with the myth he created."

5. Darrow's first successful speeches in Chicago and the defense of Eugene V. Debs gave him access to important channels of communication, stimulated him to success, and created a relationship between him and his audience

that tended to be perpetuated throughout his career.

6. During the period from the <u>Debs</u> trial to the <u>McNamara</u> case the basic elements of his career developed. The trials for bribery did not "destroy the pattern of his life, but simply altered the context of his activity."

7. As a speaker, Darrow prepared little, had a basic pattern of attack and defense, used causal argument and argument from sign in conjunction with emotional appeal and developed a convincing manner in the courtroom and on the platform.

8. His philosophy of life was based on the ideas that the world is "cruel, chaotic, and merciless"; that humans "are alone, friendless, and outcasts, consistently forced" to defend themselves against nature and human organizations; and that violence is excusable if directed against organizations.[32]

This volume will attempt to build on and explain each of these ideas by examining how they related to his trials and his activities in the public pulpit.

NOTES
1. Martin Maloney, "Clarence Darrow," in <u>A History and Criticism of American Public Address</u>, vol. 3, ed. Marie Kathryn Hochmuth (New York: Longmans, Green, 1955), pp. 263-64.
2. Maloney, "Clarence Darrow," p. 266.
3. Waldo W. Braden, "Myths in a Rhetorical Context," <u>Southern Speech Communication Journal</u> 40 (Winter 1974): 116.
4. Irving Stone, <u>Clarence Darrow for the Defense</u> (Garden City, N.Y.: Doubleday, 1941), p. 497; Kevin Tierney, <u>Darrow: A Biography</u> (New York: Thomas Y. Crowell, 1979), p. 439.
5. Arthur Weinberg and Lila Weinberg, <u>Clarence Darrow: A Sentimental Rebel</u> (New York: G. P. Putnam's Sons, 1980), pp. 10-11.
6. Stone, <u>Clarence Darrow for the Defense</u>, p.

172; Melvin Belli, quoted in Weinberg and Weinberg, Clarence Darrow, p. 27.

7. Clarence Darrow, The Story of My Life (New York: Charles Scribner's Sons, 1932), pp. 14, 7-8.

8. Darrow, quoted in Tierney, Darrow, pp. 8-9.

9. Stone, Clarence Darrow for the Defense, pp. 470-71.

10. Maloney, "Clarence Darrow," p. 265.

11. Darrow, The Story of My Life, pp. 34-35.

12. Darrow, The Story of My Life, p. 39.

13. Tierney, Darrow, pp. 35, 77.

14. Darrow, quoted in Tierney, Darrow, pp. 46-50.

15. Tierney, Darrow, p. 54; Darrow, The Story of My Life, p. 93.

16. Stone, Clarence Darrow for the Defense, p. 1.

17. Darrow, The Story of My Life, p. 74.

18. Stone, Clarence Darrow for the Defense, pp. 262, 127.

19. David H. Grover, Debaters and Dynamiters (Corvallis: Oregon State University Press, 1964), pp. 6, 111; Clarence Darrow, "Thinks Haywood Jury Hard to Get," New York Times, 7 May 1907, p. 2.

20. Weinberg and Weinberg, Clarence Darrow, p. 185.

21. Tierney, Darrow, pp. 300, 337; Stone, Clarence Darrow for the Defense, p. 404.

22. Weinberg and Weinberg, Clarence Darrow, p. 297; Tierney, Darrow, p. 347.

23. Darrow, The Story of My Life, pp. 253-54.

24. Weinberg and Weinberg, Clarence Darrow, pp. 371-72; Tierney, Darrow, p. 413.

25. Stone, Clarence Darrow for the Defense, pp. 69, 181; Darrow, quoted in Tierney, Darrow, p. 131.

26. Horace G. Rashkopf, "The Speaking of Clarence Darrow," in American Public Address, ed. Loren Reid (Columbia: University of Missouri Press, 1961), p. 33.

27. Stone, Clarence Darrow for the Defense, p.

167.
28. Stone, <u>Clarence Darrow for the Defense</u>, p.
168; Grover, <u>Debaters and Dynamiters</u>, pp.
228-29; Weinberg and Weinberg, <u>Clarence Darrow</u>,
p. 245.
29. Tierney, <u>Darrow</u>, p. 158.
30. Tierney, <u>Darrow</u>, pp. 158-59.
31. Maloney, "Clarence Darrow," p. 264.
32. Maloney, "Clarence Darrow," pp. 307-10.

2

Schoolmaster of the Courtroom

Much of the Darrow myth is based on his defense of downtrodden members of society against the rich, powerful forces who were attempting to crush them. Nowhere did this effort become more apparent or attract more attention than in his defense of workers. Darrow first captured the attention of the nation's press in a series of dramatic trials and hearings in which he defended labor leaders: Eugene V. Debs for his actions during the Pullman strike of 1894; Thomas Kidd in Oshkosh, Wisconsin, in 1894; the United Mine Workers in the anthracite arbitration in 1903; William D. Haywood, George W. Pettibone, and Charles H. Moyer, tried for murder in Boise, Idaho, in 1907; and the McNamaras in Los Angeles in 1911. Those cases made Darrow a national figure, but eventually severely damaged his career and reputation when he was charged with attempted jury bribery during the McNamara case. Those charges led to two dramatic trials of self-defense.

The speeches Darrow made during those trials are regarded as some of his best rhetorical efforts. His public statements dramatically captured the brutal fight between labor and management at the end of the nineteenth and the beginning of the twentieth centuries. As documents they provide the student of public address with insight into the ongoing conflict between labor and management and illustrate the violent, uncompromising nature of that battle.

Darrow did not set out to be a labor lawyer, but his sympathy for labor's cause led to
numerous well-paying jobs in labor's defense.
Darrow's firm "had a claim to be the first modern specialists in labor law to practice prof-
itably, and between 1897 and 1911, the practice
was very profitable indeed."[1]

Once he became a labor lawyer, Darrow developed a series of standard arguments and
ploys that he used in all of his trials.   He
built "up an inventory of original ploys, usa-
ble and reusable throughout his long career
with only a minimum of modification.   Once he
had developed an appealing argument, it was
called into aid in all sorts of contexts sub-
sequently."[2]   Even though he repeated the arguments, Darrow made them seem appropriate to the
individual situation.   Also, since each audience was new to Darrow, listeners would view
his standard arguments as fresh, new ideas.
His ability as an orator made it seem as though
he was using his arguments for the first time.

In each of the labor trials Darrow tried
to place the specific event into the larger social context of the nation.   He freely discussed the inequities in society and the need for
change.   He saw labor unions as a powerful
force in improving the lives of the downtrodden
in the nation.

As he defended labor Darrow, became more
committed to labor's views, and his attacks on
their enemies became more scathing: "up to this
time attorneys had stood apart from the labor
clients they represented, translating their
cause into the terminology of the courts so
that it was impossible for unionists to sustain
the impetus generated by the original dispute.
But from the beginning Darrow showed himself an
advocate not merely of the legal arguments in
favor of the workmen, but of the political and
economic ones as well."[3]

He was aided in many of his labor trials
by insensitive capitalists who provided him
easy targets for attack: George M. Pullman in

the Debs case, George M. Paine in the Kidd
case, George F. Baer in the anthracite hearings, and Harrison Gray Otis in the McNamara
case.   Each of these individuals was more
concerned with stamping out labor unions than
with improving the lives of individual workers.
Their attitudes were illustrated in a quotation
by Pullman. When asked whether workers who had
been loyal employees for a number of years were
not entitled to consideration, Pullman replied
that "the workers have nothing to do with the
amount of wages they shall receive; that is
solely the business of the company." He added:
"My duty is to my stockholders and to my company."   George F. Baer, the president of the
Philadelphia and Reading Coal and Iron Company,
expressed a similar view during the anthracite
arbitration hearings: "There cannot be two
masters in the management of business."[4]
     Darrow used personal attacks and much in-
vective to discredit insensitive corporation
leaders.   Although he ""protested that his
quarrels were with ideas, not men," he "used
argument and invective . . . to flay and dimin-
ish his enemies. Arguments were weapons of
psychological warfare and cross-examination
became an instrument of personal cruelty in his
hands."   He would often deliberately pick a
"'goat' to be the brunt of his attacks."[5]
     In each of the cases, Darrow referred to
his clients as universal symbols who represented causes larger than the issues involved
in their specific case. So he argued for the
causes as much or more than the individuals.
For example, in the Kidd case he said he was
arguing not for Thomas Kidd, but for "the long
line of despoiled and downtrodden people of the
earth." He went so far as to state that his
client was not his major concern; rather, the
cause of these people was more important than
that of the individual. In each of the cases
the cause was the labor movement, a movement

that would not be eliminated by prosecuting the defendant. For example, in the Haywood case he stated: "Don't be so blind in your madness as to believe that when you make three fresh new graves you will kill the labor movement of the world."[6]

THE DEBS CASE, 1894

The Debs case marked a dramatic shift in Darrow's life. As an attorney for the Chicago and Northwestern Railway he faced the internal conflict between accepting a comfortable pay-check and fighting for causes in which he real-ly believed: "It is hard enough to maintain an independent stand and freely express one's self without being handicapped by the desire for of-fice or money." There was "a stark contradic-tion in being a railroad lawyer by day and a radical by night." Eventually Darrow's beliefs won out. He chose to leave the railroad and work in defense of Debs: "I could find no suf-ficient cause, except my self interest, for refusing [to defend Debs]. So . . . I went to the president of the company and told him that I felt I should go into the case, although it would mean giving up my position; and I told him that I believed some one whose political views were more in keeping with their interests would be a much better man for the company."[7]

Once Darrow accepted the Debs case, he "worked with almost demonic enthusiasm, seeking to make up for the time he regarded as squan-dered in the service of the Chicago & North-western." He was able to use his ideological beliefs in defense of Debs: "I had never been connected with a case involving strikes, but both by education and natural tendency I had a deep-rooted feeling for the men against whom injunctions were issued." His beliefs and actions in the Debs case set the pattern for legal battles between labor and management for the next twenty years, in "which neither side gave quarter. . . . His determination not to compromise, his 'duel to the death' mentality, verged on fanaticism. . . . If every strike was a conspiracy, then every prosecution of a laboring man was a persecution.   Neither side gave the other credit for good faith."[8]

During the trial Darrow argued that men had the right to decide whether or not to leave their jobs and that the court could not stop them quitting work.   He proclaimed that "the court . . . had not enjoined the defendants from participating in a strike but simply prohibited them from committing violence."[9]

He heaped particular abuse on the government for its use of conspiracy laws as a means of destroying the labor movement.   He tried to show that the men had acted openly, not in some sort of secret conspiracy, when they refused to move trains containing Pullman cars.   He used the trial as a forum in which he tried to teach of the evils caused by such laws and as a means of damning the management of the railroads:

> This is a historic case which will count much for liberty or against liberty.   Conspiracy, from the days of tyranny in England down to the day of the General Managers' Association . . . has been the favorite of every tyrant.   It is an effort to punish the crime of thought.   If the government does not, we shall try to get the General Managers here to tell you what they know about conspiracy. These defendants published to all the world what they were doing and in the midst of a widespread strike were never so busy but that they found time to counsel against violence. For this they are brought into court by an organization which uses the government as a cloak to conceal its infamous purposes.[10]

Although he failed in getting Debs freed, the

case "marked an important turning point in the
legal relations between management and labor,
which was largely engineered by Darrow; his
defense had introduced an entirely new tone
into court, carrying the resentments of acute
industrial warfare to law as had never been
done before." The case "was notable in artic-
ulating Darrow's premise--to be developed much
further later on--that no blame or legal lia-
bility attached to those who resorted to violence for political ends. Nevertheless the
seed of the philosophy that countenanced and
even praised industrial violence are to be
found in the Pullman litigation."[11]

> The trial made Darrow a national figure:
> Darrow's defense of Debs established
> him as a leading labor attorney on
> the national scene. To his philo-
> sophical radicalism was added the
> role of radical lawyer. He became
> the movement lawyer as well as a
> criminal attorney. His reputation
> burgeoned among the poor, the weak,
> the misunderstood. His office was
> filled with representatives of labor
> unions, political dissidents, rela-
> tives of men and women charged with
> criminal offenses from petty larceny
> to robbery and murder. All sought
> his help, and seldom were any turned
> away. If there was money for a fee,
> he took it. If not, he worked with-
> out a fee. Almost half of the cases
> he undertook in his lifetime were
> without payment.[12]

THE KIDD CASE, 1894

Darrow's defense of Thomas I. Kidd "was
the first of many odysseys beyond Chicago" that
were to further build his reputation as a lawyer of national stature. The trial helped
build his image as "a dragonslayer brought in
from afar, an image he seemed to enjoy."[13]

Kidd had consulted with Darrow on legal matters on previous occasions, so he and Darrow knew each other quite well. Also, it was natural that the son of a woodworker would be asked to defend men such as Kidd and his codefendants whose livelihood is woodworking.

Although the charge against the defendants was conspiracy to interfere with interstate commerce and injure the business of the Paine company, the real attack was on the right to strike. If a crime was proved, it would in effect say that striking was illegal in Wisconsin. Obviously, such a verdict would be damaging to labor's future in Wisconsin.[14]

The climate surrounding the trial was tense. As Darrow stated: "as in all places outside of big cities and industrial centres, the feeling was very bitter on both sides. The division was, as always, the rich of the community on one side and the workers on the other."[15]

The Paine Lumber Company had done everything it could to prevent unionization and to discourage the strike. Paine had refused to negotiate or even meet with workers who had grievances. Like Pullman, Paine regarded unions "as an unmitigated evil." Unlike Pullman, Paine submitted himself to cross-examination during the trial, an event that severely damaged his reputation. Darrow's treatment of Paine might reflect a client's description of Darrow: "When he was calm, which he nearly always was, he reminded me of a lion. That majestic bearing, that leonine mane of hair. Truly the king of beasts. But when he was excited he turned instantly into a tiger--a fierce raging tiger. I'll wager that witnesses who have been raked by his fierce irony would not dispute my metaphor."[16]

As in the Pullman case, Darrow's defense was based on an attack on the prosecution. He was able to turn the conspiracy charges back on

the prosecution.   There had been little violence during the strike, so he was able to
blame the problems on Paine for lowering wages
and replacing the men in his factories with
cheaper female and child labor.   He charged
that the employers "are using the court of
justice because in their misguided cupidity,
they believe that they may be able to destroy
what little is left of the spirit of independ-
ence and manhood which they have been slowly
crushing from the breasts of those who toil for
them."[17]

Darrow's goat during the Kidd trial was
the prosecutor, F. W. Houghton.   On the first
day Paine appeared in court Houghton jumped to
his feet and escorted Paine into the courtroom.
Darrow commented: "[Houghton] would have been
glad to lick the dust from Paine's boots had he
been given the opportunity to perform this service."   During the trial Houghton used as a
precedent a case where a man had been convicted
for writing a poem praising Thomas Paine and
his Rights of Man.   Darrow attacked that
action: "How brother Houghton's mouth would
have watered if he had been given a chance to
convict Thomas Paine for daring to proclaim the
rights of man."   Throughout the trial and especially during his final speech, Darrow attacked
Houghton because he was receiving $15 a day as
a special prosecutor.   Irving Stone described
the tactic: "Darrow rubbed Houghton's nose in
the fifteen dollars a day he was getting for
this prosecution until the man should have been
so housebroken that he would never again wet
the penal code in his uncontainable excitement
at the prospect of making some extra money."[18]

The major rhetorical experiment Darrow
used in the trial was to argue from theory and
principle and deal with the evidence and facts
of the case only in passing.   His closing argument was described as being "as interesting as
a novel" and "one of the outstanding social

documents of its time, enunciating in such logical terms the rights of persons over the rights of property that it helped lead the way toward a new ordering of life in America." He attempted to speak to the entire nation on the great social issues of the day rather than just the twelve jurors on the specifics of the case. Then he stated that the issue "was not whether Kidd and his co-defendants were guilty of conspiracy, but whether labor unions were good things." Darrow even claimed, as he did in other trials, that he was not concerned about the defendant:

> Here is Thomas I. Kidd. It is a matter of the smallest consequence to him or to me what you do; and I say it as sincerely as I ever spoke a word. . . . I do not appeal for him. That cause is too narrow for me, much as I love him and long as I have worked by his side. I appeal to you, gentlemen, not for Thomas I. Kidd, but I appeal to you for the long line--the long, long line reaching back through the ages, and forward to the years to come--the long line of despoiled and down-trodden people of the earth.[19]

Throughout his summary Darrow argued that the defendants were not on trial, "that the jury system was on trial and that they could convict only the jury system by a verdict of guilty." The jury was told that their judgment would be a historic one:

> It has fallen to your lot to be leading actors in one of the great dramas of human life. For some mysterious reason Providence has placed in your charge for today, aye, for the ages, the helpless toilers, the helpless men, the despondent women and suffering children of the

world. It is a great, a tremendous
trust, and I know you will do your
duty bravely, wisely, humanely and
well; that you will render a verdict
in this case which will be a milestone in the history of the world and
an inspiration to the dumb, despair-
ing millions whose fate is in your
hands.[20]

As Stone stated, "The jury brought in a verdict
of 'not guilty'; with the weight of the centuries on their shoulders they could do no
less."[21]

Darrow's success in the trial increased
his popularity among labor. It was, however,
the last labor trial in which he appeared for
only a nominal fee. In the future he asked
labor to raise legal defense funds, and he
asked for larger fees. He made the field of
labor law a lucrative means of making a living.

The Kidd case also was significant in
building the Darrow myth. Before the trial
began, he bargained for the union to pay for
the publication of his address to the jury, a
practice he followed throughout the rest of his
career. The speech was published in a pamphlet
distributed to members of the Woodworkers Union
and sold to the general public. The pamphlet
was an effective means of getting his words
before the nation.

THE ANTHRACITE ARBITRATION, 1903

Darrow's actions and statements in the
arbitration between the United Mine Workers
(UMW) and the coal operators again focused on
the ongoing battle between labor and management. Again Darrow came down strongly on the
side of the workers: "His speeches challenged
the government's right to complain even of
murder, so long as it tolerated such working
conditions as were found in the mines. Like
many contemporary observers the world over,
Darrow found in the mining industry a dramatic

illustration of the evils of capitalism. The
combination of a high rate of physical injury
with low wages and horrible working conditions
seemed to inspire bitterness and sympathy beyond other callings."[22]

Because of the importance of coal,
national attention was focused on the strike,
with much public opinion in opposition to the
actions of the coal operators. This negative
public opinion and the interest in the arbitration provided Darrow with an arena in which
to build his national image and expand the
myth: "here was a magnificent opportunity for
Darrow: a public incensed against the coal
barons, who had combined to force up the price
of coal and force down the price of labor. . .
. There was no town or hamlet so small that one
of its newspapers would not print every word of
the hearing before the commission, and there
were few persons within reaching distance of a
newspaper who had not been so disturbed that
they would not read everything printed."[23]

Although the coal operators presented
numerous arguments to the commission in support
of their position, "the truth was in this and
many other strikes--that the employers were
less scared of giving the workers their demands
than they were of recognizing the union."
Because of the fear, many people felt that the
operators had caused the strike and prolonged
it in a manner that led to violence and a
shortage of coal in a country very dependent on
that commodity.[24]

Darrow carefully planned his case with the
help of lawyers who had worked as miners so
they had an understanding of the needs and desires of the workers. Once the case was carefully prepared, Darrow felt comfortable in
stating his views during the hearings: "I had
been in various arbitrations before; I had
found arbitration more satisfactory than
courts; there are seldom the same feelings of

hatred that accompany a court proceeding at
law. An arbitration is flexible and informal."
Darrow also believed that his side had an
advantage because "the mine owners were handicapped by too many lawyers. A large number of
corporations and individuals were involved, and
most of them came into court." The advantage
in favor of the miners came to the fore during
Darrow's final speech. Darrow summarized what
he saw as the advantages on the side of the
owners: "Their social advantages are better,
their religious privileges are better, they
speak the English language better. They are
not children. They can hire good lawyers and
expert accountants, and they have got the
advantage of us in almost every particular, and
we will admit that." At that point, the
chairman of the commission, Judge George Gray,
interjected, "Except for the lawyers."[25]

The hearings again provided Darrow with an
individual upon whom he could heap scorn,
George Baer, president of the Reading Railroad
and several coal companies. During the hearings Baer summarized the view of many capitalists when he stated that "God in his infinite
wisdom had bequeathed the management of industry to Christian gentlemen," and then added,
"We cannot interfere with the divine right of
stockholders." Obviously such statements only
supported the negative image of operators being
portrayed in the press and provided Darrow with
an opening to attack:

> These gentlemen who do not live with
> their men, who appoint their bosses
> and overseers and expect them to
> produce results--it is well for them
> to say we are Anarchists and
> criminals, that we are drunkards,
> that we are profligates, that we
> cannot speak the English language,
> that we are unruly boys. But it
> would come with far better grace from

them if they could show that even
once, even once in their adminis-
tration of these lands and of these
natural bounties which Mr. Baer
thinks the Lord gave to him to
administer--that ever once they have
considered anyone but themselves.[26]

He then castigated the coal operators for
refusing to improve conditions of work and for
employing children as laborers in the mines:
"if the civilization of this country rests upon
the necessity of leaving these starvation wages
to these miners and laborers, or if . . . it
rests upon the labor of these poor little boys
from twelve to fourteen years of age who are
picking their way through the dirt, clouds and
dust of the anthracite coal, then the sooner we
are done with this civilization and start over
anew, the better for the humanities that after
all must survive all forms of civilization,
whether good or bad."[27]

Darrow focused on the terrible working and
living conditions in the coal fields while
downplaying miner violence during the strike.
He said claims of violence were used by companies as an excuse to destroy unions: "You
will see that the proof presented by the government will be of acts brought here to inflame
your minds to convict these men in order that
their union may be destroyed by the men who are
pursuing them." Rather than criticizing men
for their actions, he felt they should be
praised: "These men are not conspirators--these
men are not criminals. . . . You and I may dis-
agree with them, may say that what they did was
unwise, but when the record is made up, that of
men laying down their tools out of sympathy for
their fellowmen as we saw last summer was one
of the proudest sublimest spectacles in the
world. Men have a right to strike; these men
did nothing more." He then argued that recognition of the United Mine Workers by the coal

companies was inevitable: "you can do just as you please about recognizing the union. If you do not recognize it, it is because you are blind. . . . It is here. It is here to stay."[28]

Due to the nature of the hearings and the evidence, Darrow attempted to keep the issues narrow.   Normally, Darrow discussed larger contexts in society and ignored the specific evidence in the case, but in the arbitration hearings, "a large part of the evidence in this case has no bearing upon the issues of the case."   He spent much of his summation attempting to refute the figures on wages introduced by the mine operators and then boiling the entire case down to how much the miners earned each year:

> So far as the demands of the mine workers are concerned, it makes no difference whether crimes have been committed or not.   If John Smith earned $600 a year, it is no answer to say that Tom Jones murdered someone in cold blood.   That does not relieve you.   It is no answer to say that some person has been boycotted.   The question is what has he earned?   Are these men entitled to more money?   Are they entitled to shorter hours?[29]

The nature of the case also brought Darrow to great flights of emotion in his speeches.   He pointed to the large numbers of textile mills in the coal region "where little girls from twelve to thirteen or fourteen years of age are working ten hours a day, twelve hours a day and twelve hours a night as well."   He then blamed the operators for exploiting the workers:

> Do not tell me that that [young children working] is due to the inhumanity of the father or mother. It is contrary to natural law.   The wolf suckles her young.   The wild

animal cares for its offspring, and
the human being is not less kind than
the wolf or the beast. The instinct
of life planted deep in all living
things provides that the old must
care for the   young.   It provides
that   the   parent,   whether   man   or
beast, must care for its offspring.
It needs no human law to enforce it.
It needs nothing but a chance for
those   common,   external   instincts
which   have   kept   the   human   race
alive.[30]

To everyone's surprise, during his final statement to the commission, Baer changed his position by offering raises to the miners.   In
effect,   he   admitted   the   miners'   argument.
Darrow   responded: "In   fact,   they   will   do
exactly that which these men demanded nine
months before, and which they in their blind-
ness,   their   ignorance   and   their   stupidity
refused."[31]

    After the hearings the arbitration board
took   several   months   to   make   its   decision.
Darrow   outlined   the   results   in   his   autobiography:

The board took the time thoroughly to
consider   the   case,   delivered   a
lengthy opinion, and granted a substantial raise of wages, better conditions and shorter hours of labor,
and found in favor of a plan offered
for   working   conditions   for   the
future. This plan was the outcome of
discussion and consideration by both
parties, and it was so well weighed
and arranged that it kept peace in
the   anthracite   regions   for   twenty-
five years. I believe that this was
the   first   agreement   reached   for
settling industrial disputes without
resorting   to   brute   force   on   both

44   Clarence Darrow

sides.   Since then it has formed the
basis   for   many   other   such
agreements.[32]

Darrow's speech to the commission again
reached a large audience.   The publishers of
the <u>Philadelphia North American</u> were offered a
dollar a line to print the closing arguments of
the operators.   Darrow agreed as long as his
speech would be printed in full with no charge
to the miners.   In printing his speech, the
paper referred to Darrow's summation as "one of
the most remarkable that has been heard in
recent years."   The victory led to much acclaim
in Chicago, and to a brief movement to convince
Darrow to run for mayor, but in the end he
refused.[33]

THE <u>HAYWOOD</u> CASE, 1907

The next major labor case marked a
dramatic change in focus and location.   In
defending Big Bill Haywood, Charles H. Moyer,
and George Pettibone, accused of the murder of
Frank Steunenberg, the   former governor of
Idaho, in Boise, Idaho, the scene shifted from
the industrial East to the mountains of the
West and from discussions of wages and the
rights of unions to murder.   Because of the
emotion surrounding the case, the trial itself
further heightened the division between labor
and management in the West.   The trial dramatically characterized the differences in opinion
and beliefs between labor and management on the
American frontier.

With the industrialization and the end of
free land in the West, which had served as a
safety valve for surplus labor, dramatic
changes were occurring in the lives of western
workers, particularly those engaged in mining.
The creation of militant organizations, such as
the Western Federation of Miners and the rise
of powerful leaders such as Haywood led to a
natural conflict: "reflecting the basic charac-
teristics of the frontier with its potential

for violence, the Idaho struggle between capital and labor--the status quo versus union recognition and a bigger share of the rewards--was
class conflict with total chaos on both sides,
each absolutely determined to achieve victory."
Darrow's description of the trial echoed the
conflict: "The whole trial was a vivid picture
of industrial warfare. . . . In all these con-
tests both sides put forth their best endeavors
to win. Not only were the employees and miners
in almost mortal combat, but all classes of
society were divided into hostile camps. There
were no disinterested people. There was no
neutrality. Each side regarded a strike as
warfare, and felt that every sort of means was
justifiable in carrying it through."[34]

Because of the dramatic nature of the
issues, the trial was described as "the most
important event that has occurred in Western
America in recent years." News coverage of the
event was immense. Over fifty magazines and
newspapers had reporters in town. The Western
Union office announced that it could handle
200,000 words a day. The trial was one of the
first covered by national wire services:
"Darrow was fortunate to come to prominence as
an advocate in the first great age of national
reporting. His rise coincided with the formation of the national wire agencies: in fact
Associated Press's single greatest reporting
success was the Haywood trial, which persuaded
many newspapers to subscribe to its services. .
. . Moreover the ability to reproduce photo-
graphs added a new dimension to newspaper jour-
nalism at the turn of the century." Darrow
used the telegraph to his advantage by sending
daily perceptions of the trial to the New York
Times. Such self-advertisement obviously
helped build his image and myth.[35]

In his summation Darrow reached out to the
country by again talking about larger issues
and his own views as well as the specific

events of the trial.   He also went on the attack, heaping scorn on the owners: "[The mine owners] reportedly hired detectives and placed them in positions of responsibilities as Secretaries or Presidents of local unions. . . . Every illegitimate child that has been born west of the Missouri River . . . has been wrapped in its swaddling clothes and hurried to Denver to be laid on the doorstep of the Western Federation of Miners."[36]

His most vitriolic attacks, however, were saved for the prosecution's major witness, Harry Orchard. He referred to Orchard as "the most perjured villain who ever sat in a court-room."   A passage in his summation about Orchard has been repeated in many sources:

Gentlemen, I sometimes think I am dreaming in this case, whether here in Idaho or anywhere in the country, broad and free, a man can be placed on trial and lawyers seriously asked to take away the life of a human being upon the testimony of Harry Orchard. . . . The juror who would take away the life of a human being upon testimony like that would place a stain which all the waters of the great seas could never wash away. . . . You had better let a thousand men go unwhipped of justice, you had better let all the criminals that come to Idaho escape scot free than to have it said that twelve men of Idaho would take away the life of a human being upon testimony like that.[37]

Much of his discussion was based on the rights and wrongs of industrial warfare. His beliefs obviously were that unions were right: "I don't care how many wrongs they committed, I don't care how many crimes these weak, rough, rugged, unlettered men who often knew no other power

but the brute force of their strong right arm,
who find themselves bound and confined and
impaired whichever way they turn, who look up
and worship the god of might as the only god
they know--I don't care how often they fail,
how many brutalities they are guilty of.   I
know their cause is just."[38]

Once he made the case that unions were
just, Darrow argued as he had in previous cases
that the death of Haywood would not end the
labor movement: "do not think for a moment that
if you hang him you will crucify the labor
movement of the world; do not think that you
will kill the hopes and the aspirations and the
desires of the weak and poor."[39]

In his peroration he again reminded the
jury of their importance in the case: "The eyes
of the world are upon you--upon you twelve men
of Idaho tonight."   He then contrasted the
possible reactions in the country to their
decision.   He told the jury that if they found
Haywood guilty, "in the railroad offices of our
great cities men will applaud your names.   If
you decree his death, amongst the spiders of
Wall Street will go up paens of praise for
these twelve good men and true.   In every bank
in the world, where men hate Haywood because he
fights for the poor and against that accursed
system upon which the favored live and grow
rich and fat--from all those you will receive
blessing and unstinted praise."   In a quote
which is often repeated he then told what would
happen if they found Haywood not guilty:

> But if your verdict should be "Not
> Guilty" in this case, there are still
> those who will reverently bow their
> heads and thank these twelve men for
> the life and reputation you have
> saved.   Out on our broad prairies
> where men toil with their hands, out
> on the wide ocean where men are
> tossed and buffeted on the waves,

through our mills and factories, and
down deep under the earth, thousands
of men, and of women and children--
men who labor, men who suffer, women
and children weary with care and
toil--these men and these women and
these children will kneel tonight and
ask their God to guide your hearts--
these men and these women and these
little children, the poor, the weak,
and the suffering of the world, are
stretching out their helpless hands
to this jury in mute appeal for Bill
Haywood's life.[40]

Although the trial featured superb oratory on
both sides, Haywood was probably found innocent
mainly because the prosecution was unable to
prove a conspiracy to commit murder. That information is often ignored, and Darrow's oratory is given credit for swaying the audience.

Reactions to Darrow's speeches were mixed.
The New York Sun called it a "vicious appeal to
class prejudice," while the Chicago Tribune referred to it as "the most unseemly, obscene,
inflammatory speech ever delivered in an American courtroom . . . the mud brawling of an
anarchist." The Idaho Statesman offered a different view: "after listening spellbound to the
eloquence of Clarence Darrow yesterday there
were many who expressed the belief that if the
jury brings in a verdict of acquittal for
William D. Haywood, that the Chicago attorney
may be the one who won the victory." Darrow
himself summarized his view: "In all my experience I never had a better opportunity, and
when I had finished I felt satisfied with the
effect I made."[41]

THE McNAMARA CASE, 1911

Haywood, Pettibone, and Moyer were found
innocent of murder, and their successful defense led to Darrow's accepting the defense of
the McNamaras. Although he did not want to

defend the McNamaras, labor leaders insisted that he take the case. They hoped he could repeat the successes of past trials. Unfortunately, the outcome of the McNamara trial was different from anything anticipated. That trial ended Darrow's career as a labor attorney and almost ended his career as a lawyer.

The Haywood case and Darrow's illness during that trial left him tired and weak. He argued that a younger, more energetic lawyer should be retained to defend the McNamaras, but Samuel Gompers and other labor leaders insisted that he take the case.

The McNamara case grew out of the bombing of the Times Building in Los Angeles. More than a score of people were killed by the blast. The owner of the Los Angeles Times, General Harrison Gray Otis, was an ardent opponent of unions. Immediately after the explosion he began a public relations campaign against the unions and called for the arrest of the bombers. Darrow also knew that Los Angeles was a violently antiunion town, that working men referred to it as "the scabbiest town on earth," and that General Otis and other prominent citizens were violently antiunion. The American Federation of Labor set up a huge defense fund "to insure a proper defense, a fair and impartial trial." Against his better judgement Darrow accepted the case.[42]

On his arrival in Los Angeles Darrow went to meet his clients: "I went to the jail and for the first time met my clients. I found both men pleasant, prepossessing, and, of course, glad to see me and the rest of the lawyers." He assembled a large staff and began to work. As time went on, however, it became clearer and clearer that the McNamaras were guilty. Yet Darrow's hatred of capital punishment kept him working:

> I have always hated capital punishment. To me it seems a cruel,

> brutal, useless barbarism. The
> killing of one individual by another
> always shows real or fancied excuse
> or reason. The cause, however poor,
> was enough to induce the act. But
> the killing of an individual by the
> State is deliberate, and is done
> without any personal grievance or
> feeling. It is the outcome of long
> premeditated hatred. It does not
> happen suddenly without warning,
> without time for the emotions to cool
> and subside, but a day is fixed a
> long time ahead, and the victim is
> kept in continued, prolonged torture
> up to the moment of execution.[43]

Eventually a settlement was reached in which
the McNamaras pleaded guilty and both were sentenced to prison: "For weeks I pondered how to
save the lives of these clients. . . . The
lawyer, if he has a deep sense of responsibility and warm sympathies, regards the human
being in his hands in the same light that a
physician views a patient in. Both try to
relieve suffering, and no one would expect a
physician to refuse to save the life of a
patient, no matter who he might be. The
lawyer's duty is just as binding; both try to
allay pain and save life. . . . And this is
what I hope to do in this case."[44]

Even though he allowed a plea of guilty,
Darrow refused to believe that the McNamaras
meant to kill people. He argued that the bomb
was planted to "scare the employees of The
Times and others in non-union shops. . . . Had
it been the intention to destroy the building,
or human life, the amount of dynamite would
have been much larger and it would have been
placed inside the building."[45]

The guilty pleas were kept secret as long
as possible. When the pleas were announced,
there was a great commotion and outpouring of

emotions. Many of those who had praised Darrow as a savior now savagely turned on him. In his autobiography Darrow movingly described what happened:

> At last I went out with the rest. It was growing dark. A few street lights were turned on. Many of our most loyal friends tore the McNamara buttons from their lapels and threw them into the street. My old friend, Billy Cavenaugh, came to my side. He was then a policeman, and still my friend. He was alarmed at the attitude of the crowd, grabbed my arm and said, "Come with me." I was not brave, but I looked him in the face and answered, "No, Billy, I shall go down the street with the crowd. I have walked with them to the courthouse when they cheered me, and I shall go back the way I came." There were some sullen faces, and threatening gestures, a few hard and cruel words, but little did these matter, little did I care. I could see only one road to take, and I never asked myself whether it led to happiness or doom.[46]

Darrow released a notice to the press: "I have known for months that our fight was hopeless. I would never have consented to their pleading guilty if I had thought there was a chance left. It was intimated to us that we must act promptly; there was danger that what was being considered would get out and make settlement impossible. We were responsible to our clients alone."[47]

Because he was perceived as harming the labor movement through his actions, Darrow never again was called to serve in a labor case, although he continued to speak for labor's cause in a variety of forums. Thus, the period that first made him famous ended, and he faced an even greater battle--a fight to keep from going to jail.

SELF-DEFENSE, 1912

The day after being charged with bribery Darrow issued a statement proclaiming his innocence: "I am innocent of the charges brought against me, and I hope that you will withhold judgement until I am given an opportunity to establish that fact. The charges that have been brought against me are too serious to treat lightly. Doubtless the district attorney's office believes that there was evidence to warrant the advice that it gave the grand jury, but in the end it will be shown that a grave error and injustice has been perpetuated."[48]

He immediately hired Earl Rogers, a successful criminal lawyer, to be his attorney. Although Rogers was the attorney of record, he and Darrow shared many of his duties in his defense. Because of the McNamara case, Darrow's labor supporters turned down his appeals for money. Therefore, the entire trial was hampered by a lack of financial resources. Also, Darrow discovered that over the years his actions and statements had offended large numbers of people, so very few came forth to help him. This lack of support sapped his energy and confidence, so he often appeared downtrodden and even beaten. Darrow's friend Lincoln Steffens described him during the trial: "at three o'clock he is a hero for courage, nerve, and calm judgement but at 3:15 he may be a coward for fear, collapse, and panicky mentality." Because of those mood swings Rogers had to constantly tell him to look confident or his moods would lead to a negative verdict by the jury.[49]

In his opening speech the district attorney, John D. Fredericks, pictured Darrow as "crooked, hypocritical, cynical, and treacherous," making as violent an attack upon Darrow's intergrity as imaginable. In his own closing speech Darrow complained about his treatment at Fredericks' hands:

> I think I can say that no one in my native town would have made to any jury any such statement as one made of me by the district attorney in opening this case. I will venture to say he could not afterward have found a companion except among detectives and crooks and sneaks in the city where I live if he had dared to open his mouth in the infamous way he did in this case.[50]

In a dramatic move, Darrow took the witness stand in his own defense. After concluding his testimony, Darrow felt that he had been a credible witness: "I had no more trouble about answering every question put to me than I would have had in reciting the multiplication table." Some observers, however, took a contrary view, saying he was a poor witness who did not answer the questions.[51]

In the final arguments, the assistant district attorney, Joe Ford, again attacked Darrow. One of the jurors stated: "Ford wrote out his speech, learned it by heart, then dressed up in his Sunday best and invited all his friends to come to court to hear him. But he laid it on too heavy; he was too bitter. He was vicious and venomous; I hated him; I couldn't bear to look at him." In that summary Ford stated: "It is one of the misfortunes of the American bar . . . that some criminal lawyers practice subornation and perjury and use bribery to win their cases. There is really no difference between the men inside the jail and those outside with men like the defendant employed to fight the case."[52]

When Darrow rose to speak, he no longer appeared weak and broken. A crowd came to "hear America's greatest pleader plead for himself: for a day and a half they heard pour from his lips words that came out of his blood and guts." In his speech "his lashing of what he called 'the criminal interests in the country' that usurp and pervert government, that carry on gigantic swindles in their account books and stock manipulations, that rob and bleed the public by extortionate price fixings; was the most passionate and ringing he had ever made. In it he made the plea of which he had deprived himself in the McNamara case."[53]

Darrow knew that there were those who believed him to be guilty so he spoke to them: "There was . . . one view that I was sure practically every one would agree on--that is, whatever the facts might be, there had been no sordid or selfish motive connected with the affair. They would know if the charge was true it was because of my devotion to a cause and my anxiety and concern over the fate of some one else." He then explained why he was on trial: "I have been a lover of the poor, a friend of the oppressed, because I have stood by labor for all these years, and have brought down upon my head the wrath of the criminal interests in this country. Whether guilty or innocent of the crime charged in the indictment, that is the reason I am here, and that is the reason I have been pursued by as cruel a gang as ever followed a man."[54]

Using an argument that he often used in defense of others, Darrow questioned his at-tackers as to whether they knew that sending him to prison will not "destroy the hopes of the poor and the oppressed. . . . Don't you know that upon my persecution and destruction would arise 10,000 men abler than I have been, more devoted than I have been, and ready to give more than I have given a righteous cause?[55]

Several times in the speech Darrow re-ferred to his thirty-five years of service as a lawyer. He argued that he had built up a reputation and that it would be foolish to destroy that reputation through such an unwise act. He then extended the argument by saying that someone with his experience certainly would not handle a bribe in such a careless, amateurish fashion. Ultimately he argued, "I am as fitted for jury bribing as a Methodist preacher for tending bar. By all my training, inclination and habit, I am about the last person in the world who could possibly have undertaken such a thing. I do not intimate for a moment that anyone else would, but in all this situation, mine was the position which needed to be guarded the most carefully, as these events have shown."[56]

He then went against Rogers' advice and talked about the McNamara case, arguing that it was a political trial, part of the ongoing battle between labor and capital: "Here is J. B. McNamara. . . . If there is no other man on earth who will raise his voice to do justice for him, I will do it, even if I am pleading for myself." He argued that the actions of the McNamaras were misunderstood:

> I would give a great portion of my
> life to have these two boys under-
> stood. . . . I want to say to this
> jury, even if it costs me my liberty,
> that the placing of dynamite in the
> Times alley was not "the crime of the
> century"; it was not even a crime as
> crimes are understood. I want to
> make myself plain upon that, if it
> costs me every man in this jury box;
> I was sorry then, and I am sorry
> today for those boys. I took my life
> in my hands to help save their lives,
> because they were my clients, and I
> understood them. And I will take my
> life in my hands again to have them
> brought back to society, as I think

some time they will be.[57]

In the speech he attacked those who condemned him, particularly Harrington:

> They used to have a steer down in the stockyards of Chicago, where Harrington came from, that had been educated; they had educated the steer to the business of climbing an incline to the shambles. There was a little door on the side so that the steer could dart through this door and not get caught in the shambles, and his business was to go out in the pen and lead the other steers up that incline to the shambles, and then just before they reached the place he would dart through the door and leave the rest to their destruction. This is Harrington.[58]

He concluded by again telling the jurors the implication of their decision: "If you should convict me, there will be people to applaud the act. But if in your judgement and your wisdom and your humanity, you believe me innocent . . . I know that from thousands and tens of thousands and yea, perhaps millions of the weak and the poor and the helpless throughout the world will come thanks to this jury for saving my liberty and my name."[59]

Reports called the speech "one of the most masterly ever heard in an American courtroom." Darrow agreed: "It was a good argument . . . I have listened to great arguments and have made many arguments myself, and consider that my judgement on the subject is sound."[60]

The jury was out for only thirty-four minutes before returning a verdict of not guilty. In an extraordinary act, the judge was one of the first to congratulate Darrow. Soon after the verdict Darrow sailed to San Francisco to speak to a Labor Day rally attended by 35,000 people. In some respect labor had forgiven him.[61]

Darrow was not cleared, however. He had to endure a second trial which ended with a hung jury. Eventually that indictment was dropped.

The question of whether Darrow did attempt to bribe a juror has created a dispute since his trial. His biographers have thoroughly explored the issue, but there seems to be no definitive answer. One conclusion cannot be disputed: with the end of the second trial Darrow's days as a labor lawyer were over.

On his return to Chicago he had no business, and no one wished to go into practice with him:

> My prolonged absence from Chicago was enough in itself to destroy my business. I had to begin anew. But then, I was already known and had a wide acquaintance. I did not sit in my office only to wait for some one to bring me a good fee; any one who came inside my door was welcome; whether he had money or not was of small concern. Neither then nor at any other time in my life did I go after business. I simply took it as it came, and the criminal courts and the jails are always crowded with the poor.[62]

In order to earn money he signed up for a series of Chautauqua appearances. He came to rely on such appearances for the rest of his life.

Although he had few clients, eventually his comeback led to even more fame. Over time, through no plan, he moved from labor lawyer to defender of criminals and his best known cases, the defense of Leopold and Loeb and the Scopes monkey trial, were in his future.

NOTES

1. Kevin Tierney, <u>Darrow: A Biography</u> (New York: Thomas Y. Crowell, 1979), p. 131.
2. Tierney, <u>Darrow</u>, p. 150.
3. Tierney, <u>Darrow</u>, pp. 103-104.
4. George M. Pullman, quoted in Irving Stone, <u>Clarence Darrow for the Defense</u> (Garden City, N.Y.: Doubleday, Inc., 1941), pp. 43, 54; George F. Baer, quoted in Arthur Weinberg and Lila Weinberg, <u>Clarence Darrow: A Sentimental Rebel</u> (New York: G. P. Putman's Sons, 1980), p. 91.
5. Tierney, <u>Darrow</u>, p. 106.
6. Darrow, quoted in Weinberg and Weinberg, <u>Clarence Darrow</u>, pp. 340, 81-82.
7. Tierney, <u>Darrow</u>, pp. 77, 60-61; Clarence Darrow, <u>The Story of My Life</u> (New York: Charles Scribner's Sons, 1934), p. 62.
8. Darrow, <u>The Story of My Life</u>, pp. 60-61; Tierney, <u>Darrow</u>, pp. 103, 107-108.
9. Darrow, quoted in Weinberg and Weinberg, <u>Clarence Darrow</u>, p. 58.
10. Darrow, quoted in Stone, <u>Clarence Darrow for the Defense</u>, p. 58.
11. Tierney, <u>Darrow</u>, pp. 107, 112.
12. Weinberg and Weinberg, <u>Clarence Darrow</u>, pp. 64-65.
13. Tierney, <u>Darrow</u>, p. 148.
14. Stone, <u>Clarence Darrow for the Defense</u>, p. 103.
15. Darrow, <u>The Story of My Life</u>, pp. 74-75.
16. Tierney, <u>Darrow</u>, pp. 149, 152-53.
17. Darrow, quoted in Weinberg and Weinberg, <u>Clarence Darrow</u>, p. 78.
18. Stone, <u>Clarence Darrow for the Defense</u>, pp. 109-10.
19. Tierney, <u>Darrow</u>, p. 153-54; William Dean Howells, quoted in Stone, <u>Clarence Darrow for the Defense</u>, p. 107; Darrow, quoted in Tierney, <u>Darrow</u>, pp. 155-56.
20. Darrow, quoted in Stone, <u>Clarence Darrow for the Defense</u>, pp. 110-11, 112.

21. Stone, <u>Clarence Darrow for the Defense</u>, p. 112.

22. Tierney, <u>Darrow</u>, p. 228.

23. Stone, <u>Clarence Darrow for the Defense</u>, p. 128.

24. Tierney, <u>Darrow</u>, p. 189.

25. Darrow, <u>The Story of My Life</u>, pp. 114-15; Clarence Darrow, "Strike, Arbitration," in <u>Attorney for the Damned</u>, ed. Arthur Weinberg (New York: Simon & Schuster, 1957), p. 337.

26. George F. Baer, quoted in Stone, <u>Clarence Darrow for the Defense</u>, p. 150; Darrow, "Strike, Arbitration," p. 351.

27. Darrow, "Strike, Arbitration," p. 345.

28. Darrow, quoted in Weinberg and Weinberg, <u>Clarence Darrow</u>, pp. 63, 103.

29. Darrow, quoted in Tierney, <u>Darrow</u>, p. 188.

30. Darrow, "Strike, Arbitration," pp. 347-48.

31. Darrow, "Strike, Arbitration," p. 332.

32. Darrow, <u>The Story of My Life</u>, p. 116.

33. Stone, <u>Clarence Darrow for the Defense</u>, p. 151; Weinberg and Weinberg, <u>Clarence Darrow</u>, p. 104.

34. Abe C. Ravitz and James N. Primm, <u>The Haywood Case</u> (San Francisco: Chandler Publishing Co., 1960), p. 1; Darrow, quoted in Weinberg and Weinberg, <u>Clarence Darrow</u>, p. 127; Darrow, <u>The Story of My Life</u>, pp. 151-52.

35. "Idaho's Great Trial About to Begin," <u>New York Times</u>, 21 April 1907, sec. 5, p. 5; Tierney, <u>Darrow</u>, p. 213.

36. Darrow, quoted in Oscar King Davis, "Haywood Defense Shrewdly Laid Out," <u>New York Times</u>, 25 June 1907, p. 2.

37. Darrow, quoted in David H. Grover, <u>Debaters and Dynamiters</u> (Corvallis: Oregon State University Press, 1964), p. 212.

38. Darrow, quoted in Tierney, <u>Darrow</u>, p. 223.

39. Clarence Darrow, "A Governor Is Murdered," in <u>Attorney for the Damned</u>, ed. Arthur Weinberg (New York: Simon & Schuster, 1957), p. 486.

40. Darrow, "A Governor Is Murdered," p. 487.

41. Quoted in Grover, <u>Debaters and Dynamiters</u>, pp. 224-25; Darrow, <u>The Story of My Life</u>, p. 153.

42. Stone, <u>Clarence Darrow for the Defense</u>, p. 262.

43. Darrow, <u>The Story of My Life</u>, p. 176, 180.

44. Darrow, <u>The Story of My Life</u>, pp. 180-181.

45. Darrow, <u>The Story of My Life</u>, p. 182.

46. Darrow, <u>The Story of My Life</u>, p. 185.

47. Darrow, quoted in Stone, <u>Clarence Darrow for the Defense</u>, pp. 306-307.

48. Darrow, quoted in Stone, <u>Clarence Darrow for the Defense</u>, p. 312.

49. Lincoln Steffens, quoted in Tierney, <u>Darrow</u>, p. 261.

50. Darrow, quoted in Tierney, <u>Darrow</u>, p. 261.

51. Darrow, quoted in Tierney, <u>Darrow</u>, p. 265.

52. Quoted in Stone, <u>Clarence Darrow for the Defense</u>, pp. 334-35.

53. Stone, <u>Clarence Darrow for the Defense</u>, p. 336.

54. Clarence Darrow, "They Tried to Get Me," in <u>Attorney for the Damned</u>, ed. Arthur Weinberg (New York: Simon & Schuster, 1957), p. 495.

55. Darrow, "They Tried to Get Me," p. 506.

56. Darrow, "They Tried to Get Me," p. 506.

57. Darrow, quoted in Weinberg and Weinberg, <u>Clarence Darrow</u>, p. 259.

58. Darrow, quoted in Tierney, <u>Darrow</u>, p. 268.

59. Darrow, "They Tried to Get Me," p. 530.

60. Darrow, "They Tried to Get Me," p. 531.

61. Weinberg and Weinberg, <u>Clarence Darrow</u>, p. 249.

62. Darrow, <u>The Story of My Life</u>, pp. 204-205.

3
The Old Lion:
Defending Leopold and Loeb

Although Darrow had an active career as a defense attorney after his bribery trials in 1911 and 1912, no trial seized the public's attention during that period of time as much as the Leopold-Loeb murder case in Chicago in 1924. The sensational nature of that trial captured national headlines, and the drama of the trial did much to build the Darrow myth: "Darrow received more national attention for his defense of Leopold and Loeb than for any of his previous cases." The combination of the Leopold-Loeb case and the Scopes trial the following year "assured his reputation as America's most famous attorney."[1]

Although much of Darrow's law practice was spent defending the poor and the downtrodden, he chose to defend Richard Loeb and Nathan Leopold, the sons of two prominent and wealthy families, for the murder of a fourteen-year-old neighbor, Bobby Franks. Although many questioned his acceptance of the case, the sensational nature of the trial gave Darrow a national platform from which to argue against the death penalty.

On the afternoon of May 21, 1924, Loeb (age eighteen) and Leopold (age nineteen) drove around their neighborhood looking for a young boy to murder. The choice of Bobby Franks was totally accidental. They offered Franks a ride and then beat him to death with a chisel. They dumped the body into a roadside culvert and then called the Franks family and faked a kidnapping by demanding a $10,000 ransom payment.

When Franks' body was discovered, a pair of eyeglasses with distinctive frames was found nearby. Those glasses led the police to Leopold. Faced with overwhelming evidence, the boys confessed to the crime.

Leopold and Loeb were seemingly unlikely killers. Both were brilliant students: Loeb had just graduated from the University of Michigan at age eighteen while Leopold had graduated from the University of Chicago and was attending law school. The boys had planned the murder to prove that they could commit a perfect crime.

The young criminals made their public image worse because neither of them seemed to feel any remorse or guilt for their actions. Loeb was quoted several weeks after the murder as saying, "I know I should feel sorry I killed that young boy and all that, but I just don't feel it. I didn't have much feeling about this from the first. That's why I could do it."[2]

Both of the young murderers underwent grueling examinations from alienists (as psychiatrists were called in the 1920s) in order to determine their mental state. Leopold was fascinated with the process of examination and eagerly participated, while Loeb was uninterested and really did not cooperate. The hearings in court later showed that the experts spent much more time talking with Leopold than Loeb: "The result has been a distorted and oversimplified picture of Richard Loeb. In the legend that would grow, Loeb is pictured as little more than a crude criminal, Leopold the evil genius. There was genius and criminality in both."[3]

Darrow was hesitant to take the case. He was sixty-seven years old, "plagued with rheumatism, neuralgia, and plain fatigue." He realized that his defense of two wealthy clients would be questioned. His critics argued that Darrow took the trial in order to make a large fee. His supporters saw the choice in a different light. He accepted the case, according to Hal Higdon, "not for any promise of wealth . . . but because he believed that in defending these two confessed killers, he would have a rare chance to strike a blow against capital punishment."[4]

Although Darrow had helped 102 other clients avoid the death penalty and had a national reputation as a defense attorney, he did not overwhelm his clients during their first meetings. Leopold described Darrow as one of the least impressive people he had ever met:

> The day was warm . . . and Darrow was wearing a light seersucker jacket. Nothing wrong with that, surely. Only this one looked as if he had slept in it. His shirt was wrinkled, too, and he must have had eggs for breakfast that morning. I could see the vestiges. Or perhaps he hadn't changed shirts since the day before. His tie was askew.
>
> He wore no hat, and his unruly shock of lusterless, almost mousy hair kept falling over his right eye. Impatiently, he'd brush it back with his hand. He looked for all the world like an innocent hayseed, a bumpkin who might have difficulty finding his way around the city. Could this scarecrow know anything about the law? He didn't look as if he knew much of anything.[5]

After observing Darrow over a period of time

and getting to know him personally, Leopold changed his mind. He then wrote Darrow a letter expressing his admiration. In part the letter said: "Intelligence has always been the one attribute of man that appealed to me more strongly than any other. And since you happen to possess more of it than any other man whom I have had the pleasure of meeting, this alone would cause me to bow down in abject hero worship." He went on to talk about the forty-six years of untiring effort that had led to the creation of Darrow's reputation, that his defense of numerous murderers had never led to a hanging verdict, that his life and actions had created a monument to his works and how now he "risks [his reputation] on a seemingly im-possible case. . . . Why does he do it? He does it for the sake of principles. Is this bravery? By God, if it isn't then the defi-nition of bravery ought to be revised. Nay, it is more than bravery, it is heroism."[6]

The "Trial of the Century" took "on the air of a Roman holiday." The murder case and upcoming trial remained the major news story in Chicago throughout the summer of 1924. On July 17 the Chicago Tribune launched a campaign to convince the public that the trial should be broadcast over its radio station, WGN. In order to create public pressure for such a broadcast, the paper asked its readers to vote on whether they felt that the trial should be broadcast. The public voted no. Even though the trial would not be broadcast, the papers continued to engage in "an orgy of sensation-alism" and "journalistic lynch law" in their coverage of the trial.[7]

Higdon described the first day of the trial:

> A bank of telegraph machines, especially equipped to transmit noiselessly and staffed by a dozen telegraph operators had been

installed.   .   .   .   the   court
accommodated   300   people.   Judge
[John]   Caverly   issued   200   pink
tickets   to   local   newsmen   and
correspondents for news agencies and
out-of-town   papers.   Reporters   had
traveled   to   Chicago   to   cover   the
hearing, but not all obtained access.
. . . Only seventy seats had been set
aside   for   the   public;   eager
spectators   would   contest   hotly   for
them each day.[8]

The sensational coverage of the trial can be
seen in how the first day was reported in one
paper:

The hangman's noose dangles in Judge
Caverly's courtroom.   It is just over
the heads of Leopold and Loeb.   Most
of the time these most talked about
of all criminals smile and seem to
feel pretty good.   Clarence Darrow,
chief counsel for the defense, paces
here and about like an old lion,
giving the noose a swift shove now
and again.   State's Attorney Crowe is
there like a panther, darting out to
put the noose where he thinks it
belongs, just over the heads of
Leopold and Loeb.[9]

On that first day of the trial on July 23,
"thousands of people" jammed "the sidewalk and
street trying to get in."   Darrow had to battle
his way through the crowd in order to enter the
courtroom.   Most of the seats in court were
occupied by lawyers and judges who had come to
hear "what they considered would be one of the
most interesting and dramatic trials of their
age."[10]

Numerous myths have grown up about this
dramatic trial.   The first major myth claims
that Darrow had a million dollars with which to
defend his clients.   That million dollars,

critics argued, made it possible for these two
rich boys to buy their way out of a death sentence.   Subsequent events proved this tale
false.

A more enduring myth was based on the impression that somehow Darrow was able to save
the boys from hanging through a clever use of
an insanity plea, a "psychiatric pardon."   In
reality, this was not the first case to use an
insanity plea, but "never before had evidence
of a defendant's mental condition been offered
to lessen a sentence. Such evidence had heretofore been used to show that a defendant was
insane, not responsible for his actions, and
thus not subject to punishment."   There was no
attempt to get the defendants set free, only to
keep them from being executed.   The trial was
based mainly on the mental condition of Leopold
and Loeb: "never before had there been so much
attention devoted to the workings of the mind,
the psychic motivation of men charged with
murder."[11]

Darrow's opening statement on July 21,
1924, provided the nation with a shock.   He
began by talking about the crime:

A death in any situation is horrible
. . . but when it comes to the question of murder, it is doubly horrible.   But there are degrees perhaps
of atrocity, and instead of this
being one of the worst of the atrocious character, it is perhaps one of
the least painful and of the smallest
inducement.   Bad, nevertheless, bad
enough of course, but anyone with any
experience of criminal trials knows
what it is to be branded, as it has
been repeatedly, as the greatest,
most important and atrocious killing
that ever happened in the State of
Illinois or in the United States.[12]

He said that the defense would not request that

the trial be removed from Chicago because "the same state of feeling exists in all the other counties" in Illinois. He went on "of course, this case has attracted very unusual attention on account of the wierd, uncanny and terrible nature of the homicide. There is in the public mind a feeling that in some manner the lawyers might succeed in getting these two defendants into an asylum and having them released."[13]

He admitted that a murder had been committed and that the crime was committed by Leopold and Loeb, but he added, "We shall insist in this case, your honor, that, terrible as this is, terrible as any killing is, it would be without precedent if two boys of this age should be hanged by the neck until dead, and it would in no way bring back Robert Franks or add to the peace and security of this community." Because the boys were defective, "we want to state frankly here that no one in this case believes that these defendants should be released or are competent to be. . . . We believe that they should be permanently isolated from society and if we as lawyers thought otherwise their families would not permit us to do otherwise." Then he dropped a verbal bomb on the court: "after long reflection and thorough discussion . . . we have determined to make a motion in this court for each of the defendants in each of the cases to withdraw our plea of not guilty and enter a plea of guilty."[14]

Darrow then noted that when a defendant pleads guilty, the judge has the decision on the nature and length of the sentence. He apologized to the court: "Your honor . . . we dislike to throw this burden upon this court or any court. We know its seriousness and its gravity, but a court can no more shirk responsibilities than attorneys. And while we wish it could be otherwise, we feel that it must be as we have chosen." The defense then asked for

permission to give evidence of the mental conditions of the defendants, "to present evidence
of their youth, and to have pleas of guilty
taken into consideration as grounds for mitigating the punishment."[15]

The prosecution was outraged, claiming
that Darrow could not both plead the boys
guilty and then prove their insanity. Judge
Caverly ruled that he would listen to evidence
from both sides: "I want to get all the
doctors' testimony about the boys I can. There
is no jury here and I'd like to be advised as
fully as possible."[16]

Even though Leopold and Loeb had pleaded
guilty, the prosecution presented a detailed
case, attempting to emphasize the brutality of
the crime. As Robert E. Crowe explained, "I
want to show their guilt clearly and conclusively, and the details of it, and ask that they
be hanged. I don't think I ought to be limit-
ed." He stated that "there is but one punishment that will satisfy the prosecution--that
they be hanged." The judge allowed him to
present his evidence in detail.[17]

Darrow described the defense's actions
during the hearing: "Whatever undue length of
time was consumed was caused by the State, and
we offered no evidence of any kind on the subject. On the other hand, the State put in all
the evidence of the killing with the greatest
minuteness and detail. None of these witnesses
were cross-examined."[18]

In his summation speech Crowe viciously
attacked the defendants, calling them perverts,
murderers, and kidnappers. His associate,
Joseph Savage, continued in the same vein in
his summation: "you have before you one of the
most cold-blooded, cruel, cowardly, dastardly
murders that was ever tried in the history of
any court. . . . it is an insult in a case of
this kind to come before the bar of justice and
beg for mercy." Not only did the prosecution

attack Leopold and Loeb, but they also questioned Darrow and his beliefs. Crowe stated:
"I want to tell you the real defense in this
case, your honor. . . . It is Clarence Darrow's
dangerous philosophy of life. . . . He said he
was looking to the future, that he was thinking
of the ten thousand young boys who in the future would fill the chairs his clients filled
and he wants to soften the law. He wants them
treated not with the severity that the law of
this state prescribes, but he wants them repaid
with kindness and consideration." He appealed
to the judge not to accept Darrow's views because such an acceptance would strike "a greater blow to our institutions than by a hundred,
yes, a thousand murders."[19]

On August 22, "a mob greater than any
other that had appeared during the previous
month" attempted to gain access to to court to
hear Darrow speak. The Daily News reported
that the "tidal wave of men and women swept
over and flattened a skirmish line of bailiffs
at the main entrance and poured up the stairs
and elevators, sweeping all obstacles away."
Two women were knocked down and trampled. The
judge had to fight to enter his own courtroom.
A little after 2:00 Clarence Darrow, "wearing
an alpaca suit and a white tie," began his
speech. He was unable to continue, however,
because of the noise. Once he was finally able
to proceed, he spoke for two hours before court
was adjourned for the day. Nathan Leopold
wrote about Darrow's speech: "That address came
through Clarence Darrow's mouth straight from
his heart. Into it he distilled a half century's penetrating observation and a half
century's profound reflection. Mr. Darrow was
pleading not so much for Dick and me as he was
pleading for the human race. For love, for
charity, for understanding. Especially for
understanding."[20]

On the next day Darrow completed his

speech. His presentation on that day has been
described in detail:

> The   newspapers   would   describe
> Darrow's summation that day as
> brilliant and bearing the marks of
> careful preparation. Lawyers who had
> followed his career would consider it
> his finest speech. The attorney had
> hinted to friends that he planned to
> make this the last speech of his
> career as a trial lawyer. He pres-
> ented a picturesque figure, this old
> warrior of the courtroom, his coat
> hung   shapelessly   over   his   bent
> shoulders, folding and unfolding his
> arms, sticking his thumbs into his
> vest pockets, wagging a forefinger to
> emphasize certain points, moving back
> and forth in the small arena between
> spectators and judge, turning now and
> then toward the former, then pivoting
> swiftly to address his audience of
> one, Judge Caverly. . . . The judge,
> hand   propped   beneath   his   chin,
> followed every word.[21]

Darrow's speech those two days contained many
of his standard arguments as well as ones
unique to this hearing. As in most previous
summation speeches, he attacked the opposition
personally. He first went after Crowe: "I
cannot   understand   the   glib,   lighthearted
carelessness of lawyers who talk of hanging two
boys as if they were taking a holiday or
visiting the races." He continued: "I have
never seen a more deliberate effort to turn the
human beings of a community into ravening
wolves as has been made in this case, and to
take advantage of anything that they might get
every mind that has to do with it into a stage
of hatred against these boys."[22]

He then turned to Savage by using a play
on his name: "did you pick him for his name or

his ability or his learning?--because my friend
Mr. Savage, in as cruel a speech as he knew how
to make, said to this court that we pleaded
guilty because we were afraid to do anything
else."   He then summarized Savage's arguments
as "Cruel; dastardly; premeditated; fiendish;
abandoned and malignant heart--sounds like a
cancer--cowardly; cold-blooded!   Now that is
what I have listened to for three days against
two minors, two children who have no right to
sign a note or make a deed."   After all these
attacks Darrow said that he could not criticize
Savage because he "is young and enthusiastic.
But has he ever read anything?   Has he ever
thought?"[23]

Darrow also questioned the integrity of
one of the prosecution's alienists, Dr. Krohn.
He compared the actions of Dick Loeb to those
of Krohn: "for sixteen years going in and out
of the courtrooms of this building and other
buildings, trailing victims without regard to
the name or sex or age or surroundings. But he
had a motive, and his motive was cash, as I
will show further.   One had the mad act of a
child; the other the cold, deliberate act of a
man getting his living by dealing in blood."[24]

Darrow believed that the actions of the
prosecution added to the already intense public
clamor calling for the hanging of the defendants: "the position of the state's attorney is
that the universe will crumble unless these two
boys are hanged. I must say that I have never
before seen the same passion and enthusiasm for
the death penalty as I have seen in this case."
He admitted that the defense was concerned
about "the almost unheard-of publicity" that
the case had received: "newspapers all over
this country have been giving it space such as
they have almost never before given to any
case. . . . And when the public is interested
and demands a punishment, no matter what the
offense, great or small, it thinks of only one

punishment, and that is death."[25]

Much of his speech focused on why his clients should not be executed. He even apologized for the length of time he spent on the issue, but felt that his appeal might do some good: "If I can succeed, my greatest reward and my greatest hope will be that I have done something for the tens of thousands of other boys, for the countless unfortunates who must tread the same road; . . . that I have done something to help human understanding, to temper justice with mercy, to overcome hate with love."[26]

He appealed to Judge Caverly not to return to the past where people were hanged for numerous petty crimes. He then described the brutality of those earlier hangings: "You can read the stories of the hangings on a high hill, and the populace for miles around coming out to the scene that everybody might be awed into goodness. Hanging for picking pockets-- and more pockets were picked in the crowd that went to the hanging than had been known before. Hangings for murder--and men were murdered on the way there and on the way home."[27]

Darrow then appealed to the judge to look to the future, a future he described: "I know the future is with me, and what I stand for here; not merely for the lives of these two unfortunate lads, but for all boys and girls. . . . I am pleading for life, understanding, charity, kindness, and the infinite mercy that considers all. I am pleading that we overcome cruelty with kindness, and hatred with love. I know the future is on my side."[28]

He then drew a picture for the judge of what would happen if the judge returned to the cruel past and hanged the boys: "I can picture them, wakened in the gray light of morning, furnished a suit of clothes by the State, led to the scaffold, their feet tied, black gowns drawn over their heads, stood on a trap door, the hangman pressing a spring so that it gives way under them; I can see them fall through space--and stopped by the rope around their necks." To Darrow, such acts make the state bloodthirsty: "You may stand them up on the trap door of the scaffold, and choke them to death, but that act will be infinitely more cold-blooded, whether justified or not, than any act that these boys have committed or can commit." Rather, let the state "set an example in consideration, kindheartedness and tenderness before they call my clients cold-blooded."[29]

Ultimately, he argued, the deaths of Leopold and Loeb will not change anything: "Robert Franks is dead, and we cannot call him back to life." He admitted that the crime was a senseless one, but if "to hang these two boys would bring him back to life, I would say let them hang, and I believe their parents would say so, too. . . . Robert Franks is dead, and we cannot call him back to life. It was all over in fifteen minutes after he got into the car, and he probably never knew it or thought of it."[30]

If the state would not accept his plea for decency, Darrow suggested that the judge think of the youth of the defendants. He argued that youth must be seen as a mitigating factor: "we have all been young, and we know that fantasies and vagaries haunt the daily life of a child. . . . We know the condition of the mind of a child. Here are two boys who are minors. The law would forbid them making contracts, forbid them marrying without the consent of their parents, would not permit them to vote. Why? Because they haven't that judgement which only comes with years, because they are not fully responsible." In order to stress their youth, Darrow referred to Loeb as Dickie and Leopold by his boyhood nickname, Babe, in all his presentations.[31]

Darrow also described the motive for the killing as a reason for the state to reject the death penalty. Darrow believed that a person's heredity, plus the circumstances under which the individual was raised, determine his/her fate. This view denied that people have free will. As Irving Stone says:

> Under this philosophy there was no room for free will; a man acted according to his equipment with which he had been endowed and in accordance with the surroundings into which he had been plunged. If, then, there was no free will, there could be no praise or blame; no man was alone responsible for his acts: his ancestors were responsible, and the state of society in which he lived was responsible, and to punish a man for having a brain, a spirit, a character, a set of action impulses that had been determined for him by powers beyond his control, was stupid, wasteful, cruel and barbaric . . . . Yet Darrow knew that there were thousands of tiny and intricate reasons behind the crime, all of them woven into the character and environment of the killers, and that the causes would be intelligible once the world could be made to understand all of the contributing factors that had made these two human machines go haywire.[32]

Based on these beliefs, Darrow attempted to convince the judge that "Loeb and Leopold were two defective human machines which had somewhere broken down because of heredity or the pressure of external environment, if he could save their lives when all the world wanted them exterminated, might he not deal a deathblow to capital punishment?" He asked the

alienists to provide the justification. Darrow
argued that their justification stated that the
murder was caused by the interplay of these
flawed personalities.[33]

Darrow outlined how the alienists found
that Loeb had spent much of his early life
reading detective novels. Eventually he began
to fantasize about engaging in crime as the
leader of a gang--Leopold filled that role.
Leopold, on the other hand, had a slave-king
fantasy in which Loeb was the king. As Dr.
Hulbert summarized the interrelationship:

> Each boy felt inadequate to carry out
> the life he most desired unless he
> had someone else in his life to
> complement him, to complete him.
> Leopold . . . wanted a superior for a
> companion. Loeb . . . wanted someone
> to adulate him for a companion. Un-
> less these two boys had their own
> individual experiences in life, the
> present crime could never have been
> committed. . . . This friendship be-
> tween the two boys was not altogether
> a pleasant one to either of them.
> The ideas that each proposed to the
> other were repulsive. Their friend-
> ship was not based so much on desire
> as on need, they being what they
> were.[34]

Darrow dealt with this unhealthy interrelationship in his speech: "These boys, neither one of
them, could possibly have committed this act
excepting by coming together. . . . It was the
act of their planning, their conniving, their
believing in each other; their thinking themselves supermen." Without their relationship
and its needs, they could not have committed
such a brutal crime.[35]

Darrow then dealt with each of the boys
and their problems individually. He pointed
out how Loeb "early developed the tendency to

mix with crime, to be a detective; as a little boy shadowing people on the street; as a little child going out with his fantasy of being the head of a band of criminals and directing them on the street." Because all detective stories end with the detective winning and the criminal failing, Loeb wanted to be the one who outwitted all detectives, to commit a crime that could not be solved. Darrow believed that Loeb had not matured beyond these childish dreams: "It is when these dreams of boyhood, these fantasies of youth still linger, and the growing boy is still a child--a child in emotion, a child in feeling, a child in hallucinations--that you can say that it is the dreams and the hallucinations of childhood that are responsible for his conduct."[36]

Even though Loeb did commit the crime, Darrow did not believe he was responsible for his actions: "Is he to blame that his machine is imperfect? Who is to blame? I do not know. . . . I am not wise enough to fix it. I know that somewhere in the past that entered into him something missed. It may be defective nerves. It may be a defective heart or liver. It may be defective endocrine glands. I know it is something. I know that nothing happens in this world without a cause."[37]

He then turned to Leopold, arguing that his extensive reading was a cause for the crime. He read the works on Nietzsche and became enamored of them: "'Here is a boy who by day and by night, in season and out, was talking of the superman, owing no obligations to anyone; whatever gave him pleasure he should do, believing it just as another man might believe a religion or any philosophical theory." He also described Leopold as having a brilliant mind, "a sort of freak in this direction . . . a boy without emotions, a boy obsessed of philosophy, a boy obsessed of learning, busy every minute of his life." But

that brilliance left him as "just a half-boy,
an intellect, an intellectual machine going
without balance and without a governor, seeking
to find out everything there was in life intellectually; seeking to solve every philosophy
but using his intellect only."[38]

To Darrow these maladjusted boys committed
a crime with no motive. The prosecution argued
that the boys had murdered Bobby Franks for the
$10,000 they had hoped to get from faking a
kidnapping. Darrow scoffed at such motives,
but admitted the prosecution's case needed some
motive: "It could not stand up a minute without
motive. Without it, it was the senseless act
of immmature and diseased children, as it was;
a senseless act of children, wandering around
in the dark and moved by some emotion that we
still perhaps have not the knowledge or the
insight into life to understand thoroughly."
He posed a question: "these two boys, neither
of whom needed a cent, scions of wealthy
people, killed this little inoffensive boy to
get ten thousand dollars?" He refused to
believe that the boys needed money to pay off
gambling debts as the prosecution charged.[39]

Ultimately, he summarized what he believed
was the motive for the killing:

Not for money, not for spite, not for
hate. They killed him as they might
kill a spider or a fly, for the
experience. They killed him because
they were made that way. Because
somewhere in the infinite processes
that go to the making up of the boy
or the man something slipped, and
those unfortunate lads sit here
hated, despised, outcasts, with the
community shouting for their blood.[40]

He saw the boys' wealth as a cause of the
crime. Their wealth had corrupted them as
surely as the slums had caused poor boys to
commit crimes. He appealed to the judge to

forget the wealth and simply treat them as he would any other boys: "had this been the case of two boys of these defendants' ages, unconnected with families supposed to have great wealth, there is not a state's attorney in Illinois who would not have consented at once to a plea of guilty and a punishment in the penitentiary for life. Not one." Ultimately he hoped that Judge Caverly would be able to get past the boys' wealth and make a decision against capital punishment:

> Your Honor, it may be hardly fair to the court; I am aware that I have helped to place a serious burden upon your shoulders. . . . I know perfectly well that where responsiblity is divided by twelve, it is easy to say: "Away with him." But, Your Honor, if these boys hang, you must do it. There can be no division of responsibility here. You can never explain that the rest overpowered you. It must be by your deliberate, cool, premeditated act, without a chance to shift responsibility.[41]

Darrow attempted to appeal to the judge on an emotional level by using the boys' age as a mitigating circumstance and by looking for legal precedents. He pointed to previous cases where defendants had pleaded guilty: "Three hundred and forty murder cases in ten years with a plea of Guilty in this country. All the young who pleaded Guilty, every one of them-- three hundred and forty in ten years with one hanging on a plea of Guilty--and that a man forty years of age. And yet they say we come here with a preposterous plea for mercy. When did any plea for mercy become preposterous in any tribunal in all the universe?"[42]

Darrow had more difficulty arguing that psychiatric testimony could be used as a mitigating factor in determining sentence. There was no precedent upon which to base the argument--this case would establish precedent. The arguments in the case therefore made legal history.

Above and beyond the legal arguments, Darrow had to counteract the belief that he had spent millions in the defense. More than once in the speech he spoke on the theme:

It was announced that there were millions of dollars to be spent on this case. Wild and extravagant stories were freely published as though they were facts. Here was to be an effort to save the lives of two boys by the use of money in fabulous amounts, amounts such as these families never even had.

We announced to the public that no excessive use of money would be made in this case, neither for lawyers nor for psychiatrists, nor in any other way. We have faithfully kept that promise.[43]

The speech lasted for two days. In his autobiography Darrow gave his view of the speech:

I endeavored in my address to make a plain, straightforward statement of the facts in the case, and I meant to apply such knowledge as we now have of the motives that move men. The argument took the largest part of two court days and was printed almost word for word in some of the Chicago papers, and very extensively by the press outside that city, so that people at the time were fairly familiar with the facts in the case, and certainly of the outcome. When I closed I had exhausted all the strength I could summon. From that day I have never gone through so protracted a strain, and could never do it again, even if I should try.[44]

One of Darrow's biographers, Kevin Tierney, described the speech's effect: "Darrow, the judge, and many in the audience were crying. Darrow had taken the case far beyond the bounds of reason and logic, moving his listeners to a pity for the human race as a whole. It was his most masterly oration, rousing his audience to display emotion openly beyond what the conventions allowed." A correspondent for the Chicago Herald-Examiner wrote: "there was scarcely any telling where his voice had finished and where silence had begun. Silence lasted a minute, two minutes. His own eyes, dimmed by years of serving the accused, the oppressed, the weak, were not the only ones that held tears."[45]

Two weeks later Judge Caverly announced that he would sentence the boys to life in prison rather than death: "In choosing imprisonment instead of death, the court is moved chiefly by the consideration of the age of the defendants, boys of eighteen and nineteen years." He explained that "life imprisonment may not, at the moment, strike the public imagination as forcible as would death by hanging; but to the offenders, particularly of the type they are, the prolonged suffering of years of confinement may well be the most severe form of retribution and expiation." Leopold later commented: "If Judge Caverly meant literally what he said in his opinion, the whole elaborate psychiatric defense presented in our behalf and the herculean efforts of our brilliant counsel were to no avail. The only thing that influenced him to choose imprisonment instead of death was our youth; we need only have introduced our birth certificates in evidence." Darrow commented: "I have always hated capital punishment. This decision at once caps my career as a criminal lawyer and starts my path in another direction.

. . . Perhaps the sentence is worse than a death penalty for the two boys, but not for their families."[46]

Even after the trial was over it continued to attract attention. The legend of the million dollars Darrow supposedly received continued to be discussed. More than a year later, Darrow received a check for $70,000--he kept half. Although Darrow complained, "it was probably a larger fee than he had received for any of his previous cases."[47]

Because of the immense attention surrounding the trial, the defendants continued to attract attention long after they went to jail. Each year the press would renew the story on the anniversary of their confinement to prison, kept track of the jobs they had in prison, and reported each time they were transferred between prisons--it was a story that would not go away. The case again gained national attention when on January 28, 1936, Loeb was killed by another prisoner named James E. Day. Although the events surrounding the death are not clear, Day claimed that Loeb made homosexual advances. Those charges again made sensational news. A writer for the Chicago Daily News, "in writing about the murder, began with what many newspapermen consider the classic lead paragraph of all time: 'Richard Loeb, a brilliant college student and master of the English language, today ended a sentence with a proposition.'"[48]

Leopold remained in prison until 1958. He spent the rest of his life as a laboratory technician in a Puerto Rican hospital. He died in 1971. Although he remained in prison for an extended period, "everything that Leopold [did was] front-page news." While in prison Leopold wrote an autobiography detailing his part in the crime and his life in prison. In that book he openly admitted his remorse for having killed Bobby Franks.[49]

One further example of the continued interest was the publication of the novel <u>Compulsion</u> by Meyer Levin which details the crime and trial in fictional form. The book was a best seller, selling over a million copies in a paperback edition. The book became a Broadway play and a movie, thus maintaining and even building the myth.

Even today the "Crime of the Century" and Darrow's role in it are of great interest. The sensational events, the lurid coverage by the media, and the brilliance of the rhetoric have made the trial an integral part of American legal history. Darrow hoped the trial would be his final one but within a year he was again at the center of a national trial--this time in Tennessee and the issue was the teaching of evolution by an obscure teacher named John Scopes.

NOTES
1. Hal Higdon, <u>The Crime of the Century</u> (New York: G. P. Putnam's Sons, 1975), p. 273.
2. Richard Loeb, quoted in Higdon, <u>The Crime of the Century</u>, p. 141.
3. Higdon, <u>The Crime of the Century</u>, pp. 219-20.
4. Higdon, <u>The Crime of the Century</u>, pp. 123-24.
5. Nathan Leopold, quoted in Higdon, <u>The Crime of the Century</u>, p. 131.
6. Nathan Leopold, <u>Life Plus 99 Years</u> (New York: Popular Library, 1958), p. 56.
7. Higdon, <u>The Crime of the Century</u>, pp. 158-171.
8. Higdon, <u>The Crime of the Century</u>, p. 169.
9. Quoted in Higdon, <u>The Crime of the Century</u>, p. 181.
10. Irving Stone, <u>Clarence Darrow for the Defense</u> (Garden City, N.Y.: Doubleday, 1941), pp. 405-406.
11. Kevin Tierney, <u>Darrow: A Biography</u> (New York: Thomas Y. Crowell, Publishers, 1979), p.

347; Higdon, _The Crime of the Century_, pp. 164-65; Arthur Weinberg and Lila Weinberg, _Clarence Darrow: A Sentimental Rebel_ (New York: G. P. Putnam's Sons, 1980), pp. 300-301.

12. Darrow, quoted in Higdon, _The Crime of the Century_, p. 174.

13. Darrow, quoted in Higdon, _The Crime of the Century_, p. 162.

14. Darrow, quoted in Higdon, _The Crime of the Century_, pp. 163-74.

15. Darrow, quoted in Higdon, _The Crime of the Century_, p. 165.

16. Judge Caverly, quoted in Stone, _Clarence Darrow for the Defense_, p. 405.

17. Robert E. Crowe, quoted in Higdon, _The Crime of the Century_, p. 180.

18. Clarence Darrow, _The Story of My Life_ (New York: Charles Scribner's Sons, 1932), p. 238.

19. Joseph Savage and Robert E. Crowe, quoted in Higdon, _The Crime of the Century_, pp. 232, 247.

20. Quoted in Higdon, _The Crime of the Century_, pp. 234, 237.

21. Higdon, _The Crime of the Century_, p. 235.

22. Darrow, quoted in Higdon, _The Crime of the Century_, p. 192.

23. Clarence Darrow, "The Crime of Compulsion," in _Attorney for the Damned_, ed. Arthur Weinberg (New York: Simon & Schuster, 1957), pp. 23, 25, 49.

24. Darrow, "The Crime of Compulsion," p. 39.

25. Darrow, quoted in Higdon, _The Crime of the Century_, p. 191.

26. Darrow, "The Crime of Compulsion," p. 87.

27. Darrow, "The Crime of Compulsion," p. 50.

28. Darrow, "The Crime of Compulsion," p. 86.

29. Darrow, "The Crime of Compulsion," pp. 42-43; 26.

30. Darrow, "The Crime of Compulsion," p. 28.

31. Darrow, quoted in Higdon, _The Crime of the Century_, p. 191.

32. Stone, _Clarence Darrow for the Defense_, p. 383.

33. Darrow, quoted in Stone, <u>Clarence Darrow for the Defense</u>, p. 383.
34. Dr. Hulbert, quoted in Higdon, <u>The Crime of the Century</u>, p. 225.
35. Darrow, "The Crime of Compulsion," p. 77.
36. Darrow, "The Crime of Compulsion," pp. 60-61.
37. Darrow, "The Crime of Compulsion," p. 55.
38. Darrow, "The Crime of Compulsion," pp. 72-73, 69.
39. Darrow, "The Crime of Compulsion," pp. 33, 30.
40. Darrow, "The Crime of Compulsion," pp. 34-35.
41. Darrow, "The Crime of Compulsion," p. 24.
42. Darrow, "The Crime of Compulsion," pp. 48-49.
43. Darrow, "The Crime of Compulsion," p. 20.
44. Darrow, <u>The Story of My Life</u>, p. 242.
45. Tierney, <u>Darrow</u>, p. 342; quoted in Stone, <u>Clarence Darrow for the Defense</u>, p. 417.
46. Judge John Caverly, quoted in Weinberg and Weinberg, <u>Clarence Darrow</u>, p. 312; Nathan Leopold, quoted in Higdon, <u>The Crime of the Century</u>, pp. 266-67.
47. Higdon, <u>The Crime of the Century</u>, p. 274.
48. Higdon, <u>The Crime of the Century</u>, p. 298.
49. Introduction by Erle Stanley Gardner in Nathan Leopold, <u>Life Plus 99 Years</u> (Garden City, N.Y.: Doubleday, 1958), p. 15.

4

Educating the Masses:
Darrow in Tennessee

Although Darrow talked of retirement after the Leopold and Loeb hearing, within a year he found himself involved in a sensational trial in the small town of Dayton, Tennessee. That dramatic trial grew out of the simple indictment of a teacher named John Thomas Scopes for unlawfully teaching "a certain theory or theories that denied the story of the divine creation of man as taught in the Bible, but did teach thereof, that man is descended from a lower order of animals."[1]

The indictment brought before the nation a debate that had been simmering in the South for many years. For a variety of social and economic reasons, a movement had arisen against the teaching of evolution in public schools. In April 1925 the American Civil Liberties Union (ACLU) released a survey that showed that "more restrictive laws had been passed in the preceding six months than at any time in the country's history." Statutes were passed that "banned the teaching of evolution, or required daily Bible reading in the schools, or forbade the employment of radical or pacifist teachers."[2]

In 1920, after William Jennings Bryan had joined the fray, the movement gained energy. Bryan traveled throughout the country speaking in favor of laws that defined the content of education. People united behind Bryan's proclamation that "the hand that writes the pay check rules the school." By 1923, Oklahoma and Florida banned the teaching of evolution in schools.[3]

As "a close observer of the American scene," Darrow was aware of these events. He observed that Bryan's message was particularly powerful in rural communities "because they were isolated from modern science and industry, because they were dependent on farming and thus likely to be dubious of the powers of human reason to solve ultimate problems--were especially subject to fundamentalism." Darrow characterized Bryan's actions during this period of time: "Bryan travelled from town to town talking against evolution, and condemning the 'infidel universities.' Some years before that he had moved from Nebraska to Florida. During the hectic days when he was campaigning to 'save the children' from getting an education . . . he was working for the 'Coral Gables Land Association' in Miami, Fla., making speeches at noon every day when the tourist crop was there, to induce investors to buy Florida real estate."[4]

The Tennessee law was sponsored by John Washington Butler, a member of the Tennessee legislature, "a modestly prosperous farmer," and "a devout man who had raised his five children on the letter of the King James Bible." In 1922, Butler heard a sermon in which the preacher told the story of a young woman "who had gone to the university and returned home believing that, instead of God creating men, he was descended from a lower order of animals." That sermon upset Butler and eventually led to his introducing a bill prohibiting the teaching of evolution in Tennessee schools. The bill made it through the legislature because the members did not dare oppose it, believing that the governor would veto it. The governor signed the bill on March 21, 1925, thinking it would never be enforced.[5]

In his autobiography Scopes described a speech by Bryan in favor of the anti-evolution bill: "His topic--'Is the Bible True'--surprised no one. His answer to that question surprised even fewer persons; the Bible was one issue on which he was never a fence straddler. Every word of the Bible was true, he argued persuasively in his best oratorical form; this gave great encouragement to the rural folk who made up the Bible Belt.   Some of the Fundamentalists printed copies of the speech and sent it to Tennessee's lawgivers."   Scopes argued that the speech had a definite effect on the eventual passage of the bill.[6]

The American Civil Liberties Union was concerned that other states would follow Tennessee's actions, so it advertised that the group would economically and legally support a test of the constitutionality of the law.   Soon thereafter George Rappelyea, an executive of a local coal company, and a group of friends met in a drug store in Dayton.   At that meeting they decided to test the law while bringing a great deal of publicity to the town.   Scopes agreed to be the defendant.   Later Scopes stated: "I don't know what Rappelyea's personal motives were.   But I am convinced that he must have had a special reason for getting the case started.   Possibly he hoped to open up the Tennessee coal business with some new industry as a result.   I didn't see how he could gain by the trial; at the same time I knew him well enough to realize he wouldn't have done the things he did if he hadn't had an angle."[7]

The Dayton group contacted the ACLU, which responded by telegraph, "we will co-operate Scopes case with financial help, legal advice and publicity."   William Jennings Bryan, three times a candidate for president and a former secretary of state, volunteered to lead the prosecution, even though he had not practiced law for thirty-six years.   For the first time in his life Darrow volunteered his services, even offering to pay his own expenses.   In his autobiography Darrow described his entrance into the trial:

In less than a year after the ending of the Loeb-Leopold case, a most uncommon series of events brought me even wider notice than any that had happened before. I cannot say that in this case I had nothing to do with the immediate cause of all the publicity. For the first, the last, the only time in my life I volunteered my services in a case; it was in the Scopes case in Tennessee that I did this because I really wanted to take part.[8]

There was much discussion among ACLU leaders as to whether or not to accept Darrow's offer. Ultimately, Scopes argued that Dayton would be filled with "screwballs, con men, and characters. It is going to be a gouging, roughhouse battle. . . . If it's going to be a gutter fight, I'd rather have a good gutter fighter," and that fighter was Darrow.[9]

Once the momentous battle between Bryan and Darrow was announced, the trial attracted immense interest. Dayton hoped to capitalize on the interest. The town's businessmen printed a pamphlet called Why Dayton of All Places? that had pictures of the town and listed all its main industries. The courthouse was repaired and painted. There was a concern that hotels would not be able to accommodate all the visitors. The United Press even incorrectly "reported that the trial would be held in a ball park where 10,000 persons could be seated" and that "Judge Raulston had agreed to have brief daily sessions of court in order to keep the extra customers in town longer."[10]

The trial in Dayton was to be "a duel to the death" in Bryan's words, but it was the culmination of a long battle of words between Darrow and Bryan. The two combatants had first met at the Democratic Convention in 1896. Darrow was in the audience when Bryan delivered

his famous "Cross of Gold" speech.   In his
autobiography Darrow described the scene that
day:

> In a few moments he had the attention
> of the great audience of twenty or
> twenty-five thousand that crowded the
> hall. . . . he was a master of
> technique; he knew exactly how to
> hold an audience in the hollow of his
> hand. . . . His voice, his person-
> ality, his knowledge of mob psycho-
> logy, his aptness for forming rhyth-
> mical sentences left him without a
> rival in the field. . . . I have
> enjoyed a great many addresses, some
> of which I have delivered myself, but
> I never listened to one that affected
> or moved an audience as that did.[11]

Although Darrow supported Bryan, he soon began
to see Bryan as a shallow individual with no
vision.   A few months after Bryan's election
defeat in 1896 Darrow confronted and pleaded
with   Bryan   to   "study   science,   history,
philosophy   .   .   .   and   quit   this   village
religious stuff. . . . You're head of the party
before you are ready and a leader should lead
with thought."   Kevin Tierney described their
conversation on that day as "the first skirmish
of a lifelong feud."[12]

In 1923 Bryan offered a hundred dollars to
anyone who would "sign an affidavit to the
effect that he was personally descended from an
ape."   He made that proposal in a letter

Darrow supported Bryan for president again
in 1900, but refused to support him in 1908.
Darrow watched as Bryan turned more and more to
religion as a means of building his power and
importance in the country.   He became more and
more concerned as Bryan worked to "organize the
Southern states into a solid anti-evolution
bloc" which could "accomplish an irreparable
harm."[13]

In 1923 Bryan offered a hundred dollars to
anyone who would "sign an affidavit to the
effect that he was personally descended from an
ape."   He made that proposal in a letter

attacking science to the <u>Chicago Tribune</u>.
Because of Bryan's fame, the letter was
published on the front page.   Darrow immediately responded with a letter in which he
"posed fifty questions at Bryan in an attempt
to find out whether Bryan thought the biblical
account of the creation of earth and of life
literally true or a poetic allegory."   Bryan
responded: "I decline to turn aside to enter
into controversy with those who reject the
Bible as Mr. Darrow does."   Two years later he
was forced to answer most of those questions on
the witness stand during the trial at Dayton.[14]

As the trial approached, the level of
excitement rose in Dayton.   Huge signs saying
"Sweetheart, Come to Jesus," "God Is Love,"
"Read Your Bible," "You Need God in Your
Business," and "Where Will You Spend Eternity?"
lined the streets.   Hot dog and lemonade stands
were opened; preachers set up tents and
"exhorted the passers-by to repent and come to
Jesus."   An article in <u>The New Republic</u>
described the scene:

> Religion, basic Bible religion, is
> the big thing in this country--the
> religion of the camp meetings and of
> the queer, violent acrobatic sects,
> creeds and faiths, all based on
> literal Bible beliefs.   The whole
> region is saturated with religion.
> Nine tenths of the people are steeped
> in it.   It is their mode of recre-
> ation as well as their means of re-
> demption, their single emotional
> outlet, the one relief from the
> deadly drabness of cut-off existence.
> It is a literal fact that, so far as
> the great bulk of the people are
> concerned, a religion, the rigidity
> of which it is difficult to exag-
> gerate, absorbs all the thought they
> have aside from their work.   In

> Dayton religion takes the place of
> golf, bridge, music, art, literature,
> the theatre, dancing, clubs.   Take
> religion away, and the desolation and
> distress would be pitiable to
> contemplate.[15]

The press focused on the sensational aspects of
religion:

> Rough wooden benches semi-circled the
> elms.   And crude teapots with fat
> white wicks crammed into their snouts
> blew opal flame into the silver of
> the moonlight night.   Night things
> all about.   The screech of the
> bobcat. . . . A whir of bats' wings,
> and the staccato of insects. . . .
> Testifying began.   An old woman of
> seventy, her gray hair straggling
> over her lean, semi-bronzed face.
> Hands at her hips, she twisted her
> sharp-boned old body into girations,
> touched the ground, shrieked and
> moaned.   Ma Ferguson "speaks with
> tongues" and testifies with strange
> and stirring words.[16]

Not all people in the community were
religious fanatics.   Darrow considered some
individuals he met in Dayton to be enlightened.
For example, there was a group that discussed
new books, and other progressive thinkers were
common in the community.

With the interest running high in the
trial, news coverage was intense.   All the wire
services were represented, two movie cameramen
and reporters were available, telegraph wires
were run, and radio equipment was installed.
The Chicago radio station WGN "covered the
trial for the express purpose of being the
first organization to make a national hookup.
It was the first remote-control broadcast,
originating in Dayton, thence to Chicago, and
from there to the nation via the radio network.

During the trial an average of 165,000 words a day--a total of two million words--were filed by telegraph.[17]

Dayton's image was not helped by the tone of the reporting. As one resident stated: "We didn't get the kind of publicity we expected out of it and I can't see that the kind we got did Dayton any good." Particularly damaging were the dispatches of H. L. Mencken of the Baltimore Sun who referred to local citizens as "morons," "hillbillies," and "peasants." His dispatches were about "degraded nonsense which country preachers are ramming and hammering into yokel skulls." Darrow described the coverage: "Most of the newspapers treated the whole case as a farce instead of a tragedy, but they did give it no end of publicity. Not only was every paper of importance in America represented, but those of many foreign lands."[18]

This whole controversy was set off by an unlikely individual, John T. Scopes. Darrow described Scopes as a "modest, studious, conscientious lad" who was a good teacher, well respected by the community. Like Darrow, Scopes had been reared by a free-thinking father. Like Darrow, his father's views rubbed off his thinking. Although Scopes became the defendant through an accident of circumstances, he firmly believed in evolution. He and Darrow were a well-matched pair. At one point Scopes even said that Darrow was the second most influential person in his life after his father.[19]

His enthusiasm for his attorney was obvious in Scopes' descriptions of Darrow. Scopes had wanted Darrow as his lawyer because the trial "was going to be a down-in-the-mud fight and I felt the situation demanded an Indian fighter rather than someone who had graduated from the proper military academy." Scopes described Darrow as "a big man, large-boned with a large head and peering blue eyes set deep under an often-frowning forehead. . . . He drawled comfortably and hadn't any airs.   He gave the impression he might have grown up in Dayton, just an unpolished, casual country lawyer, so ordinary did he act."   Although Scopes described him as a casual individual, Darrow was much different as a lawyer:

> Darrow's manner was easygoing and relaxed, almost casual.   Behind the facade of laziness operated a first-class mind always working at top speed and efficiency; on his feet he was a master of phrase-making. Afterward, it was hard to remember his precise gestures and actions in the courtroom, because one listened carefully to what he said and observed less what he did. He kept his thumbs in his colorful galluses most of the time and his gestures, rather than being motions of his arms and hands, were made with his head and shoulders. He would nod his head, he would hunch or slump his shoulders, he would thrust his face toward the court.   It was a central characteristic of Darrow that he engaged his listeners' minds, not their eyes.[20]

To Scopes, Darrow was first and foremost a teacher: "any good teacher must have an open mind, ready always to acknowledge the truth of a changed situation.   Skeptic that he was on most things, Darrow was willing to change his mind anytime there was sufficient cause for him to do so."[21]

The descriptions of Bryan also painted the picture of a powerful, successful individual. Ray Ginger described him thusly: "[a] magnificently handsome man, possessed of a voice like an organ, he was adept at caressing a crowd with the sin they loath so much."   His great popularity as an orator had made him a

relatively wealthy individual who lived in
comfort in Florida. During the winter he spoke
at noon each day to the tourists in Coral
Gables about the "advantages and pleasures" of
Florida. On Sundays between December and ay he
drew an average of 4,000 people a week to his
Bible classes. According to Ginger, Bryan
believed in absolutes--things were either all
good or all evil. For example, he had "little
respect for scientists or for humanistic
scholars." Bryan believed that the truth of
the Bible could not be in conflict with science
so he believed that the "truth that science
claimed to discover had not been discovered at
all. It was not truth, but wild guesses."[22]

His dogmatism against science was reflected in his statements: "You believe in the
age of rocks; I believe in the Rock of Ages"
and "more of those who take evolution die
spiritually than die physically from smallpox"
and "I have just as much right as the atheist
to begin with an assumption, and I would rather
begin with God and reason down than begin with
a piece of dirt and reason up."[23]

Scopes had a unique perspective on the
battle between Darrow and Bryan because he had
seen Bryan speak on several occasions before
the trial. In his book, Scopes made a comparison: "[Darrow] was not a great orator who
could stir people's emotions as Bryan did.
Darrow angled for minds rather than emotions,
realizing that reason, properly presented,
could affect a man's emotions and actions more
permanently than a blatantly emotional pitch."
He described Bryan as "probably the best orator
that America has produced. . . . Within moments
he could grip and dominate an audience and make
it respond at will." He described Bryan's
technique: "his cadence, intonation, and
gestures were exactly right for each occasion.
He could increase or decrease his volume at
will, so perfectly was his voice and his

control of it. He could reach the most distant
man in any hall without any mechanical aids."
Scopes did say that Bryan added to the "raucous
atmosphere" of the trial: "He had a truck
equipped with a loudspeaker, going about town
touting Florida real estate. It was the first
loudspeaker I had ever seen. Bryan kept busy,
managing to fight the evolutionists and sell
real estate at the same time, without any
apparent conflict."[24]

Darrow was not as kind in his descriptions
of Bryan. He saw Bryan as a man of narrow
vision who "never cared to read, much less
study. . . . To him, the most insignificant
affairs of life were controlled by Providence,
and he was sure he had been chosen for a
special work. No matter how often he was
beaten, he had the same confidence that the
Lord was on his side." Yet Darrow believed
Bryan was afraid his ideas were not totally
correct: "Mr. Bryan was like the traditional
boy passing the graveyard at night--he was
whistling to keep up his courage. His very
attitude showed that he was frightened out of
his wits lest, after all, the illusions of his
life might be only dreams."[25]

One more dominant figure needs to be
mentioned: the judge, John T. Raulston.
Raulston had never presided over a major trial,
so he saw the Scopes trial as a means of
gaining some attention. He was a religious
man, "a lay preacher in the Methodist Episcopal
Church." Therefore, his emotions and actions
tended to favor the prosecution. Raulston was
once quoted as saying: "If man, without inspiration, attempts to delve into the mysteries of
God he finds himself overwhelmed in per-
plexities. Therefore, I am much more interested that the unerring hand of Him who is the
Author of all truth and justice shall direct
every official act of mine." Raulston relished
the fact that such major figures as Darrow and

Bryan were to be in his courtroom and that media coverage of the trial would blanket the earth. He made himself available to the media, particularly the press photographers. Darrow became frustrated because the trial was often held up while the photographers took the judge's picture.[26]

Raulston's rulings also frustrated Darrow to the point that he bordered on contempt of court at one point. Scopes was less harsh on Raulston: "The judge couldn't be blamed for his rulings and pronouncements, generally. He did the best he could. . . . This trial . . . was far over his head. . . . No one expects much judicial brilliance in the lower courts anyway, especially when it frequently fails to appear in the higher courts."[27]

The prosecution in the case also seemed to follow the strong line of religious acceptance. A member of the prosecution was quoted as saying: "All we have to do . . . is to get the fact that Mr. Darrow is an atheist and does not believe in the Bible . . . across to the jury and his case is lost." This view was born out of the statement of Attorney General Stewart during the trial:

> Mr. Darrow says he is an agnostic. He is the greatest criminal lawyer in America today. His courtesy is noticeable--his ability is known--and it is a shame in my mind, in the sight of a great God, that a mentality like his has strayed so far from the natural goal that it should follow--great God, the good that a man of his ability could have done if he had aligned himself with the forces of right instead of aligning himself with that which strikes its fangs at the very bosom of Christianity.[28]

Stewart then outlined the state's contention

not that the trial is "a conflict between science and religion," but rather that "it is a case involving the fact as to whether or not a school-teacher has taught a doctrine prohibited by statute." He then made the point of again referring to Darrow as "the agnostic counsel for the defense."[29]

Always the teacher, Darrow attempted to explain his views on religion to the jury and to educate Stewart on the meaning of terms:

. . . [Stewart] is perfectly justified in saying that I am an agnostic,
for I am, and I do not consider it an
insult, but rather a compliment to be
called an agnostic. I do not pretend
to know where many ignorant men are
sure; that is all agnosticism means.
He did, however, use a word "infidel". . . . the word "infidel" has no
meaning whatever. Everybody is an
infidel that does not believe in the
prevailing religion, among the
Saracens, everybody is an infidel
that does not believe with them, and
in Mohammedean country, everybody
that is not a Mohammedean is an
infidel, and among the Christians,
everybody is an infidel that is not a
Christian, or professes to be. It
has no generic meaning, and I don't
think I am fairly classified under
it.[30]

Although Darrow was the center of attention for the defense, he was supported by very competent counsel including Dudley Field Malone. Malone provided a dramatic note to the trial in a powerful speech condemning Bryan. Scopes felt that Malone's speech shattered Bryan's "un-bounded optimism, which Darrow is commonly credited with having done later in the trial." According to Scopes, many of Bryan's later actions, including allowing himself to be put on the witness stand, were "in the vain hope of regaining some of his tarnished glory."[31]

The trial began on July 10, 1925. An observer noted that "one was hard put to it on the tenth of July to know whether Dayton was holding a camp meeting, a Chautauqua, a street fair, a carnival or a belated Fourth of July celebration. Literally, it was drunk on religious excitement." When Darrow arrived for the trial, more than a thousand people were present in a courtroom that held seven hundred, more journalists were present than on "any assignment since the Washington Arms Conference," microphones were set up to carry the trial to the nation--the first such broadcast-- and journalists from several countries were ready to send the story to European papers. The judge proclaimed, "My gavel . . . will be heard around the world." Bryan announced that the "trial uncovers an attack for a generation on revealed religion. If evolution wins Christianity goes." Darrow responded, "Scopes isn't on trial, civilization is on trial. The prosecution is opening the doors for a reign of bigotry equal to anything in the Middle Ages. No man's belief will be safe if they win."[32]

The trial opened with prayer. Then, because there was a concern that the original indictment was not valid, a new one was brought. The jury was quickly chosen because Darrow only questioned them in general terms-- the jury was far less important in this trial than in previous ones. People were happy to serve on the jury because they would have front row seats for the coming battle. The members of the jury were generally religious men with little education who made their livings as farmers.

Several events during the trial heightened the drama and therefore the interest. On July 14, for instance, Darrow objected that the trial was opened each day with a prayer by a

fundamentalist preacher: "I don't object to
the jury or anyone else praying in secret or
private. . . . But I do object to the turning
this courtroom into a meetinghouse in the trial
of this case.   This case is a conflict between
science and religion, and no attempt should be
made by means of prayer to influence the
deliberation and consideration by the jury of
the facts in this case."   Obviously he was
overruled, but the judge did appoint a
committee to chose a variety of types of
preachers to open sessions of court.[33]

Another dramatic event was the moving of
the trial from the courtroom to the lawn
outside the courthouse.   The act probably
allowed more spectators to see the trial and
served as a means of escaping the almost un-
bearable heat in the courtroom.   Once outside,
Darrow again shocked the crowd when he demanded
the removal of a large sign saying "Read Your
Bible" which "was attached to the side of a
building" not very far from where the jury
would sit.   Darrow agreed to leave up the sign
if one which said "Read Your Evolution" was
placed next to it.   The sign was removed.[34]

In order to prove the viability of evolution as a theory, the defense brought many
notable scientists and biblical scholars to
testify in the trial.   The prosecution objected
to such testimony, and the judge agreed.
Scopes described the importance of that ruling:
We hadn't expected to win our case in
Dayton; we had hoped to provide a
strong record for higher courts.   The
decision was an even greater defeat
in another way.   Admission of the
expert witnesses, testifying in open
court with reporters listening and
channeling the data all over the
country, would have given us an
unparalleled educational opportunity.
The entire nation would have got a

> short course in evolution, and in
> truth and justice.[35]

Darrow bristled at the result, raising the
potential of contempt charges when he
verbalized his frustration to the judge.
Darrow averted contempt by apologizing. Judge
Raulston accepted the apology, saying that the
people of Tennessee forgave Darrow and com-
mended "him to go back home and learn in his
heart the words of the man who said, 'If you
thirst come unto Me and I will give thee
life.'"[36]

> Denied the use of their scientific ex-
perts, the defense decided to call an expert on
religion to the stand, William Jennings Bryan.
The defense's calling of Bryan caught him in a
situation where he could not refuse:

> He had no desire to take the witness
> stand, but he was afraid not to.
> There he was, surrounded by 2,000
> people on a courthouse lawn in a
> little town in Tennessee. It was
> like an old-fashioned Southern camp
> meeting. Bryan, year after year, had
> been telling people like this what
> the Bible meant. He had written
> countless screeds on the need to do
> battle for the true faith. He had
> assured them all along that he knew
> what the true faith was. Now his
> opponents were calling on him to give
> expert testimony about the Bible. He
> could not refuse.[37]

Scopes believed that in agreeing to be a
witness, Bryan made the gravest miscalculation
of his long career: he underestimated Clarence
Darrow. Darrow had wanted to get Bryan in just
such a situation for many years. In "one of
the most unique and dramatic scenes ever
enacted in a courtroom" Darrow got his chance:

> Darrow started out casual and
> conversational in his questioning,

then became irritated, angry, disgusted.The shrug of his shoulder was more expressive than his words. Bryan, seated at a table, a glass of water near his elbow, fanned himself vigorously. He qualified some of his answers, determined to win the duel with the man who had supported him twice for the presidency of the United States and whom he now considered his foe.[38]

Bryan stated that he had taken the stand for a reason: "I am simply trying to protect the word of God against the greatest atheist or agnostic in the United States. I want the papers to know I am not afraid to get on the witness stand in front of him and let him do his worst. I want the world to know." During the exchange Darrow argued his side with equal fervor: "we have the purpose of preventing bigots and ignoramuses from controlling the education of the United States and you know it" and "you insult every man of science and learning in the world because he does not believe in your fool religion."[39]

The result of the cross-examination was devastating to Bryan. Scopes described the effect: "As [Darrow] left the courtyard, he was surrounded by admirers; his grilling of Bryan had made him the hero of the day and, for most of them, the hero of the trial. For Bryan, there was only despondency; he was left alone on that green, spacious lawn, a forgotten, forlorn man."[40]

The judge rescued Bryan by not allowing his testimony to be taken up a second day. Although upset that he could not question Bryan further, Darrow was happy because his questions "and Bryan's answers were printed in full, and the story seems to have reached the whole world."[41]

Although most coverage of the trial

focuses on the dramatic confrontation between
Darrow and Bryan during the cross-examination,
Darrow gave a significant speech earlier in the
trial.   An article in the New York Times
described him on that occasion:

> There was a craning of necks, for Mr.
> Darrow is of intense interest here-
> about. He is known as "the infidel,"
> and the crowd gazed curiously at the
> bent figure with the seamed brown
> face and the great head. He was in
> his shirt sleeves, his purple sus-
> penders standing out against his
> shirt, which had a little tear at the
> left elbow. He would stoop and brood
> a minute, hunching his shoulders
> almost up to his ears, and then they
> would drop; his head would shoot
> forward and his lower lip protrude as
> he hurled some bitter word at his
> opponents. Or he would stand swaying
> sideways at the hips, balancing him-
> self, a thunderbolt of indignation,
> words streaming from him in a torrent
> of denunciation.[42]

Irving Stone added his own description of
Darrow on the day of his speech: "He believed
that the things he had to say in these few
hours of pleading might be among the most
important of his lifetime. For this reason he
was not content to plead merely for the right
to heresy; he wanted his argument to be based
solidly on the law, for if the law of a land
will not maintain a man's intellectual freedom
the people of a country never will."[43]

Much of the basis of legal argument in the
speech started with the assumption that the
antievolution law was poorly written and that
the caption of the law and the text of the law
were unclear and contradicted each other.
Darrow pointed out the problem with having a
contradiction between the two parts of the

statute: "it would be a travesty that a caption such as this and a body such as this would be declared valid law in the state of Tennessee. . . . It is full of weird, strange, impossible and imaginary provisions.   Driven by bigotry and narrowness they come together and make this statute and bring this litigation."[44]

He then pointed out that the caption says that teachers shall not "teach the theory that denies the story of the divine creation of man, as taught in the Bible, and to teach instead that man has descended from a lower order of animals." Although the caption did not mention evolution, in reality the law attempted to outlaw the teaching of evolution.   But, Darrow argued, Tennessee "has no more divine right to teach the Bible as the divine book than that the Koran is one, or the book of Mormons, or the book of Confucius, or the Budda . . . or any one of the 10,000 books to which human souls have gone for consolation and aid in their troubles." If they were to cut out these books, the state "would have to pick the right caption at least, and they could not pick it out without violating the constitution, which is as old and as wise as Jefferson."   He concluded his discussion of the caption with a stirring passage, saying that people who read only the caption could go home "without any fear that a narrow, ignorant, bigoted shrew of religion could have destroyed their religious freedom and their right to think and act and speak," but in reality the text of the law is "a religious statute, the growth of as plain religious ignorance and bigotry as any that justified the Spanish inquisition or the hanging of the witches in New England, or the countless iniquities under the name of what some people call religion, and pursued the human race down to the last hundred years."[45]

Although Darrow believed the law invalid because it was poorly written and internally inconsistent, his main fear was an attack on learning. He described the law as a foolish, wicked, ambiguous, and ancient one which was "as brazen and as bold an attempt to destroy learning as was ever made in the middle ages, and the only difference is we have not provided that they shall be burned at the stake, but there is time for that, Your Honor, we have to approach these things gradually."[46]

Because Darrow saw the law as a threat to learning, he was concerned with the effect it would have on schools:

> Today it is the public school teachers, tomorrow the private. The next day the preachers and the lecturers, the magazines, the books, the newspapers. After a while, Your Honor, it is the setting of man against man and creed against creed until with flying banners and beating drums we are marching backward to the glorious ages of the sixteenth century when bigots lighted fagots to burn the men who dared to bring any intelligence and enlightenment and culture to the human mind.[47]

Darrow was exasperated because he believed the antievolution hysteria was caused by Bryan. Throughout the trial the prosecution had constantly pointed out that the defense lawyers were outsiders from New York and Chicago. Darrow answered that prosecution lawyers caused the problems including one "who is responsible for this foolish, mischievous and wicked act, who comes from Florida."[48]

He then turned to the Bible, saying it was not a book that had to be taken literally. He tried to teach the audience and jury about the book's history and argued that it is not a book of science: "The Bible is not one book. The Bible is made up of sixty-six books written over a period of about one thousand years, some

of them very early and some of them comparatively late.   It is a book primarily of
religion and morals.   It is not a book of
science.   Never was and was never meant to
be."[49]

Darrow sought to soften attacks on himself
by explaining his own religious views: "while I
take no offense for anybody to say in any way
that I am an agnostic, for I am . . . I think
everybody's religious rights and religious
liberties are protected under the laws of
Tennessee"; he did not "think that anybody's
religious creed should be used for the purpose
of prejudicing or influencing any action in
this case."[50]

After explaining his own views, Darrow
made it clear that he did not reject the creeds
of others, especially those who lived their
lives by the Bible: "I feel just exactly the
same toward the religious creed of every human
being who lives.   If anybody finds anything in
this life that brings them consolation and
health and happiness I think they ought to have
it whatever they get.   I haven't any fault to
find with them at all."[51]

At the conclusion of his speech the court
was adjourned for the day.   The reactions were
predictably mixed.   One woman referred to him
as "The damned infidel!" while another said,
"Mr. Darrow, if I could have heard you before,
I would never have spoken of you as I have in
the past."   Ben McKenzie, one of the prosecution attorneys, told Darrow, "It was the
greatest speech I ever heard in my life on any
subject."   A local man named Buckshot Morgan
gave his view: "I might as well have gone
fishing . . . folks ain't going to waste their
time listening to wickedness when it ain't more
interesting than that.   Do you think . . . that
a fellow could grasp more of the wickedness of
it if he had an education?"
H.L. Mencken summarized:

The net effect of Clarence Darrow's
great speech yesterday seems to be
precisely the same as if he had
bawled it up to a rainspout in the
interior of Afghanistan. . . .You
have but a dim notion of it who have
only read it.   It was not designed
for reading, but for hearing.   The
clangtint of it was as important as
the logic.   It rose like a wind and
ended like a flourish of bugles.   The
very judge on the bench, toward the
end of it, began to look uneasy.   But
the morons in the audience, when it
was over, simply hissed.

Tierney, in his biography of Darrow, gave his
analysis from a distance of time: "In vindicating John Thomas Scopes, he was vindicating
himself and his father before him, who had
asserted the right of inquiring minds to roam
where they pleased.   The backwardness of the
South, deriving from the Civil War, meant that
Dayton   resembled   spiritually   the   Ohio   of
Darrow's youth.   Darrow reveled in the scene
because his life had come full circle.   He was
finally vindicating his youthful rebellion."[52]

Darrow's great speech and his crushing of
Bryan on the witness stand did not change the
outcome of the trial.   Scopes was convicted,
but the decision was overturned on a techni-
cality   a   year   later.   The   defense   really
expected only to win on appeal anyhow--using
the trial as a showcase for ideas.

At the end of the trial each of combatants
spoke for a final time.   Bryan stated that
"this cause has stirred the world. . . . Here
has been fought out a little case of little
consequence   as   a   case,   but   the   world   is
interested because it raises an issue and that
issue will be settled right, whether it is
settled on our side or the other side."   Darrow
also spoke on the significance of the case in a

small town like Dayton: "I fancy that the place where the Magna Charta was wrestled from the barons in England was a very small place, not as big as Dayton. . . . I think this case will be remembered because it is the first case of this sort since we stopped trying people in America for witchcraft because here we have done our best to turn back the tide that has sought to force itself upon . . . this modern world, of testing every fact in science by a religious dictum."[53]

The main characters in the dramatic trial returned to their lives. Darrow and Malone returned to New York and Chicago; Judge Raulston returned to obscurity after attempting to make money on the lecture circuit; Scopes returned to his desired anonymity, although periodically rumors would surface in the press that he had a religious conversion.

Only Bryan did not return to his normal life. A few days after the trial, "Bryan did the most effective thing possible to save his fundamentalist support--he died. On Sunday, July 26 . . . after a hearty mid-day dinner . . . he went upstairs to take a nap. He died of apoplexy in his sleep." His death created a martyr for his cause. As Scopes said, "Ironically, it was Bryan's death that saved him from nearly complete disaster as a result of the Dayton trial. He died at precisely the right moment, for to many persons he became a martyr."[54]

Although Darrow expressed his regret at Bryan's death, a myth has grown up that Darrow's treatment of the trial caused his death. Scopes described the roots of the myth: "A newspaperman probably started the rumor in order to have a fresh and sensational angle, because there was less animosity in Dayton toward Darrow than one might have expected. Unfortunately, the myth of Darrow's deadly role became a popular one. It has endured through the years and its hold on the public mind is indicated by a typical letter I received recently from a young man in Tennessee. 'What was it,' he asked, 'that Darrow said to Bryan that killed him?'"[55]

That popular image has been expanded by representations of the trial in plays, in movies, and on television. In 1951 Jerome Lawrence and Robert E. Lee wrote Inherit the Wind, a dramatic version of the trial. That play has played on Broadway and has been produced by numerous theater groups; it has been made into a popular movie starring Frederick March and Spencer Tracy, and recently into a popular television movie. Toward the end of the play the fictional Darrow delivers lines that described well the career of the real Darrow: "You don't suppose this kind of thing is ever finished, do you? Tomorrow it'll be something else--and another fella will have to stand up and you've helped give him the guts to do it!"[56]

The Scopes case was the last major case for Darrow, but the trial has guaranteed him a place in American legal history and American mythology. Darrow tried to teach the country about evolution and the need for free thought. He had hoped to end the fight over the teaching of evolution in schools forever, but he was not successful. That fight continues to this very day and probably will for generations into the future, but Darrow serves as a constant inspiration to those who continue that effort.

NOTES

1. Quoted in John T. Scopes and James Presley, Center of the Storm: Memoirs of John T. Scopes (New York: Holt, Rinehart & Winston, 1967), p. 69.
2. Ray Ginger, Six Days or Forever (Boston: Beacon Press, 1958), pp. 66-67.
3. Ginger, Six Days or Forever, pp. 64-67.

4. Ginger, Six Days or Forever, pp. 62-63; Clarence Darrow, The Story of My Life (New York: Charles Scribner's Sons, 1931), p. 246.

5. Irving Stone, Clarence Darrow for the Defense (Garden City, N.Y.: Doubleday, 1941), p. 433.

6. Scopes and Presley, Center of the Storm, pp. 51-52.

7. Arthur Weinberg and Lila Weinberg, Clarence Darrow; A Sentimental Rebel (New York: G. P. Putnam's Sons, 1980), p. 318; Scopes, Center of the Storm, p. 61.

8. Darrow, quoted in Weinberg and Weinberg, Clarence Darrow, p. 318; Darrow, The Story of My Life, p. 244.

9. John T. Scopes, quoted in Weinberg and Weinberg, Clarence Darrow, p. 319.

10. Stone, Clarence Darrow for the Defense, pp. 430-31; Ginger, Six Days or Forever, p. 73.

11. Darrow, The Story of My Life, pp. 90-91.

12. Kevin Tierney, Darrow: A Biography (New York: Thomas Y. Crowell, 1979), p. 127.

13. Stone, Clarence Darrow for the Defense, pp. 448-49.

14. William Jennings Bryan, quoted in Stone, Clarence Darrow for the Defense, p. 427

15. Weinberg and Weinberg, Clarence Darrow, p. 320; an article in The New Republic, quoted in Stone, Clarence Darrow for the Defense, pp. 428-430.

16. An article in The Nation, quoted in Ginger, Six Days or Forever, p. 128.

17. Scopes and Presley, Center of the Storm, pp. 95-96; Ginger, Six Days or Forever, p. 191.

18. H. L. Mencken, quoted in Ginger, Six Days or Forever, pp. 191, 129; Darrow, The Story of My Life, p. 249.

19. Darrow, The Story of My Life, pp. 247-248.

20. Scopes and Presley, Center of the Storm, pp. 3, 70, 78, 112.

21. Scopes and Presley, Center of the Storm, p. 229.

22. Ginger, Six Days or Forever, pp.34, 38, 40.

23. William Jennings Bryan, quoted in Ginger, Six Days or Forever, p. 37.

24. Scopes and Presley, Center of the Storm, pp. 229, 26, 210, 88.

25. Darrow, The Story of My Life, pp. 94, 250.

26. Judge John Raulston, quoted in Ginger, Six Days or Forever, pp. 69, 87.

27. Scopes and Presley, Center of the Storm, p. 124.

28. Quoted in Ginger, Six Days or Forever, pp. 74-75; Attorney General Stewart, quoted in The World's Most Famous Court Trial (Cincinnati: National Book Co., 1925), p. 197.

29. Attorney General Stewart, quoted in The World's Most Famous Court Trial, p. 99.

30. Darrow, quoted in The World's Most Famous Court Trial, p. 99.

31. Scopes and Presley, Center of the Storm, p. 156.

32. Quoted in Scopes and Presley, Center of the Storm, p. 436; Ginger, Six Days or Forever, p. 103; Judge Raulston and Darrow, quoted in Stone, Clarence Darrow for the Defense, p. 437.

33. Darrow, quoted in Stone, Clarence Darrow for the Defense, p. 443.

34. Stone, Clarence Darrow for the Defense, p. 456.

35. Scopes and Presley, Center of the Storm, p. 158.

36. Judge Raulston, quoted in Weinberg and Weinberg, Clarence Darrow, p. 324.

37. Ginger, Six Days or Forever, p. 166.

38. Weinberg and Weinberg, Clarence Darrow, p. 324.

39. William Jennings Bryan and Darrow, quoted in The World's Most Famous Court Trial, pp. 299, 288-289.

40. Scopes and Presley, Center of the Storm, p. 183.

41. Darrow, The Story of My Life, p. 267.

42. Quoted in Stone, Clarence Darrow for the Defense, p. 440.

43. Stone, <u>Clarence Darrow for the Defense</u>, p. 441.

44. Darrow, quoted in <u>The World's Most Famous Court Trial</u>, p. 77.

45. Darrow, quoted in <u>The World's Most Famous Court Trial</u>, pp. 76-77.

46. Darrow, quoted in <u>The World's Most Famous Court Trial</u>, p. 75.

47. Darrow, quoted in <u>The World's Most Famous Court Trial</u>, p. 78.

48. Darrow, quoted in <u>The World's Most Famous Court Trial</u>, p. 74.

49. Darrow, quoted in <u>The World's Most Famous Court Trial</u>, p. 78.

50. Darrow, quoted in <u>The World's Most Famous Court Trial</u>, p. 99.

51. Darrow, quoted in <u>The World's Most Famous Court Trial</u>, p. 78.

52. Quoted in Weinberg and Weinberg, <u>Clarence Darrow</u>, p. 322; H. L. Mencken, quoted in Ginger, <u>Six Days or Forever</u>, p. 109; Tierney, <u>Darrow</u>, p. 368.

53. William Jennings Bryan, quoted in Scopes, <u>Center of the Storm</u>, p. 188; Darrow, quoted in <u>The World's Most Famous Court Trial</u>, p. 317.

54. Ginger, <u>Six Days or Forever</u>, pp. 192-93; Scopes, <u>Center of the Storm</u>, p. 217.

55. Scopes and Presley, <u>Center of the Storm</u>, pp. 203-204

56. Jerome Lawrence and Robert E. Lee, <u>Inherit the Wind</u> (New York: Dramatists Play Service, 1951), p. 85.

5

Speaking for the Poor and Weak

Although Darrow's career as a defense attorney is mainly remembered because of the Leopold and Loeb and the Scopes cases, some of his lesser known trials are worthy of study. Those trials reflected his concern for freedom of speech and racial ssues. His speaking in these trials reflected his consistent defense of the underdog and his belief that individuals should be able to freely voice unpopular views.

One of the inconsistencies in his record occurred during his last trial. Although the Massie case has overtures of race, Darrow did not defend either poor or downtrodden defendants, but relatively comfortable individuals who had killed a member of a racial minority. But even the memory of that trial did little to damage Darrow's reputation as a defender of the unfortunate in society.

DEFENDING THE FIRST AMENDMENT

Darrow "was a strong advocate of First Amendment rights even for those with whom he disagreed and did not admire, whether politically or on a personal level." In 1901 he successfully defended on contempt charges several newsmen who worked for the Chicago Tribune. The reporters had published an article critical of a Chicago judge, an action that led to potentially serious consequences because the judge found them in contempt of court and could have sentenced them to severe jail sentences. In the trial appealing their conviction Darrow proclaimed: "These defendants are prosecuted today, not because they have committed contempt of this court . . . but because they have dared to speak for the poor and the weak, who could not speak for them- selves." Arthur and Lila Weinberg called his speech in that trail "a classic defense of freedom of press."[1]

Darrow was not as successful in his 1903 defense of the English anarchist John Turner. Turner was arrested after a speech because he violated a law forbidding admission of anyone to the United States who opposed organized government. The case was appealed to the Supreme Court. Turner lost his right to speak in the United States when the court ruled that aliens did not have the same protection of freedom of speech as did citizens of the United States. Although he lost the case, Darrow's plea was printed in pamphlet form and "was sold as a definitive brochure on freedom of speech."[2]

These cases were but a small portion of Darrow's record in defense of unpopular positions and individuals focusing in First Amendment rights. His most difficult trials were to come, however, during and after World War I.

Darrow surprised many Americans by openly supporting World War I. Before the war Darrow had been an ardent pacifist, but changed his view when Germany invaded Belgium: "I dis- covered that pacifism is probably a good doc- trine in time of peace, but of no value in war time." Because of his fame, Darrow was invited by the government to speak in favor of the war effort. Those speeches dramatically improved his image with the general public. In his autobiography, Darrow described his role: "When we were once in the contest, I gave nearly all

my time to making speeches throughout the
United States. It was the first occasion when
I had known a war I believed in."[3]

Even though he supported the war, Darrow
was troubled by the poor treatment of those who
opposed the conflict: "public officials and the
press were encouraging the people to mob, whip,
shoot, jail or kill all dissenters." He hoped
that the end of the war would result in a more
tolerant atmosphere, but he was wrong. Pros-
ecutions of individuals continued, and Darrow
"raised his voice in some of the finest pleading of his age. Never was such good pleading
more sorely needed. Darrow described the
situation:

> No sooner had peace been declared
> than the same organization that had
> taken over the management of the war
> procured an Espionage Act, which
> forbade free discussion, either
> orally or in the press. This in-
> famous law appeared almost simul-
> taneously in Congress and in each of
> the several states of the Union. . .
> . Men were arrested, indicted and
> convicted, and sent to prison . . .
> for daring to express their opinions.
> . . . Any so-called radicalism was
> unpatriotic because [it was] contrary
> to the views of the exploiting class.

The "red raids" led by Attorney General A.
Mitchell Palmer were based on fears of communism raised by the Russian Revolution and the
distrust of foreign radical ideology. Out of
this hysteria grew three prominent cases: the
defenses of Benjamin Gitlow, Arthur Person, and
a group of Communists in Chicago. These cases
vividly illustrated Darrow's support of unpopular stands and his belief in free
expression.[4]

BENJAMIN GITLOW (1920)

Gitlow, a Communist party leader in New

York, was not indicted under the criminal syndicalism laws passed after World War I, but rather under the Criminal Anarchy Law enacted after the assassination of President McKinley. That law made it illegal to advocate in speaking or writing the overthrow of the government. Darrow took the case without even meeting Gitlow because he so strongly believed in Gitlow's right to speak freely.

Gitlow asked Darrow to defend the right of people to propose revolution. Darrow had no problem with that position because he had argued it on numerous occasions: "For a man to be afraid of revolution in America . . . would be to be ashamed of your mother. Nothing else. Revolution? There is not a drop of honest blood in a single man that does not look back to some revolution for which he would thank his God that those who revolted won." He pointed to the events leading to the founding of the United States as an example of such a revolution.[5]

In his speech in defense of Gitlow, Darrow called for no "fetters on thought and actions and dreams and ideals of men, even the most despised of them. Whatever I may think of their prudence, what I may think of their judgement, I am for dreamers. . . . I would rather that every practical man should die if the dreamer be saved." He saw Gitlow as a dreamer whose vision was made concrete in the Communist Manifesto: "The Communists believe that they seen the truth, that they have a vision of the day when there shall be real equality." He argued that society did not have the right to stop people like Gitlow from searching for their ideal: "Some time in the realm of ideas, in the realm of good emotions, in the realm of kindness and brotherly feeling, we may find truth that is higher than men, and gentlemen, no one has the right to stand in his way of finding it."[6]

Although his arguments were eloquent, Darrow failed to sway the jury. Gitlow was fined and sentenced to jail. The judge's words reflected the country's fear of people like Gitlow:

> There must be a right in organized society to protect itself. Its citizens who accept the benefits of organized government, who have the opportunity of employment because of the protection given by organized government to the conduct of business, if they do not recognize that the government that fosters them, and which is created by law and based upon law should only be overthrown by lawful methods, then it is difficult to see where civilization can be maintained and the benefits that come from civilization can be preserved.[7]

It was attitudes like these that Darrow hoped to change in later trials.

ARTHUR PERSON (1920)

Also in 1920 Darrow defended Arthur Person, a radical charged with joining an organization that called for the violent overthrow of the United States government. Person, a resident of Rockford, Illinois, was the secretary of a branch of the Communist Labor party in that community. The authorities raided his home, confiscated his records and copies of socialist pamphlets, and then arrested him.

The trial attracted a considerable amount of media attention. In speaking in defense of Person, Darrow immediately attacked the basis for indicting the defendant: "If you want to get rid of every socialist, of every communist, of every trade unionist, of every agitator, there is one way to do it, and that is to cure the ills of society. You can't do it by building jails; you can't make jails big enough or penalties hard enough to cure discontent by strangling it to death. No revolution is possible, no great discontent is possible, unless down below it all is some underlying cause for this discontent; men are naturally obedient; too almighty obedient."[8]

He accused the prosecution of "the common occupation of seeing red. These men are guilty because their platform is printed on red paper." He claimed that the real danger to the country was not the working men, but those "who are trying to send men to jail for their opinion . . . who are hastening a collapse of civilization, and we must save them from themselves." He specifically pointed to the leaders of industry as those trying to crush workers: "this mad fever has possession of them and they brook nothing that stands between them and their gold. I know that they would destroy liberty that property would live."[9]

In further attacking those who were trying to persecute Person he explained that "I am engaged in the difficult task of trying to preserve a Constitution instead of destroying it, and I am seeking to save for the people of this country such liberties as they have left." He then outlined the dangers of laws like the Espionage Act. He disliked such laws because they strangled freedom. He concluded, however, that Americans would eventually reject such statutes: "The time will come very soon when America will be ashamed of her cowardly attempt to send men to jail under laws of this kind, ashamed of the suppression of freedom of thought and freedom of speech which is making a madhouse of a once-free land."[10]

He then spoke of his client: "Now Person may be wild and crazy; I don't know. I am not here for that, and neither are you. He proposed that even if he and the jury disagreed with everything that someone believed, they should "stand for the right of every man on earth to accept his own religious faith and his own political creed and his own ideas. . . . I would be a very poor citizen and I would belong to that class of bigots who in every age have piled the fagots around their fellow men and burned them to cinders because of differences in faith."[11]

He concluded his defense with these stirring words about Person:

Arthur Person is obscure; he is unknown; he is poor; he has worked all his life, but his case is one that reaches down to the foundation of your freedom and mine. If twelve men should say that they could take a man like him and send him to prison and destroy his home, a man who is guiltless of crime and whose only stain is that he loved his fellow men; if twelve men like you should say that they would take him from his home and send him to Joliet and confine him behind prison walls, you should hang this courtroom in crepe and drape your city hall with black and wear sackcloth and ashes until his term expires.

Darrow's plea was successful. Person was found innocent.[12]

THE COMMUNIST TRIAL (1920)

In 1920 Darrow also defended unpopular political views when he accepted the case of twenty members of the Communist Labor party in Chicago. Unlike Persons, the defendants were all intellectuals, many of whom were American born, so they escaped the stigma of being foreign-born radicals. Among the defendants was William Bross Lloyd, a millionaire and son of Henry Demerest Lloyd, author of Wealth Against Commonwealth. The defendants were charged with advocating the overthrow of govenment by force. Much of the evidence

presented by the prosecution attempted to link
the defendants with a general strike in Seattle
in 1919.   The purpose of the strike supposedly
was to take political control of that city.
Ole Hanson, a former mayor of Seattle, was one
of the chief witnesses for the prosecution.

Darrow based his defense on the right of
the defendants to preach the overthrow of government under freedom of the press, speech, and
assembly.   He attacked the prosecution's case
on two fronts: that the evidence had been pro-
cured illegally through an unlawful entry into
Lloyd's home and that Mayor Hanson was not a
reputable witness.   He began by pointing out
the illegal method of gathering evidence:

> They entered his home; they had no
> search warrant.   They overhauled his
> papers. . . . What about this kind of
> patriotism that violates your right
> and mine, that violates the Consti-
> tution to get you and to get me?
> They. . . . went through his desk,
> they rifled everything he had, they
> went through his room, and they brag
> of it, in a court of justice.[13]

Then he turned his scorn on the chief witness,
former Mayor Hanson.   Although Hanson had
claimed that the Communists had tried to
politically take over Seattle, Darrow
introduced statements by Hanson during the
strike, and none of these included references
to a Communist takeover.

He detailed how Hanson had resigned as
mayor of Seattle and went on the lecture
circuit once he had gotten some media attention.   This was an indication to Darrow that
Hanson was not a dedicated public servant and
not a particularly moral one, but rather a
greedy one out for fame and money.   In his
speech Darrow questioned Hanson's morals:

> He was the mayor of Seattle, a man
> who, like everybody else, is just the

kind of fellow that the Lord makes him. You cannot add to him or take away from him. At least it would be dangerous to take much away from him, and I am afraid you cannot add to him. . . . Is Ole Hanson hard to understand? Is he? Doesn't he show, all over him, the marks of a cheap poser? Doesn't he show all over him the evidence of a lightheaded notoriety hunter?[14]

After attacking the actions of the prosecution and the credibility of its chief witness, Darrow turned to the jury. He asked them how an individual determined if certain opinions were right or wrong. He claimed that in the past he had done the best he could to discover truth, but that in the end there were no standards by which to measure it. Although there were no concrete standards, he said that people should actively continue to seek truth; "men should cling to their right to examine every question; to listen to everyone, no matter who he is; to hear the spoken words and read the written words; because if you shut men's mouths and paralyze their minds, then the greatest truth that is necessary for the human race may die." He argued that this very trial was a means of closing minds because it was "seeking to place freedom of thought and freedom of speech under such a ban that no man will ever dare speak again in a land which once was free." Ultimately he argued that his clients had the right to speak and think: "I am not here to defend their opinions. I am here to defend their right to express their opinions."[15]

He asked the jury to "protect our Constitution as our fathers gave it" by allowing people to express themselves freely; "I urge you to stand for the right of men to think; for the right to speak boldly and unafraid; the right to be masters of their

souls; the right to live free and to die free."
He argued that people cannot be free if they
fear jail; they cannot be open if police can
and will scrutinize every word they write or
speak.   As in previous trials, he argued that
eventually America "will be ashamed of her
cowardly attempt to send men to jail under laws
of this kind; ashamed of the suppression of
freedom of thought and freedom of speech which
is making a madhouse of a once free land."[16]

He believed that even if his defendants
were convicted, their actions were worthwhile
because they would be martyrs for their cause.
Darrow outlined the power of such martyrs: "the
human race has moved forward over their mangled
forms, and its path has been lighted by the
burning bodies of these devoted ones."[17]

Darrow next attempted to link the Communists to the early Christians by arguing that
those early Christians had practiced a form of
communal living and sharing.   He proposed that
communism had been a part of the world since
the time of the early Christians, but had been
ignored.

After linking the defendants to Christianity, he attempted to tie the lives of the
defendants to those of the early Americans who
brought about the American Revolution.   He
asked the jury to imagine where they would be
without rebels in American history:

> Think of the complaisant, cowardly
> people who never raise their voices
> against the powers that be.   If there
> had been only these, you gentlemen
> would be hewers of wood and drawers
> of water.   You gentlemen would have
> been slaves.   You gentlemen owe
> whatever you have and whatever you
> hope to those brave rebels who dared
> to think and dared to speak and dared
> to act; and if this jury should make
> it harder for any man to be a rebel,

you would be doing the most you could
for the damnation of the human race.[18]

Darrow concluded his defense with one of
his standard appeals, proclaiming that he was
not concerned about these particular defendants, but attempted to link them to all individuals who have been unfairly persecuted
throughout the ages:

If you want to convict these twenty
men, then do it. I ask no consideration on behalf of any one of them.
If you have any idea in your heads
that I want you to protect them or
save them, forget it. They are no
better than the millions and tens of
millions down through the ages who
have been prosecuted--yes, and
convicted, in cases like this; and if
it is necessary for my clients,
gentlemen, to show that America is
like all the rest, if it is necessary
that my clients shall go to prison to
show it, then let them go.[19]

Although the speech was a ringing defense
of free speech, Darrow failed to convince the
jury. The defendants were found guilty and
sentenced to terms of from one to five years in
prison. A juror summarized the reason for
their decision: "Although no evidence of overt
acts was presented in this case, we were certain that had the defendants carried their
revolutionary program to its logical conclusion, or had it run its course, a state of
anarchy would have been brought about."[20] The
case was appealed, but the defendants went to
jail.

DEFENSE OF BLACKS

As earlier stated, a large part of the
Darrow myth was based on the fact that he grew
up in a very tolerant home, particularly in
racial matters. The legend stated that
Darrow's childhood home was a stopping place on

the Underground Railroad that helped slaves
escape to Canada. The myth was embellished
with a story that Darrow once met the abolitionist John Brown. During that meeting Darrow
supposedly swore that he would always be a
friend of blacks. Although the story may not
be true, Darrow did grow into a champion of
blacks. As Irving Stone said, "when it came to
people, Darrow was color blind." Darrow often
spoke of the injustices blacks had suffered:
"Ever since I can remember I have been possessed of the feeling of injustice that had
been visited upon the Negro race." He often
defended blacks in court, constantly appealing
for justice: "If the Negro is a man, then all
people, high and low alike, should demand for
him all the privileges and rights of every
other citizen; should judge him for what he is,
and not on the color of his skin." He took
many cases defending blacks without compen-
sation: "For Negroes in trouble he had a
special sympathy: they were the underdogs under
the underdogs, caught in the complexities of
the white man's law and a machine age for which
their background had not prepared them."[21]

His actions in defense of blacks were returned with affection: "There was hardly a colored child over five who did not know his name
and recognize his face. When he took a driving
trip through the South with friends . . . whenever they sat down to a table, in hotel or res-
taurant, Darrow was always served the largest
portions and the choicest cuts of meat."[22]

Following his return to Chicago after his
trials of self-defense in Los Angeles, Darrow
took the case of Isaac Bond, a black man
charged with the brutal murder of a white
nurse. Most of the evidence in the case was
based on identification of Bond as the person
who had pawned several pieces of jewelry
belonging to the dead woman. Darrow questioned
the accuracy of the identification and the

evidence against Bond: "had the defendant been a white man under the same circumstances, the prosecution would not have asked for a conviction on the evidence. . . . I made the best fight I could." Although Darrow tried, Bond was convicted and sentenced to life in prison. Darrow worked for Bond's freedom, but Bond died ten years later of tuberculosis while still in prison.[23]

While Darrow tried numerous other cases involving blacks, none was more significant than the Sweet case in Detroit in 1926 and 1927. Although overshadowed by the Leopold and Loeb case and the Scopes trial, Darrow believed that the case was one of the most significant he had ever argued.

The case grew out of the large migration of blacks from the rural South to the urban North. From 1910 to 1925 the number of blacks in Detroit had grown from 6,000 to 70,000, mainly because of the availability of jobs in the automobile industry. Most of the blacks were forced into a ghetto that was grossly overcrowded. As blacks tried to move into white neighborhoods, they were opposed by white organizations "under the guise of various improvement associations and neighborhod clubs." In his autobiography Darrow described the situation: "The negro workmen could stay in the automobile factories in the daytime, but they had no place to stay at night, so they expanded the negro section, and some of them moved out to what was called the white districts."[24]

In 1924 Dr. Ossian H. Sweet, a gynecologist with a degree from Harvard, returned from Europe after studying in Vienna and France. He and his family moved in with his wife's parents and then in 1925 began searching for a home of their own. After a lengthy search the Sweets were finally able to purchase a house in a lower-middle-class white neighborhood. Sweet knew of the opposition to blacks moving into previously all-white neighborhoods, so when he moved, he brought guns, ammunition, and several other blacks to help him protect his home. On the first night a peaceful crowd gathered near the house. On the second the crowd became more threatening. Some shouted insults at Sweet and threw rocks at his home: "In the bedlam, shots were fired from several windows in the second floor, killing Leon Breiner a White man standing across the street and wounding another. Police immediately arrested the eleven Blacks in the house and charged them with first degree murder." The National Association for the Advancement of Colored People (NAACP) became involved in the case. The leaders of that organization believed that "since the case had national implications, it was essential that a white attorney of eminent reputation head the defense." Darrow agreed to take the position with support from three black Detroit lawyers.[25]

The trial of the eleven blacks began on October 30, 1925, before Judge Frank Murphy. That trial ended with no verdict. At the end of the first trial the defense asked that the defendants be tried separately in future trials. In April 1926 Henry Sweet, the younger brother of Dr. Sweet, was placed on trial. That trial was virtually identical to the first, except for Darrow's final summation.

There were two major differences between the Sweet trials and Darrow's previous trials: Darrow's appearance and his relations with the prosecuting attorney. Rather than his normal disheveled appearance, Darrow "was determined to dignify his clients before the all-white jury, and hence his dress in Detroit was way more formal than it had been in Dayton; his hair was neatly brushed. No hint of his famous galluses appeared behind his unaccustomed well-pressed jacket."[26]

The prosecutor, Robert Toms, also refused to provide Darrow with a target for his attacks: "I was quite aware of Mr. Darrow's capacity for invective and I did not propose to lay myself open by matching barbs with him." After a week of treating Darrow with respect and deference, Toms reported that Darrow said, "God damn it Toms, I can't get going. I am supposed to be mad at you and I can't even pretend that I am."   Toms did, however, occasionally take jabs at Darrow. For example, in his summation, he said, "I can't compete with this emotionalist from Chicago, neither verbally nor emotionally, but if you stick to the facts I have no fear of the outcome."[27]

As the trial progressed, an intriguing change occurred in the makeup of the spectators.   At first, the audience was mainly white with a few blacks, but as time passed, more and more blacks came until by the time of Darrow's summation, "it was a plea he was making to a white jury" and a black audience. Darrow insisted that a certain number of blacks be admitted from the beginning, even though the courtroom "was always filled, and a crowd outside waited for admission."   Yet he was stunned that whites would not sit next to blacks in the courtroom: "of course, white people do not like to sit beside colored people because they are smelly and not clean, but this in no way incapacitates them from cooking, waiting on the table, suckling the babies of the whites.   It operates only in regard to sitting together when neither are working."[28]

Although "the case missed the national attention many of his others received," Darrow felt it was the most important case in which he had ever participated. In his autobiography he explained his feelings:

> The defense of this case gave me
> about as much gratification as any
> that I have undertaken. While I was

certain that my clients were right and that they were grievously wronged, I never had any sense of resentment against the community. The people who sought to drive that colored family from their home were only a part of the product of the bitterness bred through race prejudice, for which they were not responsible. So long as this feeling lives, tragedies will result.[29]

Darrow's summation speech stated quite simply that "from the beginning of this case to the end, up to the time you write your verdict, the prosecution is based on race prejudice and nothing else." To illustrate his point he simply asked, "Would this case be in this court if these defendants were not black? . . . Would anybody be asking you to send a boy to prison for life for defending his brother's home and protecting his own life, if his face wasn't black?"[30]

Darrow argued that city officials knew there was a potential for violence because the city of Detroit had the police force there "to see that a family were permitted to move into a home that they owned without getting their throats cut by the noble Nordics who inhabit that jungle." Darrow described the scene that occurred when the Sweets were unloading their belongings. He stated that people went from home to home crying "'the Negroes are coming,' as if a foreign army was invading their homes; as if a wild beast had come down out of the mountains in the olden times."[31]

He then asked the jurors to lay aside their feelings and examine the events and evidence. He believed that no jury would take Sweet's life based on the circumstances that surrounded Breiner's death.

Darrow then placed the <u>Sweet</u> case in the long history of suffering by blacks in America.

He outlined how slaves were captured in Africa, the brutality of their transportation on slave ships from Africa, their inhuman treatment as slaves, and the riots that have occurred against blacks since they were freed. He called upon the jury not to stir up more hatred, but to help blacks and whites to learn to live together: "I would advise patience; I would advise toleration; I would advise understanding; I would advise all of those things which are necessary for men who live together."[32]

He placed the jury in the position of being able to make a momentous decision, a decision that "may mean a milestone in the progress of the human race." He pointed to the spectators who looked to a jury of twelve whites "feeling that the hopes and fears of a race are in your keeping. . . . Their eyes are fixed on you. Their hearts go out to you, and their hopes hang on your verdict." He then asked "in the name of progress and of the human race" to find Sweet not guilty.[33]

Taking the case from the larger black race, he focused on individuals. He showed how Dr. Sweet had worked his way through college, had gone through medical school, and had pursued advanced study in Europe. Yet even these accomplishments could not overcome the simple fact that he had black skin and was hated because of that skin. He pointed to the defendant, Henry Sweet, as "a decent man as any one of you twelve" who was loyal to his brother. He simply did not believe that such a fine person should be condemned to prison.[34]

Once he established the positive attributes of the Sweets, Darrow turned to the less than desirable activities of whites. He pointed to the fact that whites allowed blacks to care for their children, to be their chauffeurs, and to do other jobs that whites did not want. He charged that blacks were good enough to do the dirty work for whites, but not good enough to live next door, so they were forced into ghettos. When blacks tried to break out of the ghetto, they were then brutally attacked by mobs "seeking to tear them to bits."[35]

He asked the jury members to put themselves in the shoes of the Sweets and then asked them how they would have responded if they were in the same situation. He answered his own question, saying that they would have responded exactly as the Sweets did. After all, "every man may protect his own life. Every man has the right to protect his own property," even if that means killing in defense of his own life: "No man has a right to stop and dicker while waiting for a mob."[36]

Another undesirable action of whites, Darrow contended was that they lied on the witness stand when they declared that there had been no mob outside the Sweet home, but only a few bystanders who were attacked by the Sweets. During the trial Darrow caught the witnesses contradicting each other on the stand. Then in his summation he accused them of lying: "There isn't one of you who does not know that they lied. There isn't one of you who does not know that they tried to drive these people out and now are trying to send them to the penitentiary so that they can't move back."[37]

Because of the actions of the mob, Darrow tried to downplay the importance of the death of Breiner. He admitted that the blacks shot their guns toward the crowd, but whether "any bullets from their guns hit Breiner, I do not care. I will not discuss it." He did claim that the bullet did not come from Henry Sweet's gun. Rather than focusing on Breiner's death, he argued that there were bigger issues, such as defending one's self and one's home, and that the jury should focus on those rights.[38]

The speech received much praise. Arthur Garfield Hays stated that "In his address to

the jury Darrow showed his master hand," while
the judge, Frank Murphy, described the summation as "the greatest experience" of his life.
The NAACP published the text because "of its
historical, legal, and humanitarian value."
Darrow himself stated that "My long sympathy
for the colored people conspired to help me
make one of the strongest and most satisfactory
arguments that I ever delivered. . . . The
verdict meant simply that the doctrine that a
man's house is his castle applied to the black
man as well as to the white man. If not the
first time that a white jury had vindicted this
principle, it was the first time that ever came
to my notice."[39]

MASSIE CASE (1932)

The Darrow myth of defending the poor and
downtrodden was called into question on more
than one occasion. Like the Leopold and Loeb
trial, Darrow's final case, the defense of na-
val Lieutenant Thomas Massie; his mother-in-
law, a Mrs. Fortescue; and two sailors for the
murder of a Hawaiian, Joseph Kahahawai, in
Honolulu did not involve poor people. Massie's
wife, Thalia, claimed that Kahahawai was one of
five individuals who had raped her. The rape
case was brought to trial, but the jury could
not agree on a verdict, so the men were set
free on bail. Massie, his mother-in-law, and
the two sailors kidnapped Kahahawai in an
attempt to force him to confess to the crime.
Apparently he did confess and then was shot by
Massie.

Because there were racial overtones to the
incident, because of the ongoing friction between the native Hawaiians and the U. S. Navy
in Hawaii, and because of rumors about the
Massie marriage, there was a tremendous amount
of interest in the case. Newspapers were filled with great detail about the events surrounding the case. Darrow's entry into the trial
obviously increased interest. As Stone stated:

"Not since the Loeb-Leopold murder had the newspaper readers of the United States been so unified in their concentration on events happening in a courtroom."[40]

In his autobiography Darrow described the interest in the trial:

> The whole case was dramatic and intensely interesting, if not haunting. The courtroom was jammed with anxious listeners, day after day, many waiting outside all night so they would be sure to get in when the case opened in the morning. The Honolulu papers carried a stenographic report of the case, and the daily press on the mainlnad gave almost as full an account.[41]

As an indication of the interest, Darrow's summation to the jury was broadcast "live to the mainland--the first occasion on which this had been attempted."[42]

Although Darrow described Massie as "a kindly, sympathetic, human young man, generally liked by all who came into contact with him," his acceptance of the case raised many questions. There were rumors that race would become a major issue in the case. With his long support of racial minorities Darrow at first declined the case, but ultimately accepted partly because he claimed he wanted to see Hawaii: "I had never been to that part of the Pacific; I had heard of and read about its unusual charm, and longed sometime to see it."[43]

That reason probably was overshadowed by his need for money. As Darrow stated, "the so-called 'depression' had swept away practically all the savings that I thought I had for keeping me comfortable to the end, and I needed the fee." That fee was to be $30,000 plus expenses.[44]

Other explanations Darrow offered included the fact that the case included "psychology, philosophy, and sociology"; therefore, he could extend his previous work in those areas. Tierney added the possible explanation that Darrow had become bored with retirement and was eager to get involved in another major case. Whatever his motive, Darrow found himself in the middle of a highly emotional case among "the fantasy of many races, alien thoughts and strange tongues, unique to Hawaii." Because of that setting, he had to "mesh his own thoughts and background with the complex psychology of the various races resident on the island."[45]

Although the setting was different from any previous case, Darrow faced the standard personal attacks from the prosecution. The chief prosecutor, J. C. Kelly, brought Darrow's career into the trial: "Are you going to decide this case on the plea of a man who for fifty years has stood before the bar of justice which he belittles today, or are you going to decide this case on the law."[46]

The Darrow standing before the jury in Hawaii was also very different than in previous trials. Rear Admiral Yates Sterling provided a description of the aged defender: "Darrow, his coat hanging loosely about his bony frame, breathed kindliness and sympathy for all. . . . The courtroom seemed pervaded with this gentle, old voice. Its soothing effect upon that courtroom was miraculous to see. Slowly his voice was stamping out all bitterness."[47]

Although Stone proclaimed that "on the first morning of the case Darrow was thrilled to find that his brain was working with its old-time precision and clarity," it was obvious to most observers that he had lost much of his energy from younger days. In his summation he spoke for an hour before a recess was called so he could rest and during the lunch break he spent much of the time taking a nap. Kevin Tierney pointed out that he could no longer effectively articulate the themes or moods he had earlier evoked. Tierney concluded that it was obvious that Darrow's "time had passed."[48]

Weinberg and Weinberg described Darrow as he spoke his last summation: "His thinning shock of hair fell about his forehead as, gray and gaunt, he leaned over the jury box. His plea was without oratory or verbal polytechnics." He began his speech with a lengthy discussion of the case. This lengthy discussion of events was used to explain why Massie acted as he did. Ultimately Darrrow argued that Massie had gone temporarily insane and therefore murdered the man who had so brutally attacked his wife. That lengthy discussion also led to his standard conclusion that people are controlled by destiny: "This case illustrates the working of human destiny more than any other case I have handled. It illustrates the effect of sorrow and mishap on human minds and lives and shows us how weak and powerless human beings are in the hands of relentless powers." As always, he stated, it is "the question of free will, a will beyond people."[49]

Those outside forces led Massie and his codefendants into the court, but their lives were not hopeless because the jury had the power to do justice in the case: "Today they are in this court, in the hands of you twelve men, to settle their fate. I ask you gentlemen to consider carefully, seriously. The power is given to you to do justice in this case." He continued: I hope you will in kindness and humanity and understanding--no one else but you can do this." Ultimately, Darrow argued that these pople had suffered enough. Sending them to prison would not punish them any more than the events of recent months.[50]

Although the events had such a detrimental effect on the defendants, Darrow praised each for sticking by Mrs. Massie after her ordeal. He described how Massie "went back and forth,

nursing his wife, working all day and attending
her at night for weeks.   It was all that any
husband could do, or any man could do."   These
deeds and loyalty were admirable, but were the
kind of thing we would all do: "Do you suppose
that if you had been caught in the hands of
Fate--would you have done differently?   No, we
are not made that way."[51]

The other defendants, Mrs. Fortescue and
the sailors, likewise were praised for "human
virtues that are not common--loyalty, devotion."   That loyalty and devotion led the
defendants to do something unwise, but "[t]here
is nothing in this evidence to indicate that
they ever meant to kill--there was never any
talk about killing as far as this evidence is
concerned."[52]

He asked the members of the jury to put
themselves in Massie's place: "if you can think
of his raped wife, of his months of suffering
and mental anguish; if you can confront the
unjust, cruel fate that unrolled before him,
then you can judge--but you cannot judge any
man otherwise."   He argued that most of the
members of the jury would have done exactly as
Massie did.[53]

Although much of the interest in the case
rested on the fact that different races were
involved, Darrow argued that race was not an
issue: "I have looked at this Island, which is
a new country to me.   I've never had any prejudice against any race on earth.   I didn't
learn it, and I defy anyone to find any word of
mine to contradict what I say.   To me these
questions of race must be solved by under-
standing--not by force."   He concluded the
speech by asking for a decision that would heal
the hatred engendered by the trial:

> I'd like to think I had done my
> small part to bring peace and justice
> to an Island wracked and worn by
> strife.

You have not only the fate but
the life of these four people. What
is there for them if you pronounce a
sentence of doom on them? What have
they done?

You are a people to heal, not to
destroy. I place this in your hands
asking you to be kind and considerate
both to the living and the dead.[54]

When Darrow finished, "he appeared exhausted,"
but he held up quite well throughout. The
Honolulu Advertiser described the speech: "With
words that unfolded like the immortal pages of
a Greek tragedy, Clarence Darrow laid before
the . . . jury the reasons upon which he is
asking their freedom."[55]

After two days of deliberation the jury
found the defendants guilty of manslaughter.
Reactions on the mainland were overwhelmingly
against the verdict. Appeals were made for a
pardon. Immediately after sentencing the
governor commuted the sentences to one hour.
The Massies immediately left Hawaii.

Darrow believed that he had been
successful in the trial: "I felt . . . that we
were leaving the island more peaceful and happy
than I had found it, for which I was very
glad."[56] That conclusion was hotly debated by
his biographers.

Upon his return to Chicago, Darrow wrote a
twenty-four page description of the trial. His
autobiography had recently been published so
those pages were added as an appendix. The
addition helped sales of the book, particularly
in Hawaii, therefore again helping to further
the Darrow myth.

With the Massie trial completed, Darrow's
career as a defense attorney came to a controversial end. Although the trial was not in defense of the poor and downtrodden, it seemingly
did little to tarnish the myth. Rather, it
seems like a final small footnote to a very

diverse career, a career, that reflected consistent beliefs and actions. Aberrations like the defense of the wealthy in the Leopold and Loeb and the semiwealthy in the Massie case did not have an effect on his image as the defender of the poor--an image that continues virtually unchallenged in the present.

NOTES
1. Arthur Weinberg and Lila Weinberg, Clarence Darrow: A Sentimental Rebel (New York: G. P. Putnam's Sons, 1980), pp. 351, 81-82.
2. Weinberg and Weinberg, Clarence Darrow, p. 126.
3. Darrow, quoted in Weinberg and Weinberg, Clarence Darrow, pp. 280-81; Clarence Darrow, The Story of My Life (New York: Charles Scribner's Sons, 1932), pp. 212-13.
4. Darrow, quoted in Irving Stone, Clarence Darrow for the Defense (Garden City, N.Y.: Doubleday, Inc., 1941), p. 367; Darrow, The Story of My Life, p. 218.
5. Darrow, quoted in Weinberg and Weinberg, Clarence Darrow, p. 291.
6. Quoted in Weinberg and Weinberg, Clarence Darrow, pp. 291-92.
7. Quoted in Weinberg and Weinberg, Clarence Darrow, pp. 291-92.
8. Darrow, quoted in Stone, Clarence Darrow for the Defense, p. 371.
9. Darrow, quoted in Stone, Clarence Darrow for the Defense, p. 373; Darrow, quoted in Weinberg and Weinberg, Clarence Darrow, p. 293.
10. Darrow, quoted in Stone, Clarence Darrow for the Defense, p. 373.
11. Darrow, quoted in Stone, Clarence Darrow for the Defense, p. 372.
12. Darrow, quoted in Stone, Clarence Darrow for the Defense, p. 375.
13. Clarence Darrow, "Freedom Knows No Limits," in Attorney for the Damned, ed. Arthur Weinberg (New York: Simon & Schuster, 1957), p. 130.

14. Darrow, "Freedom Knows No Limits," pp. 155, 160.
15. Darrow, "Freedom Knows No Limits," pp. 127-28.
16, Darrow, "Freedom Knows No Limits," p. 167.
17. Darrow, "Freedom Knows No Limits," p. 171.
18. Darrow, "Freedom Knows No Limits," pp. 132-33.
19. Darrow, "Freedom Knows No Limits," pp. 123-24.
20. Quoted in Weinberg and Weinberg, Clarence Darrow, p. 295.
21. Stone, Clarence Darrow for the Defense, p. 101; Weinberg and Weinberg, Clarence Darrow, pp. 331-32.
22. Stone, Clarence Darrow for the Defense, p. 102.
23. Darrow, quoted in Stone, Clarence Darrow for the Defense, p. 102.
24. Weinberg and Weinberg, Clarence Darrow, p. 332; Darrow, The Story of My Life, p. 303.
25. Weinberg and Weinberg, Clarence Darrow, pp. 332-33.
26. Weinberg and Weinberg, Clarence Darrow, p. 335.
27. Robert Toms, quoted in Stone, Clarence Darrow for the Defense, p. 479; Weinberg and Weinberg, Clarence Darrow, p. 347.
28. Stone, Clarence Darrow for the Defense, p. 481; Darrow, The Story of My Life, p. 308.
29. Darrow, The Story of My Life, p. 311.
30. Clarence Darrow, "You Can't Live There," in Attorney for the Damned, ed. Arthur Weinberg (New York: Simon & Schuster, 1957), pp. 259, 236.
31. Darrow, "You Can't Live There!" pp. 243-46.
32. Darrow, "You Can't Live There!" p. 262.
33. Darrow, "You Can't Live There!" pp. 260, 262-63.
34. Darrow, "You Can't Live There!" p. 262.
35. Darrow, "You Can't Live There!" pp. 241-42.
36. Darrow, "You Can't Live There!" pp. 249, 252.

37. Darrow, "You Can't Live There!" pp. 240-41.
38. Darrow, "You Can't Live There!" pp. 257-58.
39. Arthur Garfield Hays and Frank Murphy, quoted in Stone, <u>Clarence Darrow for the Defense</u>, p. 483; Weinberg and Weinberg, <u>Clarence Darrow</u>, p. 348; Darrow, <u>The Story of My Life</u>, p. 311.
40. Stone, <u>Clarence Darrow for the Defense</u>, p. 505.
41. Darrow, <u>The Story of My Life</u>, p. 473.
42. Kevin Tierney, <u>Darrow: A Biography</u> (New York: Thomas Y. Crowell, 1979), p. 420.
43. Darrow, <u>The Story of My life</u>, pp. 461, 458.
44. Darrow, <u>The Story of My Life</u>, p. 459.
45. Weinberg and Weinberg, <u>Clarence Darrow</u>, pp. 369, 372; Tierney, <u>Darrow</u>, p. 414.
46. J. C. Kelly, quoted in Weinberg and Weinberg, <u>Clarence Darrow</u>, pp. 370-71.
47. Rear Admiral Yates Sterling, quoted in <u>Clarence Darrow for the Defense</u>, pp. 504-505.
48. Stone, <u>Clarence Darrow for the Defense</u>, pp. 504-505; Tierney, <u>Darrow</u>, pp. 421-22.
49. Weinberg and Weinberg, <u>Clarence Darrow</u>, p. 370; Clarence Darrow, "The Unwritten Law," in <u>Attorney for the Damned</u>, ed. Arthur Weinberg (New York: Simon & Schuster, 1957), p. 106.
50. Darrow, "The 'Unwritten Law,'" pp. 106-107.
51. Darrow, "The 'Unwritten Law,'" pp. 108-109, 111.
52. Darrow, "The 'Unwritten Law,'" pp. 113-14.
53. Darrow, "The 'Unwritten Law,'" pp. 114-15.
54. Darrow, "The 'Unwritten Law,'" pp. 116-17.
55. Quoted in "The 'Unwritten Law,'" p. 117.
56. Darrow, <u>The Story of My Life</u>, p. 481.

6

Verdicts Out of Court:
Darrow as Lecturer and Writer

Although Darrow's fame and myth are mainly based on his participation in dramatic courtroom trials, he was an active speaker in a variety of public settings. His performance in those forums helped sustain and build his public image. Even though he had an active law practice, Darrow found the time to deliver hundreds of speeches and engage in numerous debates throughout the country. Often during the course of a trial he would be invited to speak to the public or community groups in the evening. At times his career as a public speaker threatened to overshadow his legal career. At one point he was described as "the greatest box-office draw in America." Darrow outlined his extensive speaking career in his autobiography: "Probably few men in America have ever spoken to so many people over so long a stretch of time. I am satisfied that I like to speak in public, and although speaking is often a hardship, and in my case too often leads to unfriendly criticism . . . still I am sure that if I were not called upon I should feel sad and disappointed."[1]

Although he was a famous and successful speaker, there is no evidence that Darrow underwent any systematic training in the art:

"Darrow's manner of speaking was indeed effective in its own peculiar way, but there is little evidence that this effectiveness came out of any deep understanding of the processes involved or was anything more than the fortunate result of years of trial and error experience on the platform." Darrow must have done some reading on the subject, however. In his autobiography he discussed <u>Oratory</u>, written by his mentor, John Peter Altgeld, naming it the best book he had read on the subject. He commented on the need to study public speaking: "Usually a speaker is better off if he never reads books on this subject, especially one who has anything to say, for most speakers put the manner of talking above the substance; and while the manner is of considerable importance the content is really of the first concern."[2]

He came to that conclusion over a period of years. As a youngster he adopted the artificial style used by popular speakers of the day: "In those days I was rather oratorical. Like many other young men . . . I did the best, or worst, I could to cover up such ideas as I had in a cloud of sounding metrical phrases." As time went by, he changed by striving to "use simple words and shorter sentences, to make my statements plain and direct . . . I find this the better manner of expression." Ultimately he came to the conclusion that a person who "proposes to be a public speaker" must have something to say. The mature Darrow used simple words and short, simple sentences in his speeches. Most of his "illustrations were from the common experiences of daily life," and his embellishment "consisted primarily of references to literature." Darrow summarized his ideas on speaking:

> For years, before juries, on the
> platform, in conversation, I have
> tried to know what I am talking about,
> and then to make my statements clear

and simple, and the sentences short.
I am not at all sure that this is the
best method for writing and speaking.
The reader has time to consider . . .
if he misses a word or does not
understand one . . . he can look
things up in the dictionary or
encyclopaedia. But the listerner has
but one chance, and that is as the
information or opinion hastens along;
so the words must not be too long, or
too unfamiliar, nor spoken too rapid-
ly for assimilation. Some grasp spoken matter quickly, and some need time
to catch what they are not accustomed
to hear.   The speaker must aim to
reach practically every person in his
audience; therefore he must not speak
too fast or use too many uncommon
words.[3]

Much of Darrow's early life was spent in
preparation to be an orator. Part of his legend stated that his sister Mary trained him to
"speak pieces from the time he was two." As a
youth he liked to play baseball, to debate, and
to "'speak pieces' and was always keen to make
due preparation . . . no matter what the subject might be." As he grew older, Darrow took
part in Saturday night debates that were a favorite form of local entertainment in Ohio.
Darrow's success in those debates led to invitations to speak in other towns.   During those
early debates he developed many of the themes he
would use throughout his life.[4]

Darrow's interest in speaking may have been
partially responsible for his choice of law as a
career.   Early in life Darrow noticed that
lawyers were often called upon to speak on
holidays and during political campaigns. As a
youth he also observed local trials: "I enjoyed
the way the pettifoggers abused each other, and
as I grew toward maturity I developed a desire

to be a lawyer too."[5]

Part of Darrow's reason for speaking was based on his need for recognition. Both in Ohio and later in Chicago, he was "impatient to make a name for himself." He particularly craved the notice of the press: "Through the first half of my life I was anxious to get into the papers . . . in the last half I have often been eager to keep out. In neither case have I had much success."[6]

After moving to Chicago Darrow immediately joined several community clubs where he could speak and debate. Through his speaking, Darrow hoped to impress people who could advance his career. For example, at the Sunset Club he spoke on "Realism in Literature and Art," read aloud from Omar Khayyam and Robert Burns, and spoke on prohibition. Many of the topics "with which Darrow's name would become associated in the public mind were on the agenda of the club. He had not stolen his material from others, but the stock-in-trade of his lifetime of public speaking was developed there and from 1900 on would simply be polished rather than expanded."[7]

Darrow's major break came because of his speeches before the Single Tax Club. An unnamed observer described one of Darrow's speeches before that club:

> He was dressed in a cutaway and had on a white boiled shirt, a low starched collar and a narrow, black bow tie. His subject was Tolstoy's novel <u>Anna Karenina</u>. . . . Every little while during the address he hunched his wide shoulders forward and ran his hand through the long, straight, stringy, dark brown hair . . . so as to smooth it back. The lecture was full of striking, original statements, in simple language, punctuated with shafts of wit and sarcasm, which brought titters and laughter from his

audience, but it was apparent he did
not utter them to wisecrack; they were
relevant to a serious argument. . . .
This talk made a strong impression on
me and, I believe, on the audience."[8]

His dramatic speech before the Single Tax Club
in 1888 led to the desired press attention, a
job with the city of Chicago, and a variety of
speaking opportunities. He was asked to give
speeches for Democratic politicians during the
city election: "I had been asked to speak at
various meetings before, but never until then
had I been invited to choose my hall and
colleagues. This time I was asked to do both. I
named my hall, but I took no chances, and said I
would speak alone. And I did."[9]

As Darrow's fame grew, the invitations for
speaking and debates mounted. During the late
1800s and early 1900s such lectures and debates
were popular forms of entertainment and education. In his study of Darrow as a debater,
James Edward Sayer outlined the importance of
such gatherings: "Besides providing an interesting evening away from home, public debates
presented famous speakers who would do battle on
contemporary issues of the time." Because of
Darrow's fame as a courtroom speaker and his
interest in social issues, it is easy to
understand how he became involved in so many
debates. The debates also gave people the
opportunity to see and hear a famous attorney in
public: "Wherever and whenever he spoke, the
hall was packed; at times many were turned
away."[10]

Darrow enjoyed the lectures and debates
because they provided a kind of stimulation he
did not receive in his legal career. Kevin
Tierney stated:

Platform speaking did for Darrow what
Dr. Johnson believed the prospect of
hanging did for a condemned man--it
cleared the mind wonderfully. He had

a magical ability to rise to an occasion. Before an audience he became a
giant. He was less interested in
applause . . . than in attention, in
occupying many minds at one time. . .
. The pressure of performing urged him
on like nothing else, and he relied
upon it. He shared the mysterious,
obscure gift of "presence" that all
public figures have or attain.
Something brought out the best in him
and caused people to listen.[11]

The public performances also gave him an opportunity to disseminate the ideas he discussed
during trials to wider audiences.

Although Darrow enjoyed debating, there
were periods of time when he was forced to make
much of his living through his public performances. For example, the 1929 stock market
crash erased much of his fortune so he was
forced to debate and speak as a means of making
a living. As he was forced to earn his living
as a debater, he became less "the impassioned
advocate forced forward by moral outrage and
more the measured, practical reformer." Sayer
described those debates as "repetitive
patchworks of argument drawn from earlier and
greater speeches."[12]

Because the debates were so often on the
same set of topics, "he developed stock
responses to the challenges he most frequently
encountered. They appeared to some to be more
notable for their dramatic or diversionary
qualities than for their relevance or
intellectual rigor." Darrow admitted that much
of his success could be attributed to the
repetition of topics: "My debates have been on
prohibition, religion, politics, and science. .
. . In these debates, most of the speakers . . .
have very nearly echoed each other's sentiments. This of course saved me from varying my
arguments to any great extent."[13]

Tierney stated that Darrow "dressed up his public pronouncements to make them sound shocking because he enjoyed the notoriety they brought him." Often the main reason he made such shocking statements was to get the audience's attention. He claimed, however, that "I have never knowingly catered to anyone's ideas, and I have expressed what was within me, regardless of consequences." That lack of catering was reflected in the fact that Darrow often took the unpopular side of an issue; even "when his listeners were openly hostile to his unconventional ideas, he was not in the least distressed but went right on, never abandoning his good-natured, gently satirical tone and never backing away from his independent views."[14]

Because of his unconventional views, Darrow generally debated on the negative side, a position he enjoyed. As he once stated, "I can debate any question in the negative." He particularly enjoyed the negative because he was often able to make the audience angry, believing that "if he could make them mad enough he might make them mad enough to start thinking for themselves." Some of his most famous statements were attempts to make the audience respond. For example, in Miami the chair of a meeting introduced Darrow to an audience of six hundred by saying: "It gives me great pleasure to present Mr. Darrow to such a large and intelligent audience." Darrow rose and surveyed the audience; then he responded, "My friends, the chairman is mistaken. There are not this many intelligent people in the whole world." On another occasion he was introduced to a group of workers as a friend of laborers. He responded by saying, "Yes, I have always been a friend of the workingman, and I hope I always will be. I would rather be a friend of the workingman than to be a workingman."[15]

His ideas were shocking to the public because he was so far ahead of his time on most

social questions. Because of his being ahead of
his audiences, "he managed to leave to future
generations a legacy of speeches and writings
that retained their modernity for succeeding
generations."[16]

His public lectures and debates reflected
standard topics such as discussion of literary
figures, prohibition, and religion. Darrow was
an avid reader who identified with literary
figures such as Leo Tolstoy, Omar Khayyam, Walt
Whitman, and Robert Burns. He felt a kinship
with these writers because they "symbolized a
universality of man and a sensitivity to life's
trends."[17]

Darrow strongly opposed prohibition because he saw it as "a demonstration that the law
was devoid of moral content, and purely an
exercise of power." He argued that it was
unfair to the poor: "Prohibition would not
interfere with the rich; it was never meant to
interfere with them. Of course, the poor would
be shut off now and then. . . . What business is
there for a poor man to drink? It is his
business to work. Anyway, he is not able to
control his own appetite, and he needs his
money; he has no right to fool it away."[18]

His views were particularly controversial
on the subject of religion. Although his views
were often dramatically opposed to those of the
audience on the subject, he was able to win
people over because he understood them. An
opponent named Thomas G. Higgins described an
audience in Columbus, Ohio, that originally was
against Darrow, but within "a matter of minutes
. . . he seemed to have the entire audience in
the hollow of his hand. . . . As he progressed
in his talk the audience became spellbound; you
could quite literally have heard a pin drop. I
never saw such a demonstration of the power of
personality."[19]

Later in life Darrow took part in a series
of debates on religion. The debates, arranged

by a lecture manager named George Whitefield, involved having a Protestant clergyman, a prominent Catholic, and a Jewish rabbi meet with Darrow in debates in large cities in the Midwest. Most of the audiences came to see Darrow defeated, but he won them over: "any came despising him, thinking him a devil with horns. They went away liking him and feeling sorry for him." Despite the fact that he opposed organized religion, many of his opponents saw Darrow as the embodiment of Christian values. For example, one adversary proclaimed: "Here is a man who lives by Christ's teachings."[20]

Darrow's arguments in all of his debates tended to follow a similar four-step pattern: "use a backdrop of history, labelling one's opponent as a tool of some evil force, use of invective against the opponent, and the insistence that [his] position was based upon kindliness and other respectable qualities." Because he followed this pattern in all his debates, Darrow simply had to insert the issues he used for each topic into this standard format.[21]

After studying Darrow's debates, Sayer came to the conclusion that Darrow had three strengths as a debater. First of all, he used clear language that was easily understood. That language and "his conversational mode of speaking created an impression of good-natured friendliness and a 'just folks' style." Second, he used humor with "a large amount of concealed invective and sarcasm that could be devastating to the opponent's position." Finally, Darrow was philosophically consistent, so he was able to use the same lines of argument successfully throughout his career.[22]

Sayer also found three major weaknesses in Darrow's debating. First of all, his presentations lacked organization and internal development, therefore making his arguments difficult to follow at times. Second, Darrow was not good at refutation.   Rather, he tended to use his own assertions and often seemed to ignore his opponent's ideas.   Finally, Sayer found that Darrow consistently brought "peripheral and irrelevant issues into the debate."   Coupled with the lack of internal consistency, this introduction of extraneous information weakened the structure and power of his arguments.[23]

Although Darrow is best known as a speaker, he also presented his ideas to the public in writing through his autobiography, novels, and essays.   At many points in his career he expressed the desire to give up the law for a literary career. Unfortunately, he was not able to make a living as a writer, so he could only write in moments when he was free from his legal practice.   Some critics argued that Darrow was unable to write as well as he could speak because he relied on a live audience for inspiration.   Without such inspiration he was not able to produce memorable written pieces.

Darrow's autobiography and his autobiographical novel, Farmington, looked back to simpler times and the forces that shaped his life.   Both of the books were written on trips, times when he was away from home and thus free of the burdens of his legal practice. He also wrote a novel called An Eye for an Eye, an attempt to explain the lives of the poor in Chicago.   All of these books provide readers with insight into Darrow's life and his ideas.

Darrow's numerous essays appeared in pamphlets, magazines, and his own books.   Any of the ideas he expressed in lectures appeared in essay form. For example, his lectures on famous authors were reprinted in his book A Persian Pearl and Other Essays. Essays on such controversial topics as prohibition appeared in national magazines. Like his speaking, Darrow's writing "had its purpose: to correct an evil, to avert an injustice, to assuage a suffering." In their introduction to a volume of Darrow's writings, Arthur and Lila Weinberg sumarized his writings:

> In all his writings there is an antagonism toward prejudice, ignorance, hate, bigotry. He was a skeptic and a dissenter, but always in defense of what he regarded as the positive right of the individual to liberty of speech, thought, and conduct. His writings express a great love for the universal, for the understanding of man and the longing for a "better day."[24]

Over fifty years after his death Darrow is still revered by people who read his speeches and writings and support the causes he espoused. The myth of the defender of the poor and weak of society has become an important part of the American legal folklore. Much of his legend was built because of his actions, but the myth was at times a conspicuous one Darrow himself nurtured and helped grow.

Over a period of time either myths evolve and grow or they die. In Darrow's case the legend has become an accepted part of American legal lore to the point where it is unlikely to ever go away.

The man and his myth have provided inspiration for many individuals who have questioned the assumptions of American society. Perhaps that inspiration would be the sort of compliment that a nonconformist like Darrow would appreciate.

Darrow spent much of his life trying to gain and build his fame and to get people to listen to his ideas. The fact that people continue to be interested in him and his ideas would be of considerable satisfaction to him. Perhaps the teacher of the courtroom would conclude that he had taught the people of his country well.

NOTES
1. Kevin Tierney, <u>Darrow: A Biography</u> (New York: Thomas Y. Crowell, 1979), p. 399; Clarence Darrow, <u>The Story of My Life</u> (New York: Charles Scribner's Sons, 1932), p. 209.
2. Horace G. Rashkopf, "The Speaking of Clarence Darrow," in <u>American Public Address</u>, ed. Loren Reid (Columbia: University of Missiouri Press, 1961), p. 37; Darrow, <u>The Story of My Life</u>, p. 109.
3. Darrow, quoted in Tierney, <u>Darrow</u>, pp. 26-27, 141-42; Darrow, <u>The Story of My Life</u>, p. 42; Darrow, quoted in Rashkopf, "The Speaking of Clarence Darrow," p. 45.
4. Irving Stone, <u>Clarence Darrow for the Defense</u> (Garden City, N.Y.: Doubleday, Inc., 1941), p. 17.
5. Darrow, <u>The Story of My Life</u>, pp. 28-29.
6. Darrow, quoted in Arthur Weinberg and Lila Weinberg, <u>Clarence Darrow</u> (New York: G. P. Putnam's Sons, 1980), p. 37.
7. Stone, <u>Clarence Darrow for the Defense</u>, p. 29; Tierney, <u>Darrow</u>, pp. 48-49.
8. Quoted in Stone, <u>Clarence Darrow for the Defense</u>, pp. 30-31.
9. Darrow, <u>The Story of My Life</u>, p. 48.
10. James Edward Sayer, <u>Clarence Darrow: Public Advocate</u> (Dayton, Ohio: Wright State University, 1978), p. 3; Arthur Weinberg and Lila Weinberg, <u>Verdicts Out of Court</u> (Chicago: Quadrangle Books, 1963), p. 51.
11. Tierney, <u>Darrow</u>, pp. 393-94.
12. Tierney, <u>Darrow</u>, p. 394; Sayer, <u>Clarence Darrow</u>, p. 3.
13. Tierney, <u>Darrow</u>, pp. 395, 142-43.
14. Tierney, <u>Darrow</u>, p. 317; Stone, <u>Clarence Darrow for the Defense</u>, p. 171; Sayer, <u>Clarence Darrow</u>, p. 2.
15. Darrow, quoted in Weinberg and Weinberg, <u>Verdicts Out of Court</u>, p. 50; Stone, <u>Clarence Darrow for the Defense</u>, p. 168.
16. Tierney, <u>Darrow</u>, pp. 233-34.
17. Weinberg and Weinberg, <u>Clarence Darrow</u>, p.

68.

18. Tierney, <u>Darrow</u>, pp. 315-16; Darrow, quoted in Weinberg and Weinberg, <u>Verdicts Out of Court</u>, pp. 43-44.

19. Thomas G. Higgins, quoted in Tierney, <u>Darrow</u>, pp. 395-96.

20. Stone, <u>Clarence Darrow for the Defense</u>, pp. 489, 492, 423.

21. Sayer, <u>Clarence Darrow</u>, pp. 96-97.

22. Sayer, <u>Clarence Darrow</u>, p. 96.

23. Sayer, <u>Clarence Darrow</u>, p. 96.

24. Weinberg and Weinberg, <u>Verdicts Out of Court</u>, pp. 24-25.

II

COLLECTED SPEECHES

Speech in Self-Defense

Los Angeles, 1912

Gentlemen of the jury, an experience like this never came to me before, and of course I cannot say how I will get along with it. I am quite sure there are very few men who are called upon by experience of this kind, but I have felt, gentlemen, after the patience you have given this case for all these weeks, that you will be willing to listen to me, even though I might not argue it as well as I would some other case. I felt that at least I ought to say something to you twelve men besides what I have already said on the witness stand.

In the first place, I am a defendant charged with a serious crime. I have been looking into the penitentiary for six or seven months, and now I am waiting for you twelve men to say whether I shall go there or not. In the next place, I am a stranger in a strange land, 2,000 miles away from home and friends--although I am proud to say that here, so far away, there have gathered around me as good and loyal and faithful friends as any man could have upon the earth. Still I am unknown to you.

I think I can say that no one in my native town would have made to any jury any such statement as was made of me by the district attorney in opening this case. I will venture to say he could not afterward have found a com-

panion except among detectives and crooks and
sneaks in the city where I live if he had dared
to open his mouth in the infamous way he did in
this case.

But here I am in his hands.   Think of it!
In a position where he can call me a coward--and
in all my life I never saw or heard so cowardly,
sneaky and brutal an act as Ford committed in
this courtroom before this jury.   Was any
courage displayed by him?   It was only brutal
and low, and every man knows it.

I don't object to a lawyer arguing the
facts in his case and the evidence in his case,
and drawing such conclusions as he will; but
every man with a sense of justice in his soul
knows that this attack of Ford's was cowardly
and malicious in the extreme.   It was not worthy
of a man and did not come from a man.

I am entitled to some rights until you,
gentlemen, shall say differently, and I would be
entitled to some even then, and so long as I
have any, I shall assert them the best I can as
I go through the world wherever I am.

What am I on trial for, gentlemen of the
jury?   You have been listening here for three
months.   What is it all about?   If you don't
know, then you are not as intelligent as I
believe.   I am not on trial for having sought to
bribe a man named Lockwood.   There may be and
doubtless are many people who think I did seek
to bribe him, but I am not on trial for that,
and I will prove it to you.   I am on trial
because I have been a lover of the poor, a
friend of the oppressed, because I have stood by
labor for all these years, and have brought down
upon my head the wrath of the criminal interests
in this country.   Whether guilty or innocent of
the crime charged in the indictment, that is the
reason why I am here, and that is the reason
that I have been pursued by as cruel a gang as
ever followed a man.

Now, let's see if I can prove this.   If the
district attorney of this county thought a crime

had been committed, well and good, let him go
ahead and prosecute. But has he done this? Has
he prosecuted any of the bribe takers and
givers?

And who are these people back of him and
back of the organization of this county who have
been hot on my trail and whose bark I can
remember from long ago? Will you tell me,
gentlemen of the jury, why the Erectors' Association and the Steel Trust are interested in
this case way out here in Los Angeles? Will you
tell me why the Erectors' Association of
Indianapolis should have put up as vicious and
as cruel a plot to catch me as was ever used
against any American citizen?

Gentlemen, if you don't know, you are not
fit to be jurors. Are these people interested
in bribery? Why, almost every dollar of their
ill-gotten gains has come from bribery.

When did the Steel Trust--the Steel Trust,
which owns the Erectors' Association and is the
Erectors' Association--when did it become
interested in prosecuting bribery? Was it when
they unloaded a billion dollars of watered stock
upon the American people--stock that draws its
life and interest from the brawn, the brain and
the blood of the American workingman? Are they
interested in coming all the way out to this
state and to Los Angeles to prosecute a man
merely for bribery? There are a good many
states between this city and New York City?
There are a good many state's attorneys in this
broad land of ours. They can begin at home if
they would, these men who have made bribery a
profession and a fine art.

Gentlemen of the jury, it is not that any
of these men care about bribery, but it is that
there never was a chance before, since the world
began, to claim that bribery had been committed
for the poor. Heretofore, bribery, like
everything else, had been monopolized by the
rich. But now they thought there was a chance
to lay this crime to the poor and "to get" me.

Is there any doubt about it?

Suppose I am guilty of bribery, is that why I am prosecuted in this court? Is that why, by the most infamous methods known to the law and outside the law, these men, the real enemies of society, are trying to get me inside the penitentiary?

No, that isn't it, and you twelve men know it. Your faces are unfamiliar to me. There may not be a man on this jury who believes as I believe upon these great questions between capital and labor. You may all be on the other side, but I have faced the other side over and over again, and I am going to tell you the truth this afternoon. It may be the last chance that I shall ever get to speak to a jury.

These men are interested in getting me. They have concocted all sorts of schemes for the sake of getting me out of the way. Do you suppose they care what laws I might have broken? I have committed one crime, one crime which is like that against the Holy Ghost, which cannot be forgiven. I have stood for the weak and the poor. I have stood for the men who toil. And therefore I have stood against them, and now this is their chance. All right, gentlemen, I am in your hands, not in theirs, just yet.

In examining you before you were accepted as jurors, Mr. Fredericks asked you whether, if I should address you, you would be likely to be carried away by sympathy? You won't be if you wait for me to ask for sympathy. He has cautioned you against my argument. You will find I am a plain-speaking man who will try to talk to you as one man to another. I have never asked sympathy of anybody, and I am not going to ask it of you twelve. I would rather go to the penitentiary than ask for sympathy.

I have lived my life, and I have fought my battles, not against the weak and the poor--anybody can do that--but against power, against injustice, against oppression, and I have asked no odds from them, and I never shall.

I want you to take the facts of this case as they are, and consider the evidence as it is, and then if you twelve men can find on your conscience and under your oath any reason to take away my liberty, well and good, the responsibility will be on you. I would rather be in my position than in yours in the years to come.

As I have told you, I am tried here because I have given a large part of my life and my services to the poor and the weak, and because I am in the way of the interests. Those interests would stop my voice--and they have hired many vipers to help them do it. They would stop my voice--my voice which from the time I was a prattling babe, my father and mother taught me to raise for justice and freedom, and in the cause of the weak and the poor. They would stop my voice with the penitentiary. Oh, you wild, insane members of the Steel Trust and Erectors' Association! Oh, you mad hounds of detectives who are willing to do your master's will! Oh, you district attorneys! You know not what you do. Let me say to you, that if you send me to prison, within the gray, dim walls of San Quentin there will brood a silence more ominous and eloquent than any words that my poor lips could ever frame. And do you think that you could destroy the hopes of the poor and the oppressed if you did silence me? Don't you know that upon my persecution and destruction would arise 10,000 men abler than I have been, more devoted than I have been, and ready to give more than I have given in a righteous cause?

I have been, perhaps, interested in more cases for the weak and poor than any other lawyer in America, but I am pretty nearly done, anyhow. If they had taken me twenty years ago, it might have been worth their while, but there are younger men than I, and there are men who will not be awed by prison bars, by district attorneys, by detectives, who will do this work when I am done.

If you help the Erectors' Association put me into the penitentiary, gentlemen, and Mr. Ford stands outside the door licking his picturesque chops in glee at my destruction, then what? Will the labor cause be dead? Will Ford's masters ride roughshod over the liberties of men? No! Others will come to take my place, and they will do the work better than I have done it in the past.

Gentlemen, say this is not a case of bribery at all.

Will you tell me if anywhere there could be an American jury, or anywhere in the English-speaking world there could be found a jury that would for a moment lend itself to a conspiracy so obvious and foul as this? If there is, gentlemen, then send me to prison. Anyway, when I reach prison, they can do nothing more to me, and if I stay here, they will probably get me for murder after a while. I do not mean the murder of Ford, he is not worth it; but they will put up a job and get me for something else. If any jury could possibly, in a case like this, find me guilty, the quicker it is done the better. Then I will be out of my trouble.

Gentlemen, if the state of California can afford to stand it, I can. If the state of California, and the fair city of Los Angeles, can lend itself to a crime like this, the victim will be ready when the time comes. But let me tell you that if under such testimony as you have heard here, and under the sort of conspiracy you have seen laid bare here, you should send me to prison, it would leave a stain upon the fair fame of your city and your state that would last while these hills endure, and so long as the Pacific waves should wash your sandy coast. Tell me that any American jury would do it! Gentlemen, I could tell you that I did this bribery, and you would turn me loose. If I did not think so, I would not think you were

Americans of spirit or heart, or sense of justice. Gentlemen, if within this courthouse men could be bought and bribed with immunity, could be threatened and coached and browbeaten, and if the gold of the Erectors' Association could be used to destroy human life--if that could succeed, it would be better that these walls should crumble into dust. . . . I have been a busy man. I have never had to look for clients, they have come to me. I have been a general attorney of a big railroad. I have been the attorney several times, and general counsel, as it were, of the great City of Chicago. I have represented the strong and the weak--but never the strong against the weak. I have been called into a great many cases for labor unions. I have been called into a great many arbitration cases. I believe if you went to my native town, that the rich would tell you that they could trust not only my honor, but my judgement, and my sense of justice and fairness. More than once have they left their disputes with the laboring men with me to settle and I have settled them as justly as I could, without giving the working man as much as he ought to have. It will be many and many a year before he will get all he ought to have. That must be reached step by step. But every step means more in the progress of the world.

This McNamara case came like a thunderclap upon the world. What was it? A building had been destroyed, and twenty lives had been lost. It shocked the world. Whether it was destroyed by accident or violence no one knew, and yet everyone had an opinion. How did they form that opinion? Everybody who sympathized with the working man believed it was something else. All had opinions. Society was in open rupture. Upon the one hand all the powerful forces thought, "Now we have these men by the throat, and we will strangle them to death. Now we will reach out the strong arm of money and the strong arm of the law, and we will destroy the labor unions of America."

On the other hand were the weak, and the poor, and the workers, whom I had served; these were rallying to the defense of the unions and to the defense of their homes. They called on me. I did not want to go. I urged them to take someone else, but I had to lay aside my own preferences and take the case.

There was a direct cleavage in society. Upon the one hand, those who hated unions, and those who loved them. The fight was growing fiercer and bitterer day by day. It was a class struggle, gentlemen of the jury, filled with all the venom and bitterness born of a class struggle. These two great contending armies were meeting in almost mortal combat. No one could see the end.

I have loved peace all my life. I have taught it all my life. I believe that love does more than hatred. I believe that both sides have gone about the settlement of these difficulties in the wrong way. The acts of the one have cause the acts of the other, and I blame neither. Men are not perfect. They had an imperfect origin, and they are imperfect today, and the long struggle of the human race from darkness to comparative civilization has been filled with clash and discord and murder and war, and violence and wrong, and it will be, for years and years to come. But ever we are going onward and upward toward the sunshine, where the hatred and war and cruelty and violence of the world will disappear.

Men were arrayed in two great forces--the rich and the poor. None could see the end. They were trying to cure hate with hate.

I know I could have tried the McNamara case, and that a large class of the working people of America would honestly have believed, if these men had been hanged, that they were not guilty. I could have done this and have saved myself. I could have made money had I done this--if I had wanted to get money in that way.

I know if you had hanged these men and the other men, you would have changed the opinion of scarcely a man in America and you would have settled in the hearts of a great mass of men a hatred so deep, so profound, that it would never die away.

And I took the responsibility, gentlemen. Maybe I did wrong, but I took it, and the matter was disposed of and the questions set at rest. Here and there I got praise for what you called an heroic act, although I did not deserve the praise, for I followed the law of my being--that was all. I acted out the instincts that were within me. I acted according to the teachings of the parents who reared me, and according to the life I had lived. I did not deserve praise, but where I got one word of praise, I got a thousand words of blame! And I have stood under that for nearly a year.

This trial has helped clear up the McNamara case. It will all finally be cleared up, if not in time for me to profit by it, in time for my descendants to know. Some time we will know the truth. But I have gone on about my way as I always have regardless of this, without asking anything of anybody who lived, and I will go on that way to the end.

I know the mob. In one way I love it, in another way I despise it. I know the unreasoning, unthinking mass. I have lived with men and worked with them. I have been their idol and I have been cast down and trampled beneath their feet. I have stood on the pinnacle, and I have heard the cheering mob sound my praises. I have gone down to the depths of the valley, where I have heard them hiss my name--this same mob--but I have summoned such devotion and such courage as God has given me, and I have gone on--gone on my path unmoved by their hisses or their cheers.

I have tried to live my life and to live it as I see it, regarding neither praise nor blame, both of which are unjust. No man is judged rightly by his fellowman. Some look upon him as

an idol, and forget that his feet are clay, as
are the feet of every man. Others look upon him
as a devil and can see no good in him at all.
Neither is true. I have known this, and I have
tried to follow my conscience and my duty the
best I could and do it faithfully; and here I am
today in the hands of you twelve men who will
one day say to your children, and they will say
to their children, that you passed on my fate.

Gentlemen, there is not much more to say.
You may not agree with all my views of philosophy. I believe we are all in the hands of
destiny and if it is written in the book of
destiny that I shall go on to the penitentiary,
that you twelve men before me shall send me
there, I will go. If it is written that I am
now down to the depths and that you twelve men
shall liberate me, then so it will be. We go
here and there, and we think we control our
destinies, and our lives, but above us and beyond us and around us, are unseen hands, and
unseen forces that move us at their will.

I am here and I can look back to the forces
that brought me here and I can see that I had
nothing whatever to do with it, and could not
help it, any more than any of you twelve men had
to do with or could help passing on my fate.
There is not one of you that would have wished
to judge me, unless you could do it in a way to
help me in my sore distress, I know that. We
have little to do with ourselves.

As one poet has expressed it,

Life is a game of whist.   From unknown
sources
The cards are shuffled and the hands are
dealt.
Blind are our efforts to control the forces
That though unseen are no less strongly
felt.
I do not like the way the cards are
shuffled,
But still I like the game and want to play

And through the long, long night, I play unruffled
The cards I get until the break of day.

I have taken the cards as they came. I have played the best I could. I have tried to play them honestly, manfully, doing for myself and for my fellow the best I could, and I will play the game to the end, whatever that end may be.

Gentlemen, I came to this city as a stranger. Misfortune has beset me, but I never saw a place in my life with greater warmth and kindness and love than Los Angeles. Here to a stranger have come hands to help me, hearts to beat with mine, words of sympathy to encourage and cheer, and though a stranger to you twelve men and a stranger to this city, I am willing to leave this case with you. I know my life, I know what I have done. My heart has not been perfect. It has been human, too human. I have felt the heart beats of every man who lived. I have tried to be the friend of every man who lived. I have tried to help in the world. I have not had malice in my heart. I have had love for my fellow man. I have done the best I could. There are some people who know it. There are some who do not believe it. There are people who regard my name as a byword and a reproach, more for the good I have done than for the evil.

There are people who would destroy me. There are people who would lift up their hands to crush me down. I have enemies powerful and strong. There are honest men who misunderstand me and doubt me; and still I have lived a long time on earth, and I have friends--I have friends in my old home who have gathered around to tell you as best they could of the life I have lived. I have friends who have come to me here to help me in my sore distress. I have friends throughout the length and breadth of the land, and these are the poor and the weak and the helpless, to whose cause I have given voice. If you should convict me, there will be people to applaud the act.   But if in your judgement and your wisdom and your humanity, you believe me innocent, and return a verdict of not guilty in this case, I know that from thousands and tens of thousands and yea, perhaps hundreds of thousands, of the weak and the poor and the helpless throughout the world will come thanks to this jury for saving my liberty and my name.

Speech in Defense of Leopold and Loeb

Chicago, 1924

Your Honor, it has been almost three months since the great responsibility of this case was assumed by my associates and myself. I am willing to confess that it has been three months of great anxiety--a burden which I gladly would have been spared excepting my feelings of affection toward some of the members of one of these unfortunate families. This responsibility is almost too great for anyone to assume, but we lawyers can no more choose than the court can choose.

Our anxiety over this case has not been due to the facts that are connected with this most unfortunate affair, but to the almost unheard-of publicity it has received; to the fact that newspapers all over this country have been giving it space such as they have almost never before given to any case. The fact that day after day the people of Chicago have been regaled with stories of all sorts about it, until almost every person has formed an opinion.

And when the public is interested and demands a punishment, no matter what the offense, great or small, it thinks of only one punishment, and that is death.

It may not be a question that involves the

taking of human life; it may be a question of pure prejudice alone; but when the public speaks as one man it thinks only of killing.

We have been in this stress and strain for three months. We did what we could and all we could to gain the confidence of the public, who in the end really control, whether wisely or unwisely.

It was announced that there were millions of dollars to be spent on this case. Wild and extravagant stories were freely published as though they were facts. Here was to be an effort to save the lives of two boys by the use of money in fabulous amounts, amounts such as these families never even had.

We announced to the public that no excessive use of money would be made in this case, neither for lawyers nor for psychiatrists, nor in any other way. We have faithfully kept that promise.

The psychiatrists, it has been shown by the evidence in this case, are receiving a per diem, and only a per diem, which is the same as is paid by the State.

The attorneys, at their own request, have agreed to take such amount as the officers of the Chicago Bar Association may think is proper in this case.

If we fail in this defense it will not be for lack of money. It will be on account of money. Money has been the most serious handicap that we have met. There are times when poverty is fortunate.

I insist, Your Honor, that had this been the case of two boys of these defendants' ages, unconnected with families supposed to have great wealth, there is not a state's attorney in Illinois who would not have consented at once to a plea of guilty and a punishment in the penitentiary for life. Not one.

No lawyer could have justified any other attitude. No prosecution could have justified it.

We could have come into this court without
evidence, without argument, and this court
would have given to us what every judge in the
city of Chicago has given to everybody in the
city of Chicago since the first capital case
was tried. We would have had no contest.

We are here with the lives of two boys
imperiled, with the public aroused.

For what?

Because, unfortunately, the parents have
money. Nothing else.

I told Your Honor in the beginning that
never had there been a case in Chicago, where
on a plea of guilty a boy under twenty-one had
been sentenced to death. I will raise that age
and say, never has there been a case where a
human being under the age of twenty-three has
been sentenced to death. And, I think I am
safe in saying, although I have not examined
all the records and could not--but I think I am
safe in saying--that never has there been such
a case in the state of Illinois.

And yet this court is urged, aye, threatened, that he must hang two boys contrary to
precedents, contrary to the acts of every judge
who ever held court in this state.

Why?

Tell me what public necessity there is for
this.

Why need the state's attorney ask for
something that never before has been demanded?

Why need a judge be urged by every argument, moderate and immoderate, to hang two boys
in the face of every precedent in Illinois, and
in the face of the progress of the last fifty
years?

Lawyers stand here by the day and read
cases from the Dark Ages, where judges have
said that if a man had a grain of sense left
and a child if he was barely out of his cradle,
could be hanged because he knew the difference
between right and wrong. Death sentences for
eighteen, seventeen, sixteen and fourteen years

have been cited.   Brother Marshall has not half done his job.   He should read his beloved Blackstone again.

I have heard in the last six weeks nothing but the cry for blood.   I have heard from the office of the state's attorney only ugly hate.

I have heard precedents quoted which would be a disgrace to a savage race.   I have seen a court urged almost to the point of threats to hang two boys, in the face of science, in the face of philosophy, in the face of humanity, in the face of experience, in the face of all the better and more humane thoughts of the age.

Why did not my friend, Mr. Marshall, who dug up from the relics of the buried past these precedents that would bring a blush of shame to the face of a savage, read this from Blackstone:

"Under fourteen, though an infant shall be judged to be incapable of guile prima facie, yet if it appeared to the court and the jury that he was capable of guile, and could discern between good and evil, he may be convicted and suffer death."

Thus a girl thirteen has been burned for killing her mistress.

How this case would delight Dr. Krohn!

He would lick his chops over that more gleefully than over his dastardly homicidal attempt to kill these boys.

One boy of ten and another of nine years of age who had killed their companion were sentenced to death; and he of ten actually hanged?

Why?

He knew the difference between right and wrong.   He had learned that in Sunday school.

Age does not count.

Why, Mr. Savage says age makes no difference, and that if this court should do what every other court in Illinois has done since its foundation, and refuse to sentence these boys to death, no one else would ever be hanged in Illinois.

Well, I can imagine some results worse than that. So long as this terrible tool is to be used for a plaything, without thought or consideration, we ought to get rid of it for the protection of human life.

My friend Marshall has read Blackstone by the page, as if it had something to do with a fairly enlightened age, as if it had something to do with the year 1924, as if it had something to do with Chicago, with its boys' courts and its fairly tender protection of the young.

Now, Your Honor, I shall discuss more in detail a little later, and I only say it now because my friend Mr. Savage--did you pick him for his name or his ability or his learning?-- because my friend Mr. Savage, in as cruel a speech as he knew how to make, said to this court that we pleaded guilty because we were afraid to do anything else.

Your Honor, that is true.

We have said to the public and to this court that neither the parents, nor the friends, nor the attorneys would want these boys released. That they are as they are. Unfortunate though it be, it is true, and those closest to them know perfectly well that they should not be released, and that they should be permanently isolated from society. We have said that, and we mean it. We are asking this court to save their lives, which is the least and the most that a judge can do.

We did plead guilty before Your Honor because we were afraid to submit our case to a jury. I would not for a moment deny to this court or to this community a realization of the serious danger we were in and how perplexed we were before we took this more unusual step.

I can tell Your Honor why.

I have found that years and experience with life tempers one's emotions and makes him more understanding of his fellow-man.

Why, when my friend Savage is my age, or

even yours, he will read his address to this
court with horror.

I am aware that as one grows older he is
less critical.   He is not so sure.   He is
inclined to make some allowance for his
fellowman.   I am aware that a court has more
experience, more judgement and more kindliness
than a jury.

Your Honor, it may be hardly fair to the
court; I am aware that I have helped to place a
serious burden upon your shoulders.   And at
that, I have always meant to be your friend.
But that was not an act of friendship.

I know perfectly well that where responsibility is divided by twelve, it is easy to
say: "Away with him."

But, Your Honor, if these boys hang, you
must do it.   There can be no division of
responsibility here.   You can never explain
that the rest overpowered you.   It must be by
your deliberate, cool, premeditated act, without a chance to shift responsibility.

It was not a kindness to you.   We placed
this responsibility on your shoulders because
we were mindful of the rights of our clients,
and we were mindful of the unhappy families who
have done no wrong.

Now, let me see, Your Honor, what we had
to sustain us.   Of course, I have known Your
Honor for a good many years.   Not intimately, I
could not say that I could even guess from my
experience what Your Honor might do, but I did
know something.   I knew, Your Honor, that
ninety unfortunate human beings had been hanged
by the neck until dead in the city of Chicago
in our history.   We would not have civilization
except for those ninety that were hanged, and
if we cannot make it ninety-two we will have to
shut up shop.   Some ninety human beings have
been hanged in the history of Chicago, and of
those only four have been hanged on the plea of
guilty--one out of twenty-two.

I know that in the last ten years four

hundred and fifty people have been indicted for murder in the city of Chicago and have pleaded guilty in the city of Chicago, and only one has been hanged! And my friend who is prosecuting this case deserves the honor of that hanging while he was on the bench. But his victim was forty years old.

Your Honor will never thank me for unloading this responsibility upon you, but you know that I would have been untrue to my clients if I had not concluded to take this chance before a court, instead of submitting it to a poisoned jury in the city of Chicago. I did it knowing that it would be an unheard-of thing for any court, no matter who, to sentence these boys to death.

And, so far as that goes, Mr. Savage is right. I hope, Your Honor, that I have made no mistake.

I could have wished that the state's attorney's office had met this case with the same fairness that we have met it.

It seems to me as I have listened to this case, five or six times repeating the story of this tragedy, spending days to urge Your Honor that a condition of mind could not mitigate, or that tender years could not mitigate, it has seemed to me that it ought to be beneath the representative of a proud state like this to invoke the dark and cruel and bloody past to affect this court and compass these boys' death.

Your Honor, I must for a moment criticize the arguments that have preceded me. I can read you in a minute my friend Marshall's argument, barring Blackstone. But the rest of his arguments and the rest of Brother Savage's argument, I can sum up in a minute: Cruel; dastardly; premeditated; fiendish; abandoned and malignant heart--sounds like a cancer-- cowardly; cold-blooded!

Now that is what I have listened to for three days against two minors, two children who have no right to sign a note or make a deed.

Cowardly?

Well, I don't know.   Let me tell you something I think is cowardly, whether their acts were or not.   Here is Dickie Loeb, and Nathan Leopold, and the State objects to anybody calling one "Dickie" and the other "Babe" although everybody does, but they think they can hang them easier if their names are Richard and Nathan, so we will call them Richard and Nathan.

Eighteen and nineteen years old at the time of the homicide.

Here are three officers watching them. They are led out and in this jail and across the bridge waiting to be hanged.   Not a chance to get away.   Handcuffed when they get out of this room.   Not a chance.   Penned in like rats in a trap.   And for a lawyer with psychological eloquence to wave his fist in front of their faces and shout "Cowardly!" does not appeal to me as a brave act.   It does not commend itself to me as a proper thing for a state's attorney or his assistant; for even defendants not yet hanged have some rights with an official.

Cold-blooded? Why? Because they planned, and schemed, and arranged and fixed?

Yes.   But here are the officers of justice, so-called, with all the power of the state, with all the influence of the press, to fan this community into a frenzy of hate; with all of that, who for months have been planning and scheming, and contriving and working to take these two boys' lives.

You may stand them up on the trap door of the scaffold, and choke them to death, but that act will be infinitely more cold-blooded, whether justified or not, than any act that these boys have committed or can commit.

Cold-blooded!

Let the State, who is so anxious to take these boys' lives, set an example in consideration,   kindheartedness   and   tenderness before they call my clients cold-blooded.

I have heard this crime described--this most distressing and unfortunate homicide, as I would call it; this cold-blooded murder, as the State would call it.

I call it a homicide particularly distressing because I am defending.

They call it a cold-blooded murder because they want to take human lives.

Call it what you will.

I have heard this case talked of, and I have heard these lawyers say that this is the coldest-blooded murder that the civilized world has known. I don't know what they include in the civilized world. I suppose Illinois. Although they talk as if they did not. But we will assume Illinois. This is the most cold-blooded murder, says the State, that ever occurred.

Now, Your Honor, I have been practicing law a good deal longer than I should have, anyhow for forty-five or forty-six years, and during a part of that time I have tried a good many criminal cases, always defending. It does not mean that I am better. It probably means that I am more squeamish than the other fellows. It means neither that I am better nor worse. It means the way I am made. I cannot help it.

I have never yet tried a case where the state's attorney did not say that it was the most cold-blooded, inexcusable, premeditated case that ever occurred. If it was murder, there never was such a murder. If it was robbery, there never was such a robbery. If it was a conspiracy, it was the most terrible conspiracy that ever happened since the Star Chamber passed into oblivion. If it was larceny, there never was such a larceny.

Now, I am speaking moderately. All of them are the worst. Why? Well, it adds to the credit of the state's attorney to be connected with a big case. That is one thing. They can say: "Well, I tried the most cold-blooded murder case that ever was tried," and I convicted them, and they are dead," or: "I tried the worst forgery case that ever was tried, and I won that.   I never did anything that was not big."   Lawyers are apt to say that.

And then there is another thing, Your Honor: Of course, I generally try cases to juries, and these adjectives always go well with juries; bloody, cold-blooded, despicable, cowardly, dastardly, cruel, heartless--the whole litany of the state's attorney's office generally goes well with a jury.   The twelve jurors, being good themselves, think it is a tribute to their virtue if they follow the litany of the state's attorney.

I suppose it may have some effect with the court; I do not know.   Anyway, those are the chances we take when we do our best to save life and reputation.

"Here, your clients have pleaded to the most cold-blooded murder that ever took place in the history of the world.   And how does a judge dare to refuse to hang by the neck until dead two cowardly ruffians who committed the coldest-blooded murder in the history of the world?"

That is a good talking point.

I want to give some attention to this cold-blooded murder, Your Honor.

Was it cold-blooded murder?

Was it the most terrible murder that ever happened in the state of Illinois?

Was it the most dastardly act in the annals of crime?   No.

I insist, Your Honor, that under all fair rules and measurements, this was one of the least dastardly and cruel of any that I have known anything about.

Now, let me see how we should measure it.

They say that this was a cruel murder, the worst that ever happened.   I say that very few murders ever occurred that were as free from cruelty as this.

There ought to be some rule to determine whether a murder is exceedingly cruel or not.

Of course, Your Honor, I admit that I hate killing, and I hate it no matter how it is done--whether you shoot a man through the heart, or cut his head off with an ax, or kill him with a chisel or tie a rope around his neck. I hate it. I always did. I always shall.

But there are degrees, and if I might be permitted to make my own rules I would say that if I were estimating what was the most cruel murder, I might first consider the sufferings of the victim.

Now, probably the State would not take that rule. They would say the one that had the most attention in the newspapers. In that way they have got me beaten at the start.

But I would say the first thing to consider is the degree of pain to the victim.

Poor little Bobby Franks suffered very little. There is no excuse for his killing. If to hang these two boys would bring him back to life, I would say let them hang, and I believe their parents would say so, too. But:

The moving finger writes, and having writ,
Moves on; nor all your piety nor wit
Shall lure it back to cancel half a line,
Nor all your tears wash out a word of it.

Robert Franks is dead, and we cannot call him back to life. It was all over in fifteen minutes after he got into the car, and he probably never knew it or thought of it. That does not justify it. It is the last thing I would do. I am sorry for the poor boy. I am sorry for his parents. But it is done.

Of course I cannot say with the certainty of Mr. Savage that he would have been a great man if he had grown up. At fourteen years of

age I don't know whether he would or not.
Savage, I suppose, is a mind reader, and he
says that he would. He has a fantasy, which is
hanging.   So far as the cruelty to the victim
is concerned, you can scarce imagine one less
cruel.

Now, what else would stamp a murder as
being a most atrocious crime?

First, I put the victim, who ought not to
suffer; and next, I would put the attitude of
those who kill.

What was the attitude of these two boys?

It may be that the state's attorney would
think it was particularly cruel to the victim
because he was a boy.

Well, my clients are boys, too, and if it
would make more serious the offense to kill a
boy, it should make less serious the offense of
the boys who do the killing.

What was there in the conduct of these two
boys which showed a wicked, malignant and
abandoned heart beyond that of anybody else who
ever lived? Your Honor, it is simply foolish.
. . . This is a sense-less, useless, purposeless, motiveless act of two boys. Now, let me
see if I can prove it.   There was not a
particle of hate, there was not a grain of
malice, there was no opportunity to be cruel
except as death is cruel--and death is cruel.

There was absolutely no purpose in it all,
no reason in it all, and no motive for it all.

Now, let me see whether I am right or not.
. . . Your Honor, if there was every anything
so foolish, so utterly futile as the motive
claimed in this case, then I have never
listened to it.

What did Tom Marshall say?

What did Joe Savage say?

"The motive was to get ten thousand
dollars," say they.

These two boys, neither one of whom needed
a cent, scions of wealthy people, killed this
little inoffensive boy to get ten thousand

dollars? . . . On a certain day they killed
poor little Robert Franks. I will not go over
the paraphernalia, the letter demanding money,
the ransom, because I will discuss that later
in another connection. But they killed him.
These two boys. They were not to get ten
thousand dollars; they were to get five thousand dollars each. Neither one could get more
than five, and either one was risking his neck
in the job. So each one of my clients was
risking his neck for five thousand dollars, if
that had anything to do with it, which it did
not.

Did they need the money?

Why, at this very time, and a few months
before, Dickie Loeb had three thousand dollars
in a checking account in the bank. Your Honor,
I would be ashamed to talk about this except
that in all seriousness they are asking to kill
these two boys on the strength of this flimsy
foolishness.

At that time Richard Loeb had a three-
thousand-dollar checking account in the bank.
He had three Liberty Bonds, one of which was
past due, and the interest on each of them had
not been collected for three years. I said,
had not been collected; not a penny's interest
had been collected--and the coupons were there
for three years. And yet they would ask to
hang him on the theory that he committed this
murder because he needed money.

In addition to that we brought his
father's private secretary here, who swears
that whenever he asked for it, he got a check,
without ever consulting the father. She had an
open order to give him a check whenever he
wanted it, and she had sent him a check in
February, and he had lost it and had not cashed
it. So he got another in March. . . . Leopold
was in regular receipt of one hundred and
twenty-five dollars a month; he had an automobile; paid nothing for board and clothes and
expenses; he got money whenever he wanted it,

and he had arranged to go to Europe and had bought his ticket and was going to leave about the time he was arrested in this case.

He passed his examination for the Harvard Law School, and was going to take a short trip to Europe before it was time for him to attend the fall term. His ticket had been bought, and his father had given him three thousand dollars to take the trip.

Your Honor, jurors sometimes make mistakes, and courts do, too. If on this evidence the court is to construe a motive out of this case, then I insist that human liberty is not safe and human life is not safe. A motive could be construed out of any set of circumstances and facts that might be imagined.

In addition to that, these boys' families were extremely wealthy. The boys had been reared in luxury, they had never been denied anything; no want or desire left unsatisfied; no debts; no need of money; nothing.

And yet they murdered a little boy against whom they had nothing in the world, without malice, without reason, to get five thousand dollars each. All right. All right, Your Honor, if the court believes it, if anyone believes it--I can't help it.

That is what this case rests on. It could not stand up a minute without motive. Without it, it was the senseless act of immature and diseased children, as it was; a senseless act of children, wandering around in the dark and moved by some emotion that we still perhaps have not the knowledge or the insight into life to understand thoroughly.

Now, let me go on with it. What else do they claim?

I want to say to Your Honor that you may cut out every expert in this case, you may cut out every lay witness in this case, you may decide this case upon the facts as they appear here alone; and there is no sort of question that these boys were mentally diseased.

I do not know, but I do not believe that there is any man who knows this case, who does not know that it can be accounted for only on the theory of the mental disease of these two lads. . . . The State says, in order to make out the wonderful mental processes of these two boys, that they fixed up a plan to go to Ann Arbor to get a typewriter, and yet when they got ready to do this act, they went down the street a few doors from their house and bought a rope; they went around the corner and bought acid; then went somewhere else nearby and bought tape; they went down to the hotel and rented a room, and then gave it up, and went to another hotel, and rented one there. And then Dick Loeb went to the hotel room, took a valise containing his library card and some books from the library, left it two days in the room, until the hotel took the valise and took the books. Then he went to another hotel and rented another room. He might just as well sent his card with the ransom letter.

They went to the Rent-a-car place and hired a car. All this clumsy machinery was gone through without intelligence or method or rational thought. I submit, Your Honor, that no one, unless he had an afflicted mind, together with youth, could possibly have done it.

But let's get to something stronger than that. Were these boys in their right minds? Here were two boys with good intellect, one eighteen and one nineteen. They had all the prospects that life could hold out for any of the young--one a graduate of Chicago and another of Ann Arbor; one who had passed his examination for the Harvard Law School and was about to take a trip in Europe, another who had passed at Ann Arbor, the youngest in his class, with three thousand dollars in the bank. Boys who never knew what it was to want a dollar; boys who could reach any position that was given to boys of that kind of reach; boys of

distinguished and honorable families, families
of wealth and position, with all the world
before them.   And they gave it all up for
nothing, nothing!   They took a little companion
of one of them, on a crowded street, and killed
him, for nothing, and sacrificed everything
that could be of value in human life upon the
crazy scheme of a couple of immature lads.

Now, Your Honor, you have been a boy; I
have been a boy.   And we have known other boys.
The best way to understand somebody else is to
put yourself in his place.

Is it within the realm of your imagination
that a boy who was right, with all the
prospects of life before him, who could choose
what he wanted, without the slightest reason in
the world would lure a young companion to his
death, and take his place in the shadow of the
gallows?

I do not care what Dr. Krohn may say; he
is liable to say anything, except to tell the
truth, and he is not liable to do that.   No one
who has the process of reasoning could doubt
that a boy who would do that is not right.

How insane they are I care not, whether
medically or legally.   They did not reason;
they could not reason; they committed the most
foolish, most unprovoked, most purposeless,
most causeless act that any two boys ever
committed, and they put themselves where the
rope is dangling above their heads.

There are not physicians enough in the
world to convince any thoughtful, fair-minded
man that these boys are right.   Was their act
one of deliberation, of intellect, or were they
driven by some force such as Dr. White and Dr.
Glueck and Dr. Healy have told this court?

There are only two theories: one is that
their diseased brains drove them to it; the
other is the old theory of possession by
devils, and my friend Marshall could have read
you books on that, too, but it has been pretty
well given up in Illinois.

That they were intelligent and sane and
sound and reasoning is unthinkable.   Let me
call Your Honor's attention to another thing.
Why did they kill little Bobby Franks?

Not for money, not for spite, not for
hate.   They killed him as they might kill a
spider or a fly, for the experience.   They
killed him because they were made that way.
Because somewhere in the infinite processes
that go to the making up of the boy or the man
something slipped, and those unfortunate lads
sit here hated, despised, outcasts, with the
community shouting for their blood.

Are they to blame for it?   There is no man
on earth who can mention any purpose for it all
or any reason for it all.   It is one of those
things that happened; that happened, and it
calls not for hate but for kindness, for
charity, for consideration.

I heard the state's attorney talk of
mothers.

Mr. Savage is talking for the mothers, and
Mr. Crowe is thinking of the mothers, and I am
thinking of the mothers.   Mr. Savage, with the
immaturity of youth and inexperience, says that
if we hang them there will be no more killing.
This world has been one long slaughterhouse
from the beginning until today, and killing
goes on and on and on, and will forever.   Why
not read something, why not study something,
why not think instead of blindly shouting for
death?

Kill them.   Will that prevent other
senseless boys or other vicious men or vicious
women from killing?   No!

It will simply call upon every weak-minded
person to do as they have done.   I know how
easy it is to talk about mothers when you want
to do something cruel.   But I am thinking of
the mothers too.   I know that any mother might
be the mother of a little Bobby Franks, who
left his home and went to his school, and who
never came back.   I know that any mother might

be the mother of Richard Loeb and Nathan Leopold, just the same. The trouble is this, that if she is the mother of a Nathan Leopold or of a Richard Loeb, she has to ask herself the question:

"How came my children to be what they are? From what ancestry did they get this strain? How far removed was the poison that destroyed their lives? Was I the bearer of the seed that brings them to death?"

Any mother might be the mother of any of them. But these two are the victims. I remember a little poem that gives the soliloquy of a boy about to be hanged, a soliloquy such as these boys might make:

> The night my father got me
> His mind was not on me;
> He did not plague his fancy
> To muse if I should be
> The son you see.
>
> The day my mother bore me
> She was a fool and glad,
> For all the pain I cost her,
> That she had borne the lad
> That borne she had.
>
> My father and my mother
> Out of the light they lie;
> The warrant would not find them,
> And here, 'tis only I
> Shall hang so high.
>
> Oh let not man remember
> The soul that God forgot,
> But fetch the county sheriff
> And noose me in a knot,
> And I will rot.
>
> And so the game is ended,
> That should not have begun.
> My father and my mother

They had a likely son,
And I have none.

No one knows what will be the fate of the child he gets or the child she bears; the fate of the child is the last thing they consider. This weary old world goes on, begetting, with birth and with living and with death; and all of it is blind from the beginning to the end. I do not know what is was that made these boys do this mad act, but I do know there is a reason for it.   I know they did not beget themselves.   I know that any one of an infinite number of causes reaching back to the beginning might be working out in these boys' minds, whom you are asked to hang in malice and in hatred and injustice, because someone in the past has sinned against them.

I am sorry for the fathers as well as the mothers, for the fathers who give their strength and their lives for educating and protecting and creating a fortune for the boys that they love; for the mothers who go down into the shadow of death for their children, who nourish them and care for them, and risk their lives, that they may live, who watch them with tenderness and fondness and longing, and who go down into dishonor and disgrace for the children that they love.

All of these are helpless.   We are all helpless.   But when you are pitying the father and the mother of poor Bobby Franks, what about the fathers and mothers of these two unfortunate boys, and what about the unfortunate boys themselves, and what about all the fathers and all the mothers and all the boys and all the girls who tread a dangerous maze in darkness from birth to death?   Do you think you can cure it by hanging these two?   Do you think you can cure the hatreds and the maladjustments of the world by hanging them?   You simply show your ignorance and your hate when you say it.   You may here and there cure hatred with love and understanding.   But you can only add fuel to the flames by cruelty and hate.

What is my friend's idea of justice?   He says to this court, whom he says he respects-- and I believe he does--Your Honor, who sits here patiently, holding the lives of these two boys in your hands:

"Give them the same mercy that they gave to Bobby Franks."

Is that the law?   Is that justice?   Is that what a state's attorney should do?   If the state in which I live is not kinder, more humane, more considerate, more intelligent than the mad act of these two boys, I am sorry I have lived so long.

I am sorry for all the fathers and all mothers.   The mother who looks into the blue eyes of her little babe cannot help musing over the end of the child, whether it will be crowned with the greatest promises which her mind can image or whether he may meet death upon the scaffold.   All she can do is to rear him with love and care, to watch over him tenderly, to meet life with hope and trust and confidence, and to leave the rest with fate. . . . These boys, neither one of them, could possibly have committed this act excepting by coming together.   It was not the act of one; it was the act of two.   It was the act of their planning, their conniving, their believing in each other; their thinking themselves supermen. Without it they could not have done it.   It would not have happened.   Their parents happened to meet, these boys happened to meet; some sort of chemical alchemy operated so that they cared for each other, and poor Bobby Franks's dead body was found in the culvert as a result.   Neither of them could have done it alone.

I want to call your attention, Your Honor, to the two letters in this case which settle this matter to my mind conclusively; not only the condition of these boys' minds, but the terrible fate that overtook them.

Your Honor, I am sorry for poor Bobby Franks, and I think anybody who knows me knows that I am not saying it simply to talk.   I am sorry for the bereaved father and the bereaved mother, and I would like to know what they would do with these poor unfortunate lads who are here in this court today.   I know something of them, of their lives, of their charity, of their ideas, and nobody here sympathizes with them more than I.

On the twenty-first day of May poor Bobby Franks, stripped and naked, was left in a culvert down near the Indiana line.   I know it came through the act of mad boys.   Mr. Savage told us that Franks, if he lived, would have been a great man and have acomplished much.   I want to leave this thought with Your Honor now. I do not know what Bobby Franks would have been had he grown to be a man.   I do not know the laws that control one's growth.   Sometimes, Your Honor, a boy of great promise is cut off in his early youth.   Sometimes he dies and is placed in a culvert.   Sometimes a boy of great promise stands on a trap door and is hanged by the neck until dead.   Sometimes he dies of diphtheria.   Death somehow pays no attention to age, sex, prospects, wealth or intellect.

It comes, and perhaps--I can only say perhaps, for I never professed to unravel the mysteries of fate, and I cannot tell; but I can say perhaps--the boy who died at fourteen did as much as if he had died at seventy, and perhaps the boy who died as a babe did as much as if he had lived longer.   Perhaps, somewhere in fate and chance, it might be that he lived as long as he should.

And I want to say this, that the death of poor little Bobby Franks should not be in vain. Would it mean anything if on account of that death, these two boys were taken out and a rope tied around their necks and they died felons? Would that show that Bobby Franks had a purpose

in his life and a purpose in his death?   No,
Your Honor, the unfortunate and tragic death of
this young lad should mean something.   It
should mean an appeal to the fathers and
mothers, an appeal to the teachers, to the
religious guides, to society at large.   It
should mean an appeal to all of them to
appraise children, to understand the emotions
that control them, to understand the ideas that
possess them, to teach them to avoid the
pitfalls of life.

Society, too, should assume its share of
the burdens of this case, and not make two more
tragedies, but use this calamity as best
it can to make life safer, to make childhood
easier and more secure, to do something to cure
the cruelty, the hatred, the chance, and the
willfulness of life.

I have discussed somewhat in detail these
two boys separately.   Their coming together was
the means of their undoing.   Your Honor is
familiar with the facts in reference to their
association.   They had a weird, almost
impossible relationship.   Leopold, with his
obsession of the superman, had repeatedly said
that Loeb was his idea of the superman.   He had
the attitude toward him that one has to his
most devoted friend, or that a man has to a
lover.   Without the combination of these two,
nothing of this sort probably could have
happened. . . . I think all of the facts of
this extraordinary case, all of the testimony
of the alienists, all that Your Honor has seen
and heard, all their friends and acquaintances
who have come here to enlighten this court--I
think all of it shows that this terrible act
was the act of immature and diseased brains,
the act of children.

Nobody can explain it in any other way.
No one can imagine it in any other way.
It is not possible that it could have
happened in any other way.

And, I submit, Your Honor, that by every law of humanity, by every law of justice, by every feeling of righteousness, by every instinct of pity, mercy and charity, Your Honor should say that because of the condition of these boys' minds, it would be monstrous to visit upon them the vengeance that is asked by the State.

I want to discuss now another thing which this court must consider and which to my mind is absolutely conclusive in this case.   That is, the age of these boys.

I shall discuss it more in detail than I have discussed it before, and I submit, Your Honor, that it is not possible for any court to hang these two boys if he pays any attention whatever to the precedents in this county, if he pays any attention to the humane instincts which move ordinary man.

I have a list of executions in Cook County beginning in 1840, which I presume covers the first one, because I asked to have it go to the beginning.   Ninety poor unfortunate men have given up their lives to stop murder in Chicago. Ninety men have been hanged by the neck until dead, because of the ancient superstition that in some way hanging one man keeps another from committing a crime.   The ancient superstition, I say, because I defy the State to point to a criminologist, a scientist, a student, who has ever said it.   Still we go on, as if human conduct was not influenced and controlled by natural laws the same as all the rest of the universe is the subject of law. We treat crime as if it had no cause. We go on saying, "Hang the unfortunates, and it will end."   Was there ever a murder without a cause? Was there ever a crime without a cause?   And yet all punishment proceeds upon the theory that there is no cause; and the only way to treat crime is to intimidate everyone into goodness and obedience to law.   We lawyers are a long way behind.

Crime has its cause. Perhaps all crimes do not have the same cause, but they all have some cause. And people today are seeking to find out the cause. We lawyers never try to find out. Scientists are studying it; criminologists are investigating it; but we lawyers go on and on, punishing and hanging, and thinking that by general terror we can stamp out crime.

It nevers occurs to a lawyer that crime has a cause as certain as disease, and that the way to treat any abnormal condition rationally is to remove the cause.

If a doctor were called on to treat typhoid fever he would probably try to find out what kind of milk or water the patient drank, and perhaps clean out the well so that no one else could get typhoid from the same source. But if a lawyer was called on to treat a typhoid patient, he would give him thirty days in jail, and then he would think that nobody else would ever dare to take it. If the patient got well in fifteen days, he would be kept until his time was up; if the disease was worse at the end of thirty days, the patient would be released because his time was out.

As a rule, lawyers are not scientists. They have learned the doctrine of hate and fear, and they think that there is only one way to make men good, and that is to put them in such terror that they do not dare to be bad. They act unmindful of history, and science, and all the experience of the past.

Still, we are making some progress. Courts give attention to some things that they did not give attention to before.

Once in England they hanged children seven years of age; not necessarily hanged them, because hanging was never meant for punishment; it was meant for an exhibition. If somebody committed crime, he would be hanged by the head or the heels, it didn't matter much which, at the four crossroads, so that everybody could look at him until his bones were bare, and so that people would be good because they had seen the gruesome result of crime and hate.

Hanging was not necessarily meant for punishment. The culprit might be killed in any other way, and then hanged--yes. Hanging was an exhibition. They were hanged on the highest hill, and hanged at the crossroads, and hanged in public places, so that all men could see. If there is any virtue in hanging, that was the logical way, because you cannot awe men into goodness unless they know about the hanging. We have grown squeamish; we do not like to look at it, that is all. They hanged them at seven years; they hanged them again at eleven and fourteen.

We have raised the age of hanging. We have raised it by the humanity of courts, by the understanding of courts, by the progress in science which at last is reaching the law; and of ninety men hanged in Illinois from its beginning, not one single person under twenty-three was ever hanged upon a plea of Guilty-- not one. If Your Honor should do this, you would violate every precedent that has been set in Illinois for almost a century. There can be no excuse for it, and no justification for it, because this is the policy of the law which is rooted in the feelings of humanity, which are deep in every human being that thinks and feels. There have been two or three cases where juries have convicted boys younger than this, and where courts on convictions have refused to set aside the sentence. But this was because a jury had decided it.

Your Honor, if in this court a boy of eighteen and a boy of nineteen should be hanged on a plea of Guilty, in violation of every precedent of the past, in violation of the policy of the law to take care of the young, in violation of all the progress that has been made and of the humanity that has been shown in

the care of the young, in violation of the law
that places boys in reformatories instead of
prisons--if Your Honor, in violation of all
that and in the face of all the past, should
stand here in Chicago along to hang a boy on a
plea of Guilty, then we are turning our faces
backward toward the barbarism which once
possessed the world. If Your Honor can hang a
boy of eighteen, some other judge can hang him
at seventeen, or sixteen, or fourteen. Some
day, if there is any such thing as progress in
the world, if there is any spirit of humanity
that is working in the hearts of men, some day
man would look back upon this as a barbarous
age which deliberately set itself in the way of
progress, humanity and sympathy, and committed
an unforgivable act.

Now, Your Honor, I have spoken about the
war. I believed in it. I don't know whether I
was crazy or not. Sometimes I think perhaps I
was. I approved of it; I joined in the general
cry of madness and despair. I urged men to
fight. I was safe because I was too old to go.
I was like the rest. What did they do? Right
or wrong, justifiable or unjustifiable--which I
need not discuss today--it changed the world.
For four long years the civilized world was
engaged in killing men. Christian against
Christian; barbarians uniting with Christians
to kill Christians; anything to kill. It was
taught in every school, aye in the Sunday
schools. The little children played at war.
The toddling children on the street. Do you
suppose this world has ever been the same since
then? How long, Your Honor, will it take for
the world to get back the humane emotions that
were slowly growing before the war? How long
will it take the calloused hearts of men before
the scars of hatred and cruelty shall be
removed?

We read of killing one hundred thousand
men in a day. We read about it and we rejoiced
in it--if it was the other fellows who were

killed.   We were fed on flesh and drank blood.
Even down to the prattling babe.   I need not
tell Your Honor this, because you know; I need
not tell you how many upright, honorable young
boys have come into this court charged with
murder, some saved and some sent to their
death, boys who fought in this war and learned
to place a cheap value on human life.   You know
it and I know it.   These boys were brought up
in it.   The tales of death were in their homes,
their playgrounds, their schools; they were in
the newspapers that they read; it was a part of
the common frenzy.   What was a life?   It was
nothing.   It was the least sacred thing in
existence and these boys were trained to this
cruelty.

It will take fifty years to wipe it out of
the human heart, if ever.   I know this, that
after the Civil War in 1865, crimes of this
sort increased marvelously.   No one needs to
tell me that crime has no cause.   It has as
definite a cause as any other disease, and I
know that out of the hatred and bitterness of
the Civil War crime increased as America had
never known before.   I know that Europe is
going through the same experience today; I know
that it has followed every war; and I know it
has influenced these boys so that life was not
the same to them as it would have been if the
world had not been made red with blood.   I
protest against the crimes and mistakes of
society being visited upon them.   All of us
have our share of it.   I have mine.   I cannot
tell and I shall never know how many words of
mine might have given birth to cruelty in place
of love and kindness and charity.

Your Honor knows that in this very court
crimes of violence have increased, growing out
of the war.   Not necessarily by those who
fought but by those that learned that blood was
cheap, and human life was cheap, and if the
State could take it lightly why not the boy?
There are causes for this terrible crime.

There are causes, as I have said, for everything that happens in the world. War is a part
of it; education is a part of it; birth is a
part of it; money is a part of it--all these
conspired to compass the destruction of these
two poor boys.

Has the court any right to consider anything but these two boys? The State says that
Your Honor has a right to consider the welfare
of the community, as you have. If the welfare
of the community would be benefited by taking
these lives, well and good. I think it would
work evil that no one could measure. Has Your
Honor a right to consider the families of these
two defendants? I have been sorry, and I am
sorry for the bereavement of Mr. and Mrs.
Franks, for those broken ties that cannot be
healed. All I can hope and wish is that some
good may come from it all. But as compared
with the families of Leopold and Loeb, the
Franks are to be envied--and everyone knows it.

I do not know how much salvage there is in
these two boys. I hate to say it in their
presence, but what is there to look forward to?
I do not know but that Your Honor would be
merciful if you tied a rope around their necks
and let them die; merciful to them, but not
merciful to civilization, and not merciful to
those who would be left behind. To spend the
balance of their lives in prison is mighty
little to look forward to, if anything. Is it
anything? They may have the hope that as the
years roll around they might be released. I do
not know. I do not know. I will be honest
with this court as I have tried to be from the
beginning. I know that these boys are not fit
to be at large. I believe that they will not
be until they pass through the next stage of
life, at forty-five or fifty. Whether they
will be then, I cannot tell. I am sure of
this; that I will not be here to help them. So
far as I am concerned, it is over.

I would not tell this court that I do not

hope that some time, when life and age have
changed their bodies, as it does, and has
changed their emotions, as it does--that they
may once more return to life. I would be the
last person on earth to close the door to any
human being that lives, and least of all to my
clients.   But what have they to look forward
to? Nothing? And I think here of the stanza
of Housman:

> Now hollow fires burn out to black,
> And lights are fluttering low:
> Square your shoulders, lift your pack
> And leave your friends and go.
> O never fear, lads, naught's to dread,
> Look not left nor right:
> In all the endless road you tread
> There's nothing but the night.

I care not, Your Honor, whether the march
begins at the gallows or when the gates of
Joliet close upon them, there is nothing but
the night, and that is little for any human
being to expect.

But there are others to consider. Here
are these two families, who have led honest
lives, who will bear the name that they bear,
and future generations must carry it on.

Here is Leopold's father--and this boy was
the pride of his life. He watched him, he
cared for him, he worked for him; the boy was
brilliant and accomplished, he educated him,
and he thought that fame and position awaited
him, as it should have awaited. It is a hard
thing for a father to see his life's hopes
crumble into dust.

Should he be considered? Should his
brothers be considered? Will it do society any
good or make your life safer, or any human
being's life safer if it should be handed down
from generation to generation, that this boy,
their kin died upon the scaffold?

And Loeb's, the same. Here are the

faithful uncle and brother, who have watched
here day by day, while Dickie's father and his
mother are too ill to stand this terrific
strain, and shall be waiting for a message
which means more to them than it can mean to
you or me.   Shall these be taken into account
in this general bereavement?

Have they any rights?   Is there any
reason, Your Honor, why their proud names and
all the future generations that bear them shall
have this bar sinister written across them?
How many boys and girls, how many unborn
children, will feel it?   It is bad enough,
however it is.   But it's not death on the
scaffold.   It's not that.   And I ask Your
Honor, in addition to all that I have said, to
save two honorable families from a disgrace
that never ends, and which could be of no avail
to help any human being that lives.

Now, I must say a word more and then I
will leave this with you where I should have
left it long ago.   None of us are unmindful of
the public; courts are not, and juries are not.
We placed our fate in the hands of a trained
court, thinking that he would be more mindful
and considerate than a jury.   I cannot say how
people feel.   I have stood here for three
months as one might stand at the ocean trying
to sweep back the tide.   I hope the seas are
subsiding and the wind is falling, and I
believe they are, but I wish to make no false
pretense to this court.   The easy thing and the
popular thing to do is to hang my clients.   I
know it.   en and women who do not think will
applaud.   The cruel and thoughtless will
approve.   It will be easy today; but in
Chicago, and reaching out over the length and
breadth of the land, more and more fathers and
mothers, the humane, the kind and the hopeful,
who are gaining an understanding and asking
questions not only about these poor boys, but
about their own--these will join in no acclaim
at the death of my clients.   They would ask

that the shedding of blood be stopped, and that the normal feelings of man resume their sway. And as the days, the months and the years go on, they will ask it more and more. But, Your Honor, what they shall ask may not count.   I know the easy way.   I know Your Honor stands between the future and the past.   I know the future is with me, and what I stand for here; not merely for the lives of these two unfortunate lads, but for all boys and all girls; for all of the young, and, as far as possible, for all of the old.   I am pleading for life, understanding, charity, kindness, and the infinite mercy that considers all.   I am pleading that we overcome cruelty with kindness, and hatred with love.   I know the future is on my side.

Your Honor stands between the past and the future.   You may hang these boys; you may hang them by the neck until they are dead.   But in doing it you will turn your face toward the past.   In doing it you are making it harder for every other boy who, in ignorance and darkness, must grope his way through the mazes which only childhood knows.   In doing it you will make it harder for unborn children.   You may save them and make it easier for every child that sometime may stand where these boys stand.   You will make it easier for every human being with an aspiration and a vision and a hope and a fate.

I am pleading for the future; I am pleading for a time when the hatred and cruelty will not control the hearts of men, when we can learn by reason and judgement and understanding and faith that all life is worth saving, and that mercy is the highest attribute of man.

I feel I should apologize for the length of time I have taken.   This case may not be as important as I think it is, and I am sure I do not need to tell this court, or to tell my friends that I would fight just as hard for the poor as for the rich.   If I should succeed in

saving these boys' lives and do nothing for the
progress of the law, I should feel sad, indeed.
If I can succeed, my greatest reward and my
greatest hope will be that I have done
something for the tens of thousands of other
boys, for the countless unfortunates who must
tread the same road in blind childhood that
these poor boys have trod; that I have done
something to help human understanding, to
temper justice with mercy, to overcome hate
with love.

I was reading last night of the aspiration
of the old Persian poet, Omar Khayyam.   It
appealed to me as the highest that I can
vision. I wish it was in my heart, and I wish
it was in the hearts of all.

So I be written in the Book of Love,
I do not care about that Book above;
Erase my name or write it as you will,
So I be written in the Book of Love.

Speech at Scopes Trial

Dayton, Tennessee, 1925

I know my friend, McKenzie, whom I have learned not only to admire, but to love in our short acquaintance, didn't mean anything in referring to us lawyers who come from out of town. For myself, I have been treated with the greatest courtesy by the attorneys and the courtroom. . . . And I shall always remember that this court is the first one that ever gave me a great title of "Colonel" and I hope it will stick to me when I get back north. . . . But so far as coming from other cities is concerned, why, Your Honor, it is easy here. I came from Chicago, and my friend, Malone, and friend Hays, came from New York, and on the other side we have a distinguished and very pleasant gentleman who came from California and another who is prosecuting this case, and who is responsible for this foolish, mischievous and wicked act, who comes from Florida.

This case we have to argue is a case at law, and hard as it is for me to bring my mind to conceive it, almost impossible as it is to put my mind back into the sixteenth century, I am going to argue it as if it was serious, and as if it was a death struggle between two civilizations.

Let us see, now what there is about it. We have been informed that the legislature has the right to prescribe the course of study in the public schools. Within reason, they no doubt have, no doubt. They could not prescribe it, I am inclined to think, under your constitution, if it omitted arithmetic and geography and writing, neither under the rest of the constitution if it shall remain in force in the state, could they prescribe it if the course of study was only to teach religion, because several hundred years ago, when our people believed in freedom, and when no men felt so sure of their own sophistry that they were willing to send a man to jail who did not believe them. The people of Tennessee adopted a constitution, and they made it broad and plain, and said that the people of Tennessee should always enjoy religious freedom in its broadest terms, so I assume, that no legislature could fix a course of study which violated that. For instance, suppose the legislature should say, we think the religious privileges and duties of the citizens of Tennessee are much more important than education, we agree with the distinguished governor of the state, if religion must go, or learning must go, why, let learning go. I do not know how much of it would have to go, but let it go, and therefore we will establish a course in the public schools of teaching that the Christian religion as unfolded in the Bible, is true, and that every other religion, or mode or system of ethics is false and to carry that out, no person in the public schools shall be permitted to read or hear anything except Genesis, Pilgrims Progress, Baxter's Saint Rest, and In His Image. Would that be constitutional? If it is, the constitution is a lie and a snare and the people have forgot what liberty means.

I remember, long ago, Mr. Bancroft wrote this sentence, which is true: "That it is all right to preserve freedom in constitutions, but when the spirit of freedom has fled, from the hearts of the people, then its matter is easily sacrificed under law." And so it is, unless

there is left enough of the spirit of freedom
in the state of Tennessee, and in the United
States, there is not a single line of any
constitution that can withstand bigotry and
ignorance when it seeks to destroy the rights
of the individual; and bigotry and ignorance
when it seeks to destroy the rights of the
individual; and bigotry and ignorance are ever
active. Here, we find today as brazen and as
bold an attempt to destroy learning as was ever
made in the middle ages, and the only difference is we have not provided that they shall be
burned at the stake, but there is time for
that, Your Honor, we have to approach these
things gradually.

Now, let us see what we claim with
reference to this law. If this proceeding both
in form and substance, can prevail in this
court, then Your Honor, no law--no matter how
foolish, wicked, ambiguous, or ancient, but can
come back to Tennessee. All the guarantees go
for nothing. All of the past has gone, will be
forgotten, if this can succeed.

I am going to begin with some of the
simpler reasons why it is absolutely absurd to
think that this statute, indictment, or any
part of the proceedings in this case are legal,
and I think the sooner we get rid of it in
Tennessee the better for the peace of Tennessee, and the better for the pursuit of knowledge in the world, so let me begin at the
beginning.

Let us take this statute as it is, the
first point we made in this suit is that it is
unconstitutional on account of the divergence
and the difference between the statute and the
caption, and because it contains more than one
subject. Now my distinguished friend was quite
right, every constitution with which I am familiar has substantially this same provision,
that the caption and the law must correspond.
He is right in his reason. Why? Lots of
things are put through in the night-time.

Everybody does not read all of the statutes,
even members of the legislature--I have been a
member of the legislature myself, and I know
how it is--they may vote for them without
reading them, but the substance of the act is
put in the caption, so it may be seen and read,
and nothing can be in the act that is not contained in the caption. There is not any question about it, and only one subject shall be
legislated on at once. Of course the caption
may be broader than the act. My friend is
entirely right about it. They may make a
caption and the act may fall far short of it,
but the substance of the act must be in the
caption, and there can be no variance. Now,
Your Honor, that is elementary, nobody need to
brief on that, it is a sufficient brief to read
the constitution, that one section, it is very
short.

Now, let us see what they have done, there
is not much dispute about the English language.
I take it, here is the caption, "Public act,
Chapter 37, 1925. An act prohibiting the
teaching of the evolution theory in all the
universities, normals and all the public
schools of Tennessee which are supported in
whole or in part by the public school funds of
the state, and to prescribe penalties for the
violation thereof."

Now what is it, an act to prohibit the
teaching of the evolution theory in Tennessee?
Well, if that the act? Is this statute to
prevent the teaching of the evolutionary theory? There is not a word said in the statute
about evolution, there is not a word said in
the statute about preventing the teaching of
the theory of evolution--not a word. This
statute contains nothing whatever in reference
to teaching the theory of evolution in the
public schools of Tennessee. And, Your Honor,
the caption contains nothing else--nothing
else. Does the caption say anything about the
Bible? Oh! no, does it say anything about the

divine account contained in the Bible? Oh! no.
If a man was interested in the peace and har-
mony and welfare of the citizens of Tennessee,
if he was interested in intellectual freedom
and religious freedom, if he was interested in
the right to worship God as he saw fit, but he
found out that chaos and disorder and riot
would follow in the wake of this caption, and
he found out that every religious prejudice
inherent in the breast of man could be appealed
to, by the law the legislature was about to
pass--there is not a single word in it. This
caption says that what follows is an act forbidding the teaching of evolution, and the
Catholic could have gone home without any
thought that his faith was about to be attacked, the Protestant could have gone home without
any thought that his religion could be attacked, the intelligent scholarly Christian, who by
the millions in the United States, find no in-
consistency between evolution and religion,
could have gone home without any fear that a
narrow, ignorant, bigoted shrew of religion
could have destroyed their religious freedom
and their right to think and act and speak, and
the nation and the state could have laid down
peacefully to sleep that night without the
slightest fear that religious hatred and
bigotry was to be turned loose in a great
state. Any question about it? Anything in
this caption whatever about religion, or
anything about measuring science and knowledge
and learning by the book of Genesis, written
when everybody thought the world was flat!
Nothing. They went to bed in peace, probably,
and they woke up to find this, which has not
the slightest reference to it, which does not
refer to evolution in any way, which is as
claimed a religious statute, the growth of as
plain religious ignorance and bigotry as any
justified the Spanish inquisition or the hanging of the witches in New England, or the
countless iniquities under the name of what

some people called religion, and pursued the human race down to the last hundred years. That is what they found, and here is what it is: "Be it enacted by the general assembly of the state of Tennessee, that it shall be unlawful for any teacher in any of the universities, normals and all other public schools in the state, which are supported in part by the public school funds of the state, to teach"--what, teach evolution? Oh! no--"to teach the theory that denies the story of the divine creation of man, as taught in the Bible, and to teach instead that man has descended from a lower order of animals." That is what was foisted on the people of this state, under a caption which never meant it, and could give no hint of it, that it should be a crime in the state of Tennessee to teach any theory of the origin of man, except that contained in the divine account as recorded in the Bible. But the state of Tennessee under an honest and fair interpretation of the constitution has no more divine right to teach the Bible as the divine book than that the Koran is one, or the book of Mormons, or the book of Confucius, or the Budda, or the Essays of Emerson, or any one of the 10,000 books to which human souls have gone for consolation and aid in their troubles. Are they going to cut them out? They would have to pick the right caption at least, and they could not pick it out without violating the constitution, which is as old and as wise as Jefferson. . . . Now, as to the statute itself. It is full of weird, strange, impossible and imaginary provisions. Driven by bigotry and narrowness they come together and make this statute and bring this litigation. I cannot conceive anything greater.

What is this law? What does it mean? . . . The statute should be comprehensible. It should not be written in Chinese anyhow. It should be in passing English. As you say, so that common, human beings would understand what

it meant, and so a man would know whether he is
liable to go to jail when he is teaching, not
so ambiguous as to be a snare or a trap to get
someone who does not agree with you. It should
be plain, simple and easy. Does this statute
state what you shall teach and what you shall
not? Oh, no! Oh, no! Not at all. Does it
say you cannot teach the earth is round?
Because Genesis says it is flat? No. Does it
say you cannot teach that the earth is millions
of ages old, because the account in Genesis
makes it less than six thousand years old? Oh,
no. It doesn't state that. If it did you
could understand it. It says you shan't teach
any theory of the origin of man that is contrary to the divine theory contained in the
Bible.

Now let us pass up the word "divine!" No
legislature is strong enough in any state in
the Union to characterize and pick any book as
being divine. Let us take it as it is. What
is the Bible? Your Honor, I have read it myself. I might read it more or more wisely.
Others may understand it better. Others may
think they understand it better when they do
not. But in a general way I know what it is.
I know there are millions of people in the
world who look on it as being a divine book,
and I have not the slightest objection to it.
I know there are millions of people in the
world who derive consolation in their times of
trouble and solace in times of distress from
the Bible. I would be pretty near the last one
in the world to do anything or take any action
to take it away. I feel just exactly the same
toward the religious creed of every human being
who lives. If anybody finds anything in this
life that brings them consolation and health
and happiness I think they ought to have it
whatever they get. I haven't any fault to find
with them at all. But what is it? The Bible
is not one book. The Bible is made up of
sixty-six books written over a period of about

one thousand years, some of them very early and some of them comparatively late. It is a book primarily of religion and morals. It is not a book of science. Never was and was never meant to be. Under it there is nothing prescribed that would tell you how to build a railroad or a steamboat or to make anything that would advance civilization. It is not a textbook or a text on chemistry. It is not big enough to be. It is not a book on geology; they knew nothing about geology. It is not a book on biology; they knew nothing about it. It is not a work on evolution; that is a mystery. It is not a work on astronomy. The man who looked out at the universe and studied the heavens had no thought but that the earth was the center of the universe. But we know better than that. We know that the sun is the center of the solar system. And that there are an infinity of other systems around us. They thought the sun went around the earth and gave us light and gave us night. We know better. We know the earth turns on its axis to produce days and nights. They thought the earth was created 4,004 before the Christian Era. We know better. I doubt if there is a person in Tennessee who does not know better. They told it the best they knew. And while suns may change all you may learn of chemistry, geometry and mathematics, there are no doubt certain primitive, elemental instincts in the organs of man that remain the same, he finds out what he can and yearns to know more and supplements his knowledge with hope and faith.

That is the province of religion and I haven't the slightest fault to find with it. . . . Can Your Honor tell what is given as the origin of man as shown in the Bible? Is there any human being who can tell us? There are two conflicting accounts in the first two chapters. There are scattered all through it various acts and ideas, but to pass that up for the sake of argument no teacher in any school in the state

of Tennessee can know that he is violating a
law, but must test every one of its doctrines
by the Bible must he not? You cannot say two
times two equals four or a man an educated man
if evolution is forbidden. It does not specify
what you cannot teach, but says you cannot
teach anything that conflicts with the Bible.
Then just imagine making it a criminal code
that is so uncertain and impossible that every
man must be sure that he has read everything in
the Bible and not only read it but understands
it, or he might violate the criminal code. Who
is the chief mogul that can tell us what the
Bible means? He or they should write a book
and make it plain and distinct, so we would
know. Let us look at it. There are in America
at least five hundred different sects or
churches, all of which quarrel with each other
and the importance or nonimportance of certain
things or the construction of certain passages.
All along the line they do not agree among
themselves and cannot agree among themselves.
They never have and probably never will. There
is a great division between the Catholics and
the Protestants. There is such a disagreement
that my client, who is a school-teacher, not
only must know the subject he is teaching, but
he must know everything about the Bible in reference to evolution. And he must be sure that
he expresses his right or else some fellow will
come along here, more ignorant perhaps than he
and say "You made a bad guess and I think you
have committed a crime." No criminal statute
can rest that way. There is not a chance for
it, for this criminal statute and every criminal statute must be plain and simple. If Mr.
Scopes is to be indicted and prosecuted because
he taught a wrong theory of the origin of life
why not tell him what he must teach. Why not
say that you must teach that man was made of
the dust; and still stranger not directly from
the dust, without taking any chances on it,
whatever, that Eve was made out of Adam's rib.

You will know what I am talking about. . . . I
am reading from a newspaper.   I forget what
newspaper it was, but I am sure it was right:
"That John Thomas Scopes on April, 1925, did
unlawfully and willfully teach in the public
schools of Rhea County, Tennessee, which public
schools are supported in part and in whole"--I
don't know how that is possible, but we will
pass that up--"In part or in whole by the
public school funds of the state a certain
theory and theories that deny the story of the
divine creation of man as taught in the Bible
and did teach instead there that man is descended from a lower order of animals."   Now,
then there is something that is very elementary.   That is one of them and very elementary,
because the constitution of Tennessee provides
and the constitutions of pretty near every
other state in the United States provide that
an indictment must state in sufficient terms so
that a man may be appraised of what is going to
be the character of charge against him.   Tennessee said that my friend the attorney-general
says that John Scopes knows what he is here
for.   Yes, I know what he is here for.   Because
the fundamentalists are after everybody that
thinks.   I know why he is here.   I know he is
here because ignorance and bigotry are rampant,
and it is a mighty strong combination, Your
Honor, it makes him fearul.   But the state is
bringing him here by indictment, and several
things must be stated in the indictment: in-
dictments must state facts, not law nor conclusions of law. . . . It is not enough in this
indictment to say that John Scopes taught something contrary to the divine account written by
Moses--maybe--that is not enough.   There are
several reasons for it.   First it is good and
right to know.   Secondly, after the shooting is
all over here and Scopes has paid his fine if
he can raise the money, or has gone to jail if
he cannot, somebody else will come along and
indict him over again.   But there is one thing

I cannot account for, that is the hatred and
the venom and feeling and the very strong religious combination.   That I never could account
for. . . . Now, Mr. Scopes on April 24 did unlawfully and willfully teach in a public school
of Rhea County, Tennessee, which public school
is supported in whole or in part by the public
school funds of the state, certain theories
that deny the story of the divine creation of
man.   What did he teach?   What did he teach?
Who is it that can tell us that John Scopes
taught certain theories that denied the story
of the divine--the divine story of creation as
recorded in the Bible.   How did he know what
textbooks did he teach from?   Who did he teach?
Why did he teach?   Not a word--all is silent.
He taught, oh yes, the place mentioned is Rhea
County.   Well, that is some county--Maybe all
over it, I don't know where he taught, he might
have taught in a half a dozen schools in Rhea
county on the one day and if he is indicted
next year after this trial is over, if it is,
for teaching in district No. 1, in Rhea county,
he cannot plead that he has already been convicted, because this was over here in another
district and at another place.   What did he
teach?   What was the horrible thing he taught
that was in conflict with Moses and what is it
that is not in conflict with Moses?   What
shouldn't he have taught?   What is the account
contained in the Bible which he ignored, when
he taught the doctrine of evolution which is
taught by every--believed by every scientific
man on earth.   Joshua made the sun stand still.
The fundamentalists will make the ages roll
back.   He should have been informed by the
indictment what was the doctrine he should have
taught and he should have been informed what he
did teach so that he could prepare, without
reading a whole book through, and without
waiting for witnesses to testify--we should
have been prepared to find out whether the
thing he taught was in conflict with the Bible

or what the Bible said about it.   Let me call
attention, Your Honor, to one case they have
heralded here--I don't know why.   I will refer
to it later.   Let me show you a real indictment, gentlemen, in case you ever need to draw
another one.   You don't mind a little pleas-
antry, do you?   Here is the case we have heard
so much about . . . .

Leeper vs. State.   My fellow is a leper,
too, because he taught evolution.   I am going
to discuss this case a moment later to show
that it has nothing to do with the subject.
This man was indicted because under the school
book law of this state the commission had
decided certain books should be taught, and
amongst the rest they decided that Frye's
geography should be taught.   That any teacher
did not follow the law and taught something
else should be fined $25.   Of course, it wasn't
so bad as to teach evolution, although the
statute doesn't say anything about evolution.
Now they indicted him and this is what they
said in the indictment.   This is their leading
case.   "The grand jury for the State of Tennessee, upon their oaths present that Edward
Leeper, heretofore, to-wit: On the 5th day of
October, 1899, in the state and county aforesaid, being then and there a public school-
teacher and teaching the public school known as
school No. 5, Sixth district, Blount county"--
they pick that out all right--"did unlawfully
use and permit to be used in said public
school, after the state textbook commission had
adopted and prescribed for use in the public
schools of the state Frye's introductory
geography as a uniform textbook another and
different textbook on that branch than the one
so adopted aforesaid, to-wit: Butler's geography and the new Eclectic elementary geography
against the peace and dignity of the state."
Now, Your Honor, would that have been a good
indictment, if they had left all that out and
said he taught some book not authorized by the

board?   He has got a right to know what he
taught and where he taught it and all the necessary things to convict him of crime.   Your
Honor, he cannot be convicted in this case unless they prove what he taught and where he
taught it, and we have got a right to know all
that before we go into court--every word of it.
The indictment isn't any more than so much
blank paper.   I insist, Your Honor, that no
such indictment was ever returned before on
land or sea.   Some men may pull one on me but I
don't think so--I don't think so.   You might
just as well indict a man for being no good--
and we could probably find a lot of them down
here probably and if we couldn't I could bring
them down from Chicago--but only a man is held
to answer for a specific thing and he must be
told what that specific thing is before he gets
into court.   The statute is absolutely void,
because they have violated the constitution in
its caption and it is absolutely uncertain--the
indictment is void because it is uncertain, and
gives no fact or information and it seems to me
the main thing they did in bringing this case
was to try to violate as many provisions of the
constitution as they could, to say nothing
about all the spirit of freedom and independ-
ence that has cost the best blood in the world
for ages, and it looks like it will cost some
more.   Let's see what else we got.   This legis-
lation--this legislation and all similar legislation that human ingenuity and malice can con-
coct, is void because it violates Section 13,
Section 12 and Section 3.   I want to call attention to that, Your Honor, Section 12 is the
section providing that the state should cherish
science, literature and learning.   Now, Your
Honor, I make it a rule to try not to argue
anything that I do not believe in, unless I am
caught in a pretty close corner and I want to
say that the construction of the attorney--
general given to that, I think, is correct and
the court added a little to it, which I think

makes your interpretation correct for what it
is good for. It shows the policy of the state.
It shows what the state is committed to. I do
not believe that a statute could be set aside
as unconstitutional simply because the legislature did not see fit to pass proper acts to
enlighten and educate the yeomen of Tennessee.

The state by constitution is committed to
the   doctrine   of   education,   committed   to
schools.   It is committed to teaching and I
assume when it is committed to teaching it is
committed to teaching the truth--ought to be
anyhow--plenty of people to do the other.   It
is committed to teaching literature and science. My friend has suggested that literature
and science might conflict. I cannot see how,
but   that   is   another   question.   But   that
indicates the policy of the state of Tennessee
and wherever it is used in construing the un-
constitutionality of this act it can only be
used as an indication of what the state meant
and you could not pronounce a statute void on
it, but we insist that this statute is absolutely void because it contravenes Section 3,
which is headed "the right of worship free."
Now, let's see, Your Honor, there isn't any
court in the world that can uphold the spirit
of the law by simply upholding its letters.   I
read somewhere--I don't know where--that the
letter killeth, but the spirit giveth life.   I
think I read it out of "The Prince of Peace."
I don't know where I did, but I read it.   If
this section of the constitution which guarantees religious liberty in Tennessee cannot be
sustained in the spirit it cannot be sustained
in the letter. What does it mean? I know two
intelligent people can agree only for a little
distance, like a company walking along in a
road. They may go together a few blocks and
then one branches off. The remainder go together a few more blocks and another branches
off and still further some one else branches
off and the human minds are just that way, pro-

vided they are free, of course, the fundamentalists may be put in a trap so they cannot
think differently if at all, probably not at
all, but leave two free minds and they may go
together a certain distance, but not all the
way together. There are no two human machines
alike and no two human beings have the same
experiences and their ideas of life and philosophy grow out of their construction of the
experiences that we meet on our journey through
life. It is impossible, if you leave freedom
in the world, to mold the opinions of one man
upon the opinions of another--only tyranny can
do it--and your constitutional provision, providing a freedom of religion, was meant to meet
that emergency. I will go further--there is
nothing else--since man--I don't know whether I
dare say evolved--still, this isn't a school--
since man was created out of the dust of the
earth--out of hand--there is nothing else Your
Honor that has caused the difference of opinion, of bitterness, of hatred, of war, of cruelty, that religion has caused. With that, of
course, it has given consolation to millions.

But it is one of those particular things
that should be left solely between the individual and his Maker, or his God, or whatever
takes expression with him, and it is no one
else's concern.

How many creeds and cults are there this
whole world over? No man could enumerate them?
At least as I have said, 500 different Christian creeds, all made up of differences, your
Honor, every one of them, and these subdivided
into small differences, until they reach every
member of every congregation. Because to think
is to differ, and then there are any number of
creeds older and any number of creeds younger,
than the Christian creed, any number of them,
the world has had them forever. They have come
and they have gone, they have abided their time
and have passed away, some of them forever, but
there has been a multitude, due to the multi-

tude and manifold differences in human beings,
and it was meant by the constitutional convention of Tennessee to leave these questions of
religion between man and whatever he worshiped,
to leave him free.   Has the Mohammedan any
right to stay here and cherish his creed? Has
the Buddist a right to live here and cherish
his creed? Can the Chinaman who comes here to
wash our clothes, can he bring his joss and
worship it?   Is there any man that holds a
religious creed, no matter where he came from,
or how old it is or how false it is, is there
any man that can be prohibited by any act of
the legislature of Tennessee? Impossible? The
constitution of Tennessee, as I understand, was
copied from the one that Jefferson wrote, so
clear, simple, direct, to encourage the freedom
of religious opinion, said in substance, that
no act shall ever be passed to interfere with
complete religious liberty. Now is this it or
is not this it? What do you say? What does it
do? We will say I am a scientist, no, I will
take that back, I am a pseudo-scientist, because I believe in evolution, pseudo-scientist
named by somebody, who neither knows or cares
what science is except to grab it by the throat
and throttle it to death. I am a pseudo-scientist, and I believe in evolution. Can a leg-
islative body say, "You cannot read a book or
take a lesson, or make a talk on science until
you first find out whether you are saying
against Genesis. It can unless that constitutional provision protects me. It can. Can
it say to the astronomer, you cannot turn your
telescope upon the infinite planets and suns
and stars that fill space, lest you find that
the earth is not the center of the universe and
there is not any firmament between us and the
heaven. Can it? It could--except for the work
of Thomas Jefferson, which has been woven into
every state constitution of the Union, and has
stayed there like the flaming sword to protect
the rights of man against ignorance and bigot-

ry, and when it is permitted to overwhelm them, then we are taken in a sea of blood and ruin that all the miseries and tortures and carnion in the middle ages would be as nothing. They would need to call back these men once more. But are the provisions of the constitutions that they left, are they enough to protect you and me, and every one else in a land which we thought was free?   Now, let us see what it says: "All men have a natural and indefeasible right to worship Almighty God according to the dictates of their own conscience."

That takes care even of the despised modernist, who dares to be intelligent. "That no man can of right be compelled to attend, erect or support any place of worship, or to maintain any minister against his consent; that no human authority can in any case whatever control or interfere with the rights of con- science in any case whatever"--that does not mean whatever, that means, "barring fundamen- talist propaganda." It does not mean whatever at all times, sometimes may be--and that "no preference shall be given by law to any relig- ious establishment or mode of worship." Does it? Could you get any more preference, Your Honor, by law? Let us see. Here is the state of Tennessee, living peacefully, surrounded by its beautiful mountains, each one of which con- tains evidence that the earth is millions of years old--people quiet, not all agreeing upon any one subject, and not necessary. If I could not live in peace with people I did not agree with . . . I could not live. . . .

Let us look at this act, Your Honor. Here is a law which makes it a crime to teach evolution in the caption. I don't know whether we have discussed that or not, but it makes it a crime in the body of the act to teach any theory of the origin of man excepting that contained in the divine account which we find in the Bible. All right. Now that act applies to what? Teachers in the public schools. Now

I have seen somewhere a statement of Mr.
Bryan's that the fellow that made the pay check
had a right to regulate the teachers.   All
right, let us see. I do not question the right
of the legislature to fix the courses of study,
but the state of Tennessee has no right under
the police power of the state to carve out a
law which applies to school-teachers, a law
which is a criminal statute and nothing else;
which makes no effort to prescribe the school
law or course of study.   It says that John
Smith who teaches evolution is a criminal if he
teaches it in the public schools. There is no
question about this act; there is no question
where it belongs; there is no question of its
origin. Nobody would claim that the act could
be passed for a minute excepting that teaching
evolution was in the nature of a criminal act;
that it smacked of policemen and criminals and
jails and grand juries; that it was in the
nature of some thing that was criminal and,
therefore, the state should forbid it.

It cannot stand a minute in this court on
any theory than that it is a criminal act,
simply because they say it contravenes the
teaching of Moses without telling us what those
teachings are. Now, if this is the subject of
a criminal act, then it cannot make a criminal
out of a teacher in the public schools and
leave a man free to teach it in a private
school.   It cannot make it criminal for a
teacher in the public schools to teach evolution, and for the same man to stand among the
hustings and teach it.   It cannot make it a
criminal act for this teacher to teach evolution and permit books upon evolution to be sold
in every store in the state of Tennessee and to
permit the newspapers from foreign cities to
bring into your peaceful community the horrible
utterances of evolution. Oh, no, nothing like
that. If the state of Tennessee has any force
in this day of fundamentalism, in this day when
religious bigotry and hatred is being kindled

all over our land, see what can be done?

Now, Your Honor, there is an old saying that nits make lice. I don't know whether you know what it makes possible down here in Tennessee? I know, I was raised in Ohio. It was a good idea to clear the nits, safer and easier.

To strangle puppies is good when they grow up into mad dogs, maybe. I will tell you what is going to happen, and I do not pretend to be a prophet, but I do not need to be a prophet to know. Your Honor knows the fires that have been lighted in America to kindle religious bigotry and hate. You can take judicial notice of them if you cannot of anything else. You know that there is no suspicion which possesses the minds of men like bigotry and ignorance and hatred. . . . If today you can take a thing like evolution and make it a crime to teach it in the public school, tomorrow you can make it a crime to teach it in the private schools, and the next year you can make it a crime to teach it on the hustings or in the church. At the next session you may ban books and newspapers. Soon you may set Catholic against Protestant and Protestant against Protestant, and try to foist your own religion upon the minds of men. If you can do one you can do the other. Ignorance and fanaticism is ever busy and needs feeding. Always, it is feeding and gloating for more. Today it is the public school teachers, tomorrow the private. The next day the preachers and the lecturers, the magazines, the books, the newspapers. After a while, Your Honor, it is the setting of man against man and creed against creed until with flying banners and beating drums we are marching backward to the glorious ages of the sixteenth century when bigots lighted fagots to burn the men who dared to bring any intelligence and enlightenment and culture to the human mind.

Speech at Sweet Trial

If the court please, gentlemen of the jury: You have listened so long and patiently that I do not know whether you are able to stand much more. I want to say, however, that while I have tried a good many cases in the forty-seven or forty-eight years that I have lived in courthouses, that in one way this has been one of the pleasantest trials I have been in. The kindness and consideration of the Court is such as to make it easy for everybody, and I have seldom found as courteous, gentlemanly and kind opponents as I have had in this case. I appreciate their friendship. Lawyers are apt to look at cases from different standpoints, and I sometimes find it difficult to understand how a lawyer on the other side can think as he thinks and say what he says; I, being an extremely reasonable man and extremely free from all kinds of prejudices myself, find this hard to comprehend.

My friend Mr. Moll says, gentlemen, that this isn't a race question. This is a murder case. We don't want any prejudice; we don't want the other side to have any. Race and color have nothing to do with this case. This is a case of murder.

I insist that there is nothing but prejudice in this case; that if it was reversed and eleven white men had shot and killed a black

while protecting their home and their lives
against a mob of blacks, nobody would have
dreamed of having them indicted. I know what I
am talking about, and so do you. They would
have been given medals instead. Ten colored
men and one women are in this indictment, tried
by twelve jurors, gentlemen. Every one of you
are white, aren't you. At least you all think
so. We haven't one colored man on this jury.
We couldn't get one. One was called and he was
disqualified. You twelve white men are trying
a colored man on race prejudice.

Now, let me ask you whether you are not
prejudiced. I want to put this square to you,
gentlemen. I haven't any doubt but that every
one of you is prejudiced against colored people. I want you to guard against it. I want
you to do all you can to be fair in this case,
and I believe you will. A number of you have
answered the question that you are acquainted
with colored people. One juror I have in mind,
who is sitting here, said there were two or
three families living on the street in the
block where he lives, and had lived there for a
year or more, but he didn't know their names
and had never met them. Some of the rest of
you said that you had employed colored people
to work for you, are even employing them now.
All right. You have seen some colored people
in this case. They have been so far above the
white people that live at the corner of Garland
and Charlevoix that they can't be compared,
intellectually, morally and physically, and you
know it. How many of you have invited them to
dinner in your house? Probably not one of you.
Now, why, gentlemen? There isn't one of you
men but what knows just from the witnesses you
have seen in this case that there are colored
people who are intellectually the equal of all
of you. Am I right? Colored people living
right here in the city of Detroit are intellectually the equals and some of them superior
to most of us. Is that true? Some of them are

people of more character and learning than most
of us.

Now, why don't you individually, and why
don't I, and why doesn't every white person
whose chances have been greater and whose
wealth is larger, associate with them?   There
is only one reason, and that is prejudice.   Can
you give any other reason for it?   They would
be intellectual companions.   They have good
manners.   They are clean.   They are all of them
clean enough to wait on us, but not clean e-
nough to associate with.   Is there any reason
in the world why we don't associate with them
excepting prejudice?   I think not one man of
this jury wants to be prejudiced.   It is forced
into us almost from our youth, until somehow or
other we feel we are superior to these people
who have black faces.

Now, gentlemen, I say you are prejudiced.
I fancy every one of you is, otherwise you
would have some companions amongst these colored people.   You will overcome it, I believe, in
the trial of this case.   But they tell me there
is no race prejudice, and it is plain nonsense,
and nothing else.

Who are we, anyway?   A child is born into
this world without any knowledge of any sort.
He has a brain which is a piece of putty; he
inherits nothing in the way of knowledge or of
ideas.   If he is white, he knows nothing about
color.   He has no antipathy to the black.   The
black and white both will live together and
play together, but as soon as the baby is born
we begin giving him ideas.   We begin planting
seeds in his mind.   We begin telling him he
must do this and he must not do that.   We tell
him about race and social equality and the
thousands of things that men talk about until
he grows up.   It has been trained into us, and
you, gentlemen, bring that feeling into this
jury box.

You need not tell me you are not prejudiced.   I know better.   We are not very much

but a bundle of prejudices anyhow. We are prejudiced against other people's color. Prejudiced against other men's religions; prejudiced against other people's politics. Prejudiced against people's looks. Prejudiced about the way they dress. We are full of prejudices. You can teach a man anything beginning with the child; you can make anything out of him, and we are not responsible for it. Here and there some of us haven't any prejudices on some questions, but if you look deep enough you will find them; and we all know it.

All I hope for, gentlemen of the jury, is this: that you are strong enough and honest enough, and decent enough to lay it aside in this case and decide as you ought to. And I say, there is no man in Detroit that doesn't know that these defendants, every one of them, did right. There isn't a man in Detroit who doesn't know that the defendant did his duty, and that this case is an attempt to send him and his companions to prison because they defended their constitutional rights. It is a wicked attempt, and you are asked to be party to it. You know it. I don't need to talk to this jury about the facts in this case. There is no man who can read or understand that does not know the facts. Is there prejudice in it?

Now, let's see. I don't want to lean very much on your intelligence. I don't need much. I just need a little. Would this case be in this court if these defendants were not black? Would anyone be asking you to send a boy to prison for life for defending his brother's home and protecting his own life, if his face wasn't black? What were the people in the neighborhood of Charlevoix and Garland streets doing on that fatal night? There isn't a child that doesn't know. Have you any doubt as to why they were there? Was Mr. Moll right when he said that color has nothing to do with the case? There is nothing else in this case but the feeling of prejudice which has been carefully nourished by the white man until he doesn't know that he has it himself.   While I admire and like my friend Moll very much, I can't help criticizing his argument.   I suppose I may say what old men are apt to say, in a sort of patronizing way, that his zeal is due to youth and inexperience.   That is about all we have to brag about as we get older, so we ought to be permitted to do that.   Let us look at this case.

Mr. Moll took particular pains to say to you, gentlemen, that these eleven people here are guilty of murder; he calls this a cold-blooded, deliberate and premeditated murder; that is, they were there to kill.   That was their purpose.   Eleven, he said.   I am not going to discuss the case of all of them just now, but I am starting where he started.   He doesn't want any misunderstanding.   Amongst the eleven is Mrs. Sweet, the wife of Dr. Sweet. She is a murderer, gentlemen?   The state's attorney said so, and the assistant state's attorney said so.   The state's attorney would have to endorse it because he himself stands by what his assistant says.   Pray, tell me what has Mrs. Sweet done to make her a murderer? She is the wife of Dr. Sweet.   She is the moth-er of his little baby.   She left the child at her mother's home while she moved into this highly cultured community near Goethe Street. Anyway, the baby was to be safe; but she took her own chance, and she didn't have a gun; none was provided for her.   Brother Toms drew from the witnesses that there were ten guns, and ten men.   He didn't leave any for her.   Maybe she had a penknife, but there is no evidence on that question.   What did she do gentlemen?   She is put down here as a murderer.   She wasn't even upstairs.   She didn't even look out of a window.   She was down in the back kitchen cook-ing a ham to feed her family and friends, and a white mob came to drive them out of their home before the ham was served for dinner.   She is a murderer, and all of those defendants who were driven out of their home must go to the penitentiary for life if you can find twelve jurors somewhere who have enough prejudice in their hearts, and hatred in their minds. Now, that is this case, gentlemen, and all there is to this case. Take the hatred away, and you have nothing left. Moll says that this is a case between Breiner and Henry Sweet. . . . The question here is whether these defendants or this defendant is guilty of murder. It has nothing to do with Breiner. He says that I wiggled and squirmed every time they mentioned Breiner. Well, now, I don't know. Did I? Maybe I did. I didn't know it. I have been around courtrooms so long that I fancy I could listen to anything without moving a hair. Maybe I couldn't.

I rather think that my friend is pretty wise. He said that I don't like to hear them talk about Breiner. I don't gentlemen, and I might have shown it. This isn't the first case I was ever in. I don't like to hear the state's attorney talk about the blood of a victim. It has such a mussy sound. I wish they would leave it out. I will be frank with you about it. I don't think it has any place in this case. I think it tends to create prejudice and feeling and it has no place, and it is always dangerous. And perhaps--whether I showed it or not, my friend read my mind. I don't like it. Now, gentlemen, as he talked about Breiner, I am going to talk about him, and it isn't easy, either. It isn't easy to talk about the dead, unless you "slobber" over them and I am not going to "slobber" over Breiner. I am going to tell you the truth about it. Why did he say that he held a brief for Breiner, and ask you to judge between Breiner and Henry Sweet? You know why he said it? Had it any place in this case? Henry Sweet never knew that such a man lived as Breiner. Did he? He didn't shoot at him.

Somebody shot out into that crowd and Breiner got it. Nobody had any feeling against him. But who was Breiner, anyway? I will tell you he was. I am going to measure my words when I state it, and I am going to make good before I am through in what I say.

Who was he? He was a conspirator in as foul a conspiracy as was ever hatched in a community; in a conspiracy to drive from their homes a little family of black people. Not only that, but to destroy these blacks and their home. Now, let me see whether I am right. What do we know of Breiner? He lived two blocks from the Sweet home. On the fourteenth day of July, seven hundred people met at the schoolhouse and the schoolhouse was too small, and they went out into the yard. This schoolhouse was right across the street from the Sweet house.

Every man in the community knew all about it. Every man in that community understood it. And it that schoolhouse a man rose and told what they had done in his community; that by main force they had driven Negro families from their homes, and that when a Negro moved to Garland Street, their people would be present to help. That is why Mr. Breiner came early to the circus on September 9, 1925. He went past that house, back and forth, two or three times that night. What was he doing? "Smoking his pipe." What were the rest of them doing? They were a part of a mob and they had no rights, and the Court will tell you so, I think. And, if he does, gentlemen, it is your duty to accept it.

Gentlemen, it is a reflection upon anybody's intelligence to say that everyone did not know why this mob was there. You know! Every one of you know why. They came early to take their seats at the ringside. Didn't they? And Breiner sat at one point where the stones were thrown, didn't he? Was he a member of that mob? Gentlemen, that mob was bent not only on making an assault upon the rights of the owners of that house, not only making an assault upon their persons and their property, but they were making an assault on the constitution and the laws of the nation and the state under which they live.

Gentlemen, my friend said that he wasn't going to mince matters. I think I will, because I know the prejudice is the other way. You can pick twelve men in these black faces that are watching your deliberations and have throughout all these weary days, and with them I would not need to mince matters; but I must be very careful not to shock your sensibilities. I must state just as much or as near the facts as I dare to state without shocking you and be fair to my client.

It was bad enough for a mob, by force and violation of law, to attempt to drive these people from their house but, gentlemen, it is worse to send them to prison for life for defending their home. Think of it. That is this case. Are we human? Hardly.

Did the witnesses for the State appearing here tell the truth? You know they did not. I am not going to analyze the testimony of every one of them. But they did not tell the truth and they did not mean to tell the truth. Let me ask you this question, gentlemen: Mr. Moll says that these colored people had a perfect right to live in that house. He did not say it was an outrage to molest them. Oh, no, he said they had a perfect right to live in that house. But the mob met there to drive them out. That is exactly what they did, and they have lied and lied and lied to send these defendants to the penitentiary for life, so that they will not go back to their home.

Now, you know that the mob met there for that purpose. They violated the Constitution and the law; they violated every human feeling, and threw justice and mercy and humanity to the winds, and they made a murderous attack upon

their neighbor because his face was black.
Which is the worse, to do that or lie about it?
In describing this mob, I heard the word "few"
from the State's witnesses so many times that I
should hear it in my sleep, and I presume that
when I am dying I will hear that "few," "few,"
"few" stuff that I heard in Detroit from people
who lied and lied and lied.   What was this
"few"?   And who were they, and how did they
come from there?

I can't tell you about every one of these
witnesses, but I can tell you about some of
them.   Too many, I can't even carry all of
their names in my mind and I don't want to.
There are other things more interesting--bugs,
for instance. Anything is more interesting to
carry in your mind than the names of that
bunch, and yet I am going to say something for
them, too, because I know something about human
nature and life; and I want to be fair, and if
I did not want to, I think perhaps it would pay
me to be.

Are the people who live around the corner
of Charlevoix and Garland worse than other
people?   There isn't one of you who doesn't
know that they lied.   There isn't one of you
who does not know that they tried to drive
those people out and now are trying to send
them to the penitentiary so that they can't
move back, all in violation of the law, and are
trying to get you to do the job.   Are they
worse than other people? I don't know as they
are.   How much do you know about prejudice?
Race prejudice.   Religious prejudice.   These
feelings that have divided men and caused them
to do the most terrible things.   Prejudices
have burned men at the stake, broken them on
the rack, torn every joint apart, destroyed
people by the million. Men have done this on
account of some terrible prejudice which even
now is reaching out to undermine this republic
of ours and to destroy the freedom that has
been the most cherished past of our institu-

tions. These witnesses honestly believe that
they are better than blacks. I do not. They
honestly believe it is their duty to keep colored people out. They honestly believe that
blacks are an inferior race and yet if they
look at themselves, I don't know how they can.

Gentlemen, lawyers are very intemperate in
their statements. My friend, Moll, said that
my client here was a coward. A coward, gentlemen. Here, he says, were a gang of gunmen, and
cowards--shot Breiner through the back. Nobody
saw Breiner, of course. If he had his face
toward the house, while he was smoking there,
waiting for the shooting to begin, it wasn't
our fault. It wouldn't make any difference
which way he turned. I suppose the bullet
would have killed him just the same, if he had
been in the way of it. If he had been at home,
it would not have happened. Who are the cowards in this case? Cowards, gentlemen! Eleven
persons with black skins, eleven people, gentlemen, whose ancestors did not come to America
because they wanted to, but were brought here
in slave ships, to toil for nothing, for the
whites--whose lives have been taken in nearly
every state in the Union--they have been victims of riots all over this land of the free.
They have had to take what is left after
everybody else had grabbed what he wanted. The
only place where he has been put in front is on
the battlefield. When we are fighting we give
him a chance to die, and the best chance. But
everywhere else, he has been food for the
flames, and the ropes, and the knives, and the
guns and hate of the white, regardless of law
and liberty, and the common sentiments of
justice that should move men. Were they
cowards?

No, gentlemen, they may have been gunmen.
They may have tried to murder. But they were
not cowards. Eleven people, knowing what it
meant, with the history of the race behind
them, with the knowledge of shooting and kill-

ing and insult and injury without end, elev en of them go into a house, gentlemen, with no police protection, in the face of a mob, and the hatred of a community, and take guns and ammunition and fight for their rights, and for your rights and for mine, and for the rights of every being that lives. They went in and faced a mob seeking to tear them to bits. Call them something besides cowards. The cowardly curs were in the mob gathered there with the backing of the law. A lot of children went in front and threw the stones. They stayed for two days and two nights in front of this home, and by their threats and assault were trying to drive the Negroes out. Those were the cowardly curs, and you know it. I suppose there isn't any ten of them that would come out in the open daylight against those ten. Oh no, gentlemen, their blood is too pure for that. They can only act like a band of coyotes baying some victim who has no chance. And then my clients are called cowards.

All right, gentlemen, call them something else. These blacks have been called many names along down through the ages, but there have been those through the sad years who believed in justice and mercy and charity and love and kindliness, and there have been those who believed that a black man should have some rights, even in a country where he was brought in chains. There are those even crazy enough to hope and to dream that sometime he will come from under this cloud and take his place amongst the people of the world. If he does, it will be through his courage and his culture. It will be by his intelligence and his scholarship and his effort, and I say, gentlemen of the jury, no honest, right-feeling man, whether on a jury or anywhere else, would place anything in his way in this great struggle behind him and before him.

What are you, gentlemen? And what am I? I don't know. I can only go a little way to-

ward the source of my own being. I know my father and I know my mother., I know my grandmothers and my grandfathers on both sides, but
I don't know my great-grandfathers and great-
grandmothers on either side, and I don't know
who they were. All that a man can do in this
direction is but little. He can only slightly
raise the veil that hangs over all the past.
He can peer into the darkness just a little way
and that is all. I know that somewhere around
1600, as the record goes, some of my ancestors
came from England. Some of them. I don't know
where all of them came from, and I don't think
any human being knows where all his ancestors
came from. But back of that, I can say nothing. What do you know of yours? I will tell
you what I know, or what I think I know, gentlemen. I will try to speak as modestly as I
can, knowing the uncertainty of human knowledge, because it is uncertain. The best I can
do is to go a little way back. I know that
back of us all and each of us is the blood of
all the world. I know that it courses in your
veins and mine. It has come out of the infinite past, and I can't pick out mine and you
can't pick out yours, and it is only the ignorant who know, and I believe that back of that-
-back of that--is what we call the lower order
of life; back of that there lurks the instinct
of the distant serpent, of the carnivorous tiger. All the elements have been gathered together to make the mixture that is you and I
and all the race, and nobody knows anything a-
bout his own. Gentlemen, I wonder who we are
anyhow, to be so proud of our ancestry? We had
better try to do something kindly, something
humane, to some human being, than to brag about
our ancestry, of which none of us know
anything.
    Now, let us go back to the street again.
I don't know. Perhaps I weary you. Perhaps
these things that seem important to me are un-
important, but they are all a part of the great

human tragedy that stands before us. And if I could do something, which I can't, to make the world better, I would try to have it more tolerant, more kindly, more understanding; could I do that and nothing else, I would be glad.

The police department went up there on the morning of the eighth, in the city of Detroit, in the state of Michigan, U.S.A., to see that a family were permitted to move into a home that they owned without getting their throats cut by the noble Nordics who inhabit that jungle. Fine, isn't it? No race question in this? Oh, no, this is a murder case, and yet, in the forenoon of the eighth, they sent four policemen there, to protect a man and his wife, with two little truckloads of household furniture, who were moving into that place. Pretty tough, isn't it? Aren't you glad you are not black? You deserve a lot of credit for it, don't you, because you didn't choose black ancestry? People ought to be killed who chose black ancestry. The policemen went there to protect the lives and the small belongings of these humble folks who moved into their home. What are these black people to do?

I seem to wander from one thing to another without much sequence. I must get back again to the colored man. You don't want him. Perhaps you don't want him next to you. Suppose you were colored. Did any of you ever dream that you were colored? Did you ever wake up out of a nightmare when you dreamed you were colored? Would you be willing to have my client's skin? Why? Just because somebody is prejudiced! Imagine yourselves colored gentlemen. Imagine yourselves back in the Sweet house on that fatal night. That is the only right way to treat this case, and the Court will tell you so. Would you move there? Where would you move? Dancy says there were six or seven thousand colored people here sixteen years ago. And seventy-one thousand five years

ago. Gentlemen, why are they here? They came
here as you came here, under the laws of trade
and business, under the instincts to live; both
the white and the colored, just the same; the
instincts of all animals to propagate their
kind, the feelings back of life and on which
life depends. They came here to live. Your
factories were open for them. Mr. Ford hired
them. They were all willing to give them work,
weren't they? Every one of them. You and I
are willing to give them work, too. We are
willing to have them in our houses to take care
of the children and do the rough work that we
shun ourselves. They are not offensive, either. We invited them; pretty nearly all the
colored population has come to Detroit in the
last fifteen years; most of them, anyhow. They
have always had a corner on the meanest jobs.
The city must grow, or you couldn't brag about
it. The colored people must live somewhere.
Everybody is willing to have them live somewhere else. The people at the corner of
Garland and Charlevoix would be willing to have
them go to some other section. Everybody would
be willing to have them go somewhere else.

Somewhere they must live. Are you going
to kill them? Are you going to say that they
can work, but they can't get a place to sleep?
They can toil in the mill, but they can't eat
their dinner at home. We want them to build
automobiles for us, don't we? We even let them
become our chauffeurs. Oh, gentlemen, what is
the use! You know it is wrong. Every one of
you knows it is wrong. You know it is wrong.
You know that no man in conscience could blame
a Negro for almost anything. Can you think of
these people without shouldering your own responsibility? Don't make it harder for them, I
beg you.

They sent four policemen in the morning to
help this little family move in. They had a
bedstead, a stove and some bedding, ten guns
and some ammunition, and they had food to last

them through a siege. I feel that they should have taken less furniture and more food and guns.

Gentlemen, nature works in a queer way. I don't know how this question of color will ever be solved, or whether it will be solved. Nature has a way of doing things. There is one thing about nature, she has plenty of time. She would make broad prairies so that we can raise wheat and corn to feed men. How does she do it? She sends a glacier plowing across a continent, and takes fifty thousand years to harrow it and make it fit to till and support human life. She makes a man. She tries endless experiments before the man is done. She wants to make a race and it takes an infinite mixture to make it. She wants to give us some conception of human rights, and some kindness and charity, she makes pain and suffering and sorrow and death. It all counts. That is a rough way, but it is the only way. It all counts in the great, long, broad scheme of things. I look on a trial like this with a feeling of disgust and shame. I can't help it now. It will be after we have learned in the terrible and expensive school of human experience that we will be willing to find each other and understand each other.

Now let us get to the bare facts of this case. The city of Detroit had the police force there to help these people move into their home. When they unloaded their goods, men and women on the street began going from house to house. They went from house to house to sound the alarm, "the Negroes are coming," as if a foreign army was invading their homes; as if a wild beast had come down out of the mountains in the olden times. Can you imagine those colored people? They didn't dare move without thinking of their color. Where we go into a hotel unconsciously, or a church, if we choose, they do not. Of course, colored people belong to a church, and they have a YMCA. That is, a

Jim Crow YMCA. The black Christians cannot mix
with the white Christians. They will probably
have a Jim Crow Heaven where the white angels
will not be obliged to meet the black angels,
except as servants.

Gentlemen, they say there is nothing to
justify this shooting; it was an orderly,
neighborly crowd. They came there for a purpose and intended to carry it out. How long,
pray, would you wait? The very presence of the
crowd was a mob, as I believe the Court will
tell you. Suppose a crowd gathers around your
house; a crowd which doesn't want you there; a
hostile crowd, for a part of two days and two
nights, until the police force of this city is
called in to protect you. How long, tell me,
are you going to live in that condition with a
mob surrounding your house and the police force
standing in front of it? How long should these
men have waited? You wouldn't have waited.
Counsel say that they had just as good reason
to shoot on the eighth as on the ninth. Con-
cede it. They did not shoot. They waited and
hoped and prayed that in some way this crowd
would pass them by and grant them the right to
live. The mob came back the next night and the
colored people waited while they were gathering; they waited while they were coming from
every street and every corner, and while the
officers were supine and helpless and doing
nothing. And they waited until dozens of
stones were thrown against the house on the
roof, probably--I don't know how many. Nobody
knows how many. They waited until the windows
were broken before they shot. Why did they
wait so long? I think I know. How much chance
had these people for their lives after they
shot, surrounded by a crowd as they were? They
would never take a chance unless they thought
it was necessary to take a chance. Eleven
people penned up in the face of a mob. What
chance did they have?

Suppose they shot before they should.

What is the theory of counsel in this case? Nobody pretends there is anything in this case to prove that our client Henry fired the fatal shot. There isn't the slightest. It wasn't a shot that would fit the gun he had. The theory of this case is that he was part of a combination to do something. Now, what was that combination, gentlemen? Your own sense will tell you what it was. Did they combine to go there and kill somebody? Were they looking for somebody to murder? Dr. Sweet scraped together his small earnings by his industry and put himself through college, and he scraped together his small earnings of three thousand dollars to buy that home because he wanted to kill somebody?

It is silly to talk about it. He bought that home just as you buy yours, because he wanted a home to live in, to take his wife and to raise his family. There is no difference between the love of a black man for his offspring and the love of a white. He and his wife had the same feeling of fatherly and motherly affection for their child that you gentlemen have for yours, and that your father and mother had for you. They bought that home for that purpose; not to kill somebody. They might have feared trouble, as they probably did, and as the evidence shows that every man with a black face fears it, when he moves into a home that is fit for a dog to live in. It is part of the curse that, for some inscrutable reason, has followed the race--if you call it a race--and which curse, let us hope, sometime the world will be wise enough and decent enough and human enough to wipe out.

They went there to live. They knew the dangers. Why do you suppose they took these guns and this ammunition and these men there? Because they wanted to kill somebody? It is utterly absurd and crazy. They took them there because they thought it might be necessary to defend their home with their lives and they were determined to do it. They took guns there that in case of need they might fight, fight even to the death for their home, and for each other, for their people, for their race, for their rights under the Constitution and the laws under which all of us live; and unless men and women will do that, we will soon be a race of slaves, whether we are black or white. "Eternal vigilance is the price of liberty," and it has always been so and always will be. Do you suppose they were in there for any other purpose?

Gentlemen, there isn't a chance that they took arms there for anything else. They did go there knowing their rights, feeling their responsibility, and determined to maintain those rights if it meant death to the last man and the last woman, and no one could do more. No man lived a better life or died a better death than fighting for his home and his children, for himself, and for the eternal principles upon which life depends. Instead of being here under indictment, for murder, they should be honored for the brave stand they made for their rights and ours. Some day, both white and black, irrespective of color, will honor the memory of these men, whether they are inside prison walls or outside, and will recognize that they fought not only for themselves, but for every man who wishes to be free. . . . This isn't a case of a man who trespasses upon the ground of some other man and is killed. It is the case of an unlawful mob, which is itself a crime; a mob bent on mischief; a mob that has no rights. They are too dangerous. It is like a fire. One man may do something. Two will do much more; three will do more than three times as much; a crowd will do something that no man ever dreamed of doing. The law recognizes it. It is the duty of the officers to disperse them. It was the duty of the inmates of the house, even though they had to kill somebody to do it.

Now, gentlemen, I wouldn't ask you to take

the law on my statement. The Court will tell
you the law. A mob is a criminal combination
of itself. Their presence is enough. You need
not wait until it spreads. It is there, and
that is enough. There is no other law; there
hasn't been for years, and it is the law which
will govern this case. . . . Here is Henry
Sweet, the defendant in this case, a boy. How
many of you know why you are trying him? What
had he to do with it? Why is he in this case?
A boy, twenty-one years old, working his way
through college, and he is just as good a boy
as the boy of any juror in this box; just as
good a boy as you people were when you were
boys, and I submit to you, he did nothing whatever that was wrong. Of course, we lawyers
talk and talk, as if we feared results.   I
don't mean to trifle with you. I always fear
results. When life and liberty is in the hands
of a lawyer, he realizes the terrible responsibility that is on him, and he fears that some
word will be left unspoken, or some thought
will be forgotten. I would not be telling you
the truth if I told you that I did not fear the
result of this important case; and when my
judgement and my reason come to my aid and take
counsel with my fears, I know, and I feel
perfectly well that no twelve American jurors,
especially in any Northern land, could be
brought together who would dream of taking a
boy's life or liberty under circumstances like
this. That is what my judgement tells me, but
my fears perhaps cause me to go further and to
say more when I should not have said as much.
    Now, let me tell you when a man has the
right to shoot in self-defense, and in defense
of his home; not when these vital things in
life are in danger, but when he thinks they
are. These despised blacks did not need to
wait until the house was beaten down above
their heads. They didn't need to wait longer
for that mob to grow more inflamed. There is
nothing so dangerous as ignorance and bigotry

when it is unleashed as it was here. The Court will tell you that these inmates of this house had the right to decide upon appearances, and if they did, even though they were mistaken, they are not guilty.   I don't know but they could safely have stayed a little longer. I don't know but it would have been well enough to let this mob break a few more windowpanes. I don't know but it would have been better and been safe to let them batter down the house before they shot. I don't know. How am I to tell, and how are you to tell?

You are twelve white men, gentlemen. You are twelve men sitting here eight months after all this occurred, listening to the evidence, perjured and otherwise, in this court, to tell whether they acted too quickly or too slowly. A man may be running an engine on the railroad. He may stop too quickly or too slowly. In an emergency he is bound to do one or the other, and the jury a year after, sitting in cold blood, may listen to the evidence and say that he acted too quickly. What do they know about it? You must sit out there upon a moving engine with your hand on the throttle and facing danger and must decide and act quickly. Then you can tell.

Cases often occur in the courts, which doesn't speak very well for the decency of courts, but they have happened, where men have been shipwrecked at sea, a number of men having left the ship and gone into a small boat to save their lives; they have floated around for hours and tossed on the wild waves of an angry sea; their food disappearing, the boat heavy and likely to sink and no friendly sail in sight. . . . What are they to do? Will they throw some of their companions off the boat and save the rest? Will they eat some to save the others? If they kill anybody, it is because they want to live. Every living thing wants to live. The strongest instinct in life is to keep going. You have seen a tree upon a rock

send a shoot down for ten or fifteen or twenty
feet, to search for water, to draw it up, that
it may still survive; it is a strong instinct
with animals and with plants, with all sentient
things, to keep alive.   Men are out in a boat,
in an angry sea, with little food and less water.   No hope in sight.   What will they do?
They throw a companion overboard to save themselves, or they kill somebody to save themselves.   Juries have come into court and passed
on the question of whether they should have
waited longer, or not.   Later, the survivors
were picked up by a ship and perhaps, if they
had waited longer, all would have been saved.
Yet a jury, months after it was over, sitting
safely in their jury box, pass upon the question of whether they acted too quickly or not.
Can they tell?   No.   To decide that case, you
must be in a small boat, with little food and
water; in a wild sea, with no sail in sight,
and drifting around for hours or days in the
face of the deep, beset by hunger and darkness
and fear and hope.   Then you can tell; but, no
man can tell without it.   It can't be done,
gentlemen, and the law says so, and this Court
will tell you so.

Let me tell you what you must do, gentlemen.   It is fine for lawyers to say, naive-
ly, that nothing happened.   No foot was set
upon that ground; as if you had to put your
foot on the premises.   You might put your hand
on.   The foot isn't sacred.   No foot set
upon their home.   No shot was fired, nothing
except that the house was stoned and windows
broken, and an angry crowd was outside seeking
their destruction.   That is all.   That is all,
gentlemen.   I say that no American citizen,
unless he is black, need wait until an angry
mob sets foot upon his premises before he
kills.   I say that no free man need wait to see
just how far an aggressor will go before he
takes life.   The first instinct a man has is to
save his life.   He doesn't need to experiment.

He hasn't time to experiment. When he thinks
it is time to save his life, he has the right
to act. There isn't any question about it. It
has been the law of every English-speaking
country as long as we have had law. Every
man's home is his castle, which even the king
may not enter. Every man has a right to kill,
to defend himself or his family, or others,
either in the defense of the home or in the
defense of themselves. So far as that branch
of the case is concerned, there is only one
thing that this jury has a right to consider,
and that is whether the defendants acted in
honest fear or danger. That is all. . . . Now
let us look at these fellows. Here were eleven
colored men, penned up in the house. Put yourselves in their place. Make yourselves colored
for just a little while, long enough, gentlemen, to judge them, and before any of you want
to be judged, you would want your juror to put
himself in your place. That is all I ask in
this case, gentlemen. They were black, and
they knew the history of the black. Our friend
makes fun of Dr. Sweet and Henry Sweet talking
these things all over in the short space of two
months. Well, gentlemen, let me tell you something, that isn't evidence. This is just theory, and nothing else. I should imagine that
the only thing that two or three colored people
talk of when they get together is race. I
imagine that they can't rub color off their
faces or rub it out of their minds. I imagine
that it is with them always. I imagine that
the stories of lynchings, the stories of murders, the stories of oppression is a topic of
constant conversation. I imagine that everything that appears in the newspapers on this
subject is carried from one to another until
every man knows what others know, upon the
topic which is the most important to all of
their lives.

What do you think about it? Suppose you
were black. Do you think you would forget it

even in your dreams?   Or would you have black
dreams?   Suppose you had to watch every point
of contact with your neighbor and remember your
color, and you knew your children were growing
up under this handicap.   Do you suppose you
would think of anything else?   Do you suppose
this boy coming in here didn't know all about
the conditions, and did not learn all about
them?   Did he not know about Detroit?   Do you
suppose he hadn't read the story of his race?
He is intelligent.   He goes to school.   He
would have been a graduate now, except for this
long hesitation, when he is waiting to see
whether he goes back to college or goes to
jail.   Do you suppose that black students and
teachers are discussing it?   Anyhow, gentlemen,
what is the use?   The jury isn't supposed to be
entirely ignorant.   They are supposed to know
something.   These black people were in the
house with the black man's psychology, and with
the black man's fear, based on what they had
heard and what they had read and what they
knew.   I don't need to go far.   I don't need to
travel to Florida.   I don't even need to talk
about the Chicago riots.   The testimony showed
that in Chicago a colored boy on a raft had
been washed to a white bathing beach, and men
and boys of my race stoned him to death.   A
riot began, and some hundred and twenty were
killed.   I don't need to go to Washington or to
St. Louis.   Let us take Detroit.   I don't need
to go far either in space or time.   Let us take
this city.   Now, gentlemen, I am not saying
that the white people of Detroit are different
from the white people of any other city.   I
know what prejudice growing out of race and
religion has done the world over, and all
through time.   I am not blaming Detroit.   I am
stating what has happened, that is all.   And I
appeal to you, gentlemen, to do your part to
save the honor of this city, to save its reputation, to save yours, to save its name, and to
save the poor colored people who cannot save

themselves.

I was told there had not been a lynching of a colored man in thirty years or more in Michigan. All right. Why, I can remember when the early statesmen of Michigan cared for the colored man and when they embodied the rights of the colored men in the constitution and statutes. I can remember when they laid the foundation that made it possible for a man of any color or religion, or any creed, to own his home wherever he could find a man to sell it. I remember when civil rights laws were passed that gave the Negro the right to live where the white man went and as he went. There are some men who seem to think those laws were wrong. I do not. Wrong or not, it is the law, and if you were black you would protest with every fiber of your body your right to live. Michigan used to protect the rights of colored people. There were not many of them here, but they have come in the last few years, and with them has come prejudice. Then, too, the Southern white man has followed his black slave. But that isn't all. Black labor has come in competition with white. Prejudices have been created where there was no prejudie before. We have listened to the siren song that we are a superior race and have superior rights, and that the black man has none. It is a new idea in Detroit that a colored man's home can be torn down about his head because he is black. There are some eighty thousand blacks here now, and they are bound to reach out. They have reached out in the past, and they will reach out in the future. Do not make any mistake, gentlemen. I am making no promises. I know the instinct for life. I know it reaches black and white alike. I know that you cannot confine any body of people to any particular place; and, as the population grows, the colored people will go farther. I know it, and you must change the law or you must take it as it is, or you must invoke the primal law of nature and

get back to clubs and fists, and if you are
ready for that, gentlemen, all right, but do it
with your eyes open. That is all I care for.
You must have a government of law or blind
force, and if you are ready to let blind force
take the place of law, the responsibility is on
you, not on me.

Now, let us see what has happened here.
So far as I know, there had been nothing of the
sort happened when Dr. Sweet bought his home.
He took an option on it in May, and got his
deed in June; and in July, in that one month,
while he was deliberating on moving, there were
three cases of driving Negro families out of
their homes in Detroit. This was accomplished
by stones, clubs, guns, and mobs. Suppose you
were colored and had bought a house on Garland
Avenue. Take this just exactly as it is. You
bought it in June, intending to move in July,
and you read and heard about what happened in
another part of the city. Would you have waited? Would you have waited a month, as Sweet
did?

Remember, these men didn't have any too
much money. Dr. Sweet paid three thousand
dollars on his home, leaving a loan on it of
sixteen thousand dollars more. He had to
scrape together some money to buy his furniture, and he bought fourteen hundred dollars'
worth the day after he moved in and paid two
hundred dollars down. Gentlemen, it is only
right to consider Dr. Sweet and his family. He
has a little child. He has a wife. They must
live somewhere. If they could not, it would be
better to take them out and kill them, and kill
them decently and quickly. Had he any right to
be free? They determined to move in and to
take nine men with them. What would you have
done, gentlemen? If you had courage, you would
have done as Dr. Sweet did. You would have
been crazy or a coward if you hadn't. Would
you have moved in alone? No, you would not
have gone alone. You would have taken your

wife.   If you had a brother or two, you would have taken them because you would know that you could rely on them, and you would have taken those nearest to you.   And you would have moved in just as Dr. Sweet did.   Wouldn't you?   He didn't shoot the first night.   He didn't look for trouble.   He kept his house dark so that the neighbors wouldn't see him.   He didn't dare have a light in his house, gentlemen, for fear of the neighbors.   Noble neighbors, who were to have a colored family in their neighborhood. He had the light put out in the front of the house, so as not to tempt any of the mob to violence.

Now, let us go back a little.   What happened before this?   I don't need to go over the history of the case.   Everybody who wants to understand knows it, and many who don't want to understand it.   As soon as Dr. Sweet bought this house, the neighbors organized the "Water Works Park Improvement Association."   They were going to aid the police.   They didn't get a chance to try to aid them until that night. They were going to regulate automobile traffic. They didn't get any chance to regulate automobile traffic until that night.   They were going to protect the homes and make them safe for children.   The purpose was clear, and every single member reluctantly said that they joined it to keep colored people out of the district. They might have said it first as well as last. People, even in a wealthy and aristocratic neighborhood like Garland and Charlevoix, don't give up a dollar without expecting some profit; not a whole dollar.   Sometimes two in one family, the husband and wife, joined.   They got in quick.   The woods were on fire.   Something had to be done, as quick as they heard that Dr. Sweet was coming; Dr. Sweet, who had been a bellhop on a boat, and a bellhop in hotels, and fired furnaces and sold popcorn and worked his way with his great handicap through college, and graduated as a doctor, and gone to Europe

and taken another degree; Dr. Sweet who knew
more than any man in the neighborhood ever
would know or ever want to know. He deserved
more for all he had done. When they heard he
was coming, then it was time to act, and act
together, for the sake of their homes, their
families and their firesides, and so they got
together. . . . Gentlemen, these black men
shot. Whether any bullets from their guns hit
Breiner, I do not care. I will not discuss it.
It is passing strange that the bullet that went
through him, went directly through, not as if
it were shot from some higher place. It was
not the bullet that came from Henry Sweet's
rifle; that is plain. It might have come from
the house; I do not know, gentlemen, and I do
not care. There are bigger issues in this case
than that. The right to defend your home, the
right to defend your person, is as sacred a
right as any human being could fight for, and
as sacred a cause as any jury could sustain.

That issue not only involves the defendants in this case, but it involves every man
who wants to live, every man who wants freedom
to work and to breathe; it is an issue worth
fighting for, and worth dying for, it is an
issue worth the attention of this jury, who
have a chance that is given to few juries to
pass upon a real case that will mean something
in the history of a race.

These men were taken to the police station. Gentlemen, there was never a time that
these black men's rights were protected in the
least; never once. They had no rights--they
are black. They were driven out of their home
under the law's protection. When they defended
their home, they were arrested and charged with
murder. They were taken to a police station,
manacled. And they asked for a lawyer. And,
every man, if he has any brains at all, asks
for a lawyer when he is in the hands of the
police. If he does not want to have a web
woven around him, to entangle and ensnare him,

he will ask for a lawyer.   And, the lawyer's
first aid to the injured always is, "Keep your
mouth shut."   It is not a case of whether you
are guilty or not guilty.   That makes no difference.   "Keep your mouth shut."   The police
grabbed them, as is their habit.   They got the
county attorney to ask questions.   What did
they do?   They did what everybody does, helpless, alone, and unadvised.   They did not know,
even, that anybody was killed.   At least there
is no evidence that they knew.   But, they knew
that they had been arrested for defending their
own rights to live; and they were there in the
hands of their enemies; and they told the best
story they could think of at the time--just as
ninety-nine men out of a hundred always do.
Whether they are guilty or not guilty makes no
difference.   But lawyers and even policemen
should have protected their rights.

Some things that these defendants said
were not true, as is always the case.   The
prosecutor read a statement from this boy,
which is conflicting.   In two places he says
that he shot "over them."   In another he said
that he shot "at them."   He probably said it in
each place but the reporter probably got one of
them wrong.   But Henry makes it perfectly ex-
plicit, and when you go to your jury room and
read it all, you will find that he does.   In
another place he said he shot to defend his
brother's home and family.   He says that in two
or three places.   You can also find he said
that he shot so that they would run away and
leave them to eat their dinner.   They are both
there.   These conflicting statements you will
find in all cases of this sort.   You always
find them, where men have been sweated, without
help, without a lawyer, groping around blindly,
in the hands of the enemy, without the aid of
anybody to protect their rights.   Gentlemen,
from the first to the last, there has not been
a substantial right of these defendants that
was not violated.

We come now to lay this man's case in the hands of a jury without peers--the first defense and the last defense is the protection of home and life as provided by our law. We are willing to leave it here. I feel, as I look at you, that we will be treated fairly, and decently, even understandingly and kindly. You know what this case is. You know why it is. You know that if white men had been fighting their way against colored men, nobody would ever have dreamed of a prosecution. And you know that, from the beginning of this case to the end, up to the time you write your verdict, the prosecution is based on race prejudice and nothing else.

Gentlemen, I feel deeply on this subject; I cannot help it. Let us take a little glance at the history of the Negro race. It only needs a minute. It seems to me that the story would melt hearts of stone. I was born in America. I could have left it if I had wanted to go away. Some other men, reading about this land of freedom we brag about on the Fourth of July, came voluntarily to America. These men, the defendants, are here because they could not help it. Their ancestors were captured in the jungles and on the plains of Africa, captured as you capture wild beasts, torn from their homes and their kindred; loaded into slave ships, packed like sardines in a box, half of them dying on the ocean passage; some jumping into the sea in their frenzy, when they had a chance to choose death in place of slavery. They were captured and brought here. They could not help it. They were brought and sold as slaves, to work without pay, because they were black. They were subjected to all of this for generations, until finally they were given their liberty, so far as the law goes--and that is only a little way, because, after all, every human being's life in this world is inevitably mixed with every other life and, no matter what laws we pass, no matter what precautions we

take, unless the people we meet are kindly and
decent and human and liberty-loving, then there
is no liberty. Freedom comes from human beings, rather than from laws and institutions.

Now, that is their history. These people
are the children of slavery. If the race that
we belong to owes anything to any human being,
or to any power in this universe, it owes it to
these black men. Above all other men, they owe
an obligation and a duty to these black men
which can never be repaid. I never see one of
them, that I do not feel I ought to pay part of
the debt of my race--and if you gentlemen feel
as you should feel in this case, your emotions
will be like mine.

Gentlemen, you were called into this case
by chance. It took us a week to find you, a
week of culling out prejudice and hatred.
Probably we did not cull it all out at that;
but we took the best and the fairest that we
could find. It is up to you.

Your verdict means something in this case.
It means something more than the fate of this
boy. It is not often that a case is submitted
to twelve men where the decision may mean a
milestone in the progress of the human race.
But this case does. And I hope and I trust
that you have a feeling of responsibility that
will make you take it and do your duty as
citizens of a great nation, and, as members of
the human family, which is better still.

Let me say just a parting word for Henry
Sweet, who has well nigh been forgotten. I am
serious, but it seems almost like a reflection
upon this jury to talk as if I doubted your
verdict. What has this boy done? This one boy
now that I am culling out from all the rest,
and whose fate is in your hands--can you tell
me what he has done? Can I believe myself? Am
I standing in a court of justice, where twelve
men on their oaths are asked to take away the
liberty of a boy twenty-one years of age, who
has done nothing more than what Henry Sweet has

done?

Gentlemen, you may think he shot too quick; you may think he erred in judgement; you may think Dr. Sweet should not have gone there, prepared to defend his home. But what of this case of Henry Sweet? What has he done? I want to put it up to you, each of you, individually. Dr. Sweet was his elder brother. He had helped Henry through school. He loved him. He had taken him into his home. Henry had lived with him and his wife; he had fondled his baby. The doctor had promised Henry money to go through school. Henry was getting his education, to take his place in the world, gentlemen--and this is a hard job. With his brother's help, he had worked himself through college up to the last year. The doctor had bought a home. He feared danger. He moved in with his wife and he asked this boy to go with him. And this boy went to help defend his brother and his brother's wife and his child and his home.

Do you think more of him or less of him for that? I never saw twelve men in my life-- and I have looked at a good many faces of a good many juries--and I never saw twelve men in my life, that, if you could get them to understand a human case, were not true and right.

Should this boy have gone along and helped his brother? Or should he have stayed away? What would you have done? And yet, gentlemen, here is a boy, and the president of his college came all the way from Ohio to tell you what he thinks of him. His teachers have come here, from Ohio, to tell you what they think of him.

So, gentlemen, I am justified in saying that this boy is as kindly, as well disposed, as decent a man as any one of you twelve. Do you think he ought to be taken out of his school and sent to the penitentiary? All right, gentlemen, if you think so, do it. It is your job, not mine. If you think so, do it. It is your job, not mine. If you think so, do it. But if you do, gentlemen, if you should

ever look into the face of your own boy, or
your own brother, or look into your own heart,
you will regret it in sackcloth and ashes. You
know, if he committed any offense, it was being
loyal and true to his brother whom he loved. I
know where you will send him, and it will not
be the penitentiary.

Now, gentlemen, just one more word, and I
am through with this case. I do not live in
Detroit. But I have no feeling against this
city. In fact, I shall always have the kindest
remembrance of it, especially if this case results as I think and I feel that it will. I am
the last one to come here to stir up race hatred, or any other hatred. I do not believe in
the law of hate. I may not be true to my
ideals always, but I believe in the law of
love, and I believe that you can do nothing
with hatred. I would like to see a time when
man loves his fellow-man, and forgets his color
and his creed. We will never be civilized
until that time comes. I know the Negro race
has a long road to go. I believe the life of
the Negro race has been a life of tragedy, of
injustice, of oppression. The law has made him
equal, but man has not. And, after all, the
last analysis is, what has man done?--and not
what has the law done? I know there is a long
road ahead of him, before he can take the place
which I believe he should take. I know that
before him there is suffering, sorrow, tribula-
tion and death among the blacks, and perhaps
the whites. I am sorry. I would do what I
could to avert it. I would advise patience; I
would advise toleration; I would advise understanding; I would advise all of those things
which are necessary for men who live together.

Gentlemen, what do you think is your duty
in this case? I have watched day after day,
these black, tense faces that have crowded this
court. These black faces that now are looking
to you twelve whites, feeling that the hopes
and fears of a race are in your keeping.

This case is about to end, gentlemen.   To them, it is life.   Not one of their color sits on this jury.   Their fate is in the hands of twelve whites.   Their eyes are fixed on you. Their hearts go out to you, and their hopes hang on your verdict.

This is all.   I ask you, on behalf of this defendant, on behalf of these helpless ones who turn to you, and more than that--on behalf of this great state, and this great city which must face this problem, and face it fairly--I ask you, in the name of progress and of the human race, to return a verdict of Not Guilty in this case!

Speech at Massie Trial

Honolulu, 1932

Gentlemen: We are getting close to the end of this case.   It has been a long, serious, tedious trial, and you of the jury probably have had the worst of it.

This case illustrates the working of human destiny more than any other case I have handled.   It illustrates the effect of sorrow and mishap on human minds and lives, and shows us how weak and powerless human beings are in the hands of relentless powers.

Eight months ago Mrs. Fortescue was in Washington, respected and known like any other woman.

Eight months ago Lieutenant Massie worked himself up to the rank of lieutenant in the navy, respected, courageous and intelligent.

His young wife, handsome and attractive, was known and respected and admired by the community.

In that short space of time they are in a criminal court and the jury asked to send them to prison for life.

What has happened is a long series of events, beginning at a certain time, ending we don't know where.

A whole family--their life, future, name-- bound up in a criminal act committed by someone else in which they had no part.

About eight months ago Massie and his wife

went to a dance. They were young, happy. He was following the profession he had chosen, and she was the wife of a Navy officer--brave, courageous and fearless.

Today they are in this court, in the hands of you twelve men, to settle their fate. I ask you gentlemen to consider carefully, seriously. The power is given to you to do justice in this case.

We contend that for months Massie's mind had been affected by all that was borne upon him: grief, sorrow, trouble, day after day, week after week, and month after month. What do you think would have happened to any of you under the same condition? We measure other people by ourselves. We place ourselves in their place and say, "How would we have acted?" We have no further way of telling, except perhaps from the conditions of the life in which we live.

As to the early history of this case--they went to a dance with their friends. About half-past eleven in the evening, Mrs. Massie, who didn't especially care for these festivities, went out for a walk intending to go down the street and come back and join her husband again at the dance. It was only a few steps from safety to destruction.

What did Massie learn from her a few hours later? An unbelievable story--almost--at least an unthinkable one about which even my friend who opened this argument for the State said: "It was a terrible story"--so terrible that he pitied them. Still, he asked you to send these people to prison.

She had gone but a short way when four or five men drove up behind her in an automobile, dragged her into it, beat her, and broke her jaw in two places. They were ruffians, unknown to her. And after that they dragged her into the bushes, and she was raped by four or five men.

Can you imagine anything worse that could

have happened or any greater calamity that
could have fallen upon that family? They had
nothing to do with it--not the slightest.

    She was going on her way as she had a
right to go, and in the twinkling of an eye her
whole life, the life of the family, was changed
and they are now here in this court for you to
say whether they will go to prison--for life!

    Is there a more terrible story in litera-
ture? I don't know whether there is--or who it
was--or where I can find that sad tale but
right here. You and all the other people in
the city have been chosen to take care of their
fate. I hope you will in kindness and humanity
and understanding--no one else but you can do
this.

    She was left on that lonely road in pain
and agony and suffering. In this Mrs. Massie
suffered the greatest humiliation that a woman
can suffer at the hands of man. She had done
nothing! Massie had done nothing! So far,
suffering has been inflicted on them. Suffering that few people encounter in their lives.

    Massie dances until the dance is nearly
over. He is ready to go home. He looks for
his wife. She is not there. He calls home,
and she isn't there. He looks wherever he can
and he calls home again and she sobs out a part
of the story over the telephone, part of the
story as terrible, as cruel, as any story I
ever heard: "Hurry home, something terrible has
happened to me!"

    Tommy (Lieutenant Massie) rushes home!
She meets him at the door and sobs and tells
him this terrible story--isn't that enough to
unsettle any man's mind? Suppose you heard
it!--then and there--what effect would it have
had on your mind--what effect would it have had
on anybody's mind!

    Shock, grief, and sorrow, at times pro-
tracted, sometimes at once, causes a human mind
to break down in the end. This was only the
beginning--here was his wife: she told him that

they had broken her jaw, that she thought they had knocked out her teeth, that they had hit her on the jaw, that they had beaten her, taken her into the machine, dragged her into the bushes, ravished her and left her by the road to find her way home.

Do you remember the subsequent story? The police were called to pick up the trail. No one raised even a doubt about this story, except the originators of a few vile slanders which were carried from tongue to tongue. Has anybody placed their finger upon a single fact to contradict the saddest tale that was ever brought to a husband?

What did Mrs. Massie do? All of this she told her husband. They had reason to believe and fear infection and that she might be placed in a family way from these men who dragged her into the bushes and ravished her. She took the best precautions she could. She gave her information to the police and they jested and hinted and quarreled and haggled about what should be done.

There have been people who spread around in this community stories I don't believe. They concocted these terrible stories and what effect did they have on Massie? May I ask what effect they would have had on you, and how you would have stood them? Massie attended to his day's duties as best he could. He went back and forth, nursing his wife, working all day and attending her at night for weeks. It was all that any husband could do, or any man could do. He lost sleep. He lost courage. He lost hope. He was distraught! And all this load was on his shoulders!

Any cause for it? Our insane institutions are filled with men and women who have less cause for insanity than he had. Everyone knows it. The mind isn't too easy to understand at the best. But what happens to the human mind? It does one thing with one person and another thing with another. You know what it did to

Massie's.   Do you think he is responsible, or
has been, from that terrible night?

What could he do?   Days he worked.   At
night he nursed his wife.   Could anyone do
more?   The slow, long, terrible times.   The
doctor attending her helped Massie too.
Gentlemen, just think how much is involved here
now.   Here was the assault, the rape, the pain,
the days and nights, and what else?   Dr.
Withington told them that they must take the
greatest pain to guard against disease and
pregnacy.   So he watched her day by day.   Day
by day Tommy tended to his duties.   He nursed
his wife at night.   Well, how would it affact
you?   Finally, the doctor said, "You must have
an operation to prevent Pregnancy."

Here is a man--his wife--she is bearing
inside her the germs of--who?   Does anybody
know?   Not he, but someone of the four ruffians
who assaulted her and left a wreck of her.   The
doctor was not only a physician, but a friend.
He asked no question.   He didn't even read the
statutes.   He wasn't afraid the district attorney would indict him for abortion.   You know
what a friend would do, what an intelligent
physician did do.   So he took away what was
there.   He did it out of kindness and consider-
ation--and prescribed for Massie, too.

Now, gentlemen, don't you suppose all this
trouble might have been what ailed him?   Would
you take a chance on your own mind or any other
person's, strong or weak?

It is almost inconceivable that so much
could happen to one family.   In time, four men
were indicted for the crime.   Tommy was away on
duty some of the time.   Part of the time he was
in the courtroom during the trial of the as-
sailants.   A strange circumstance, indeed, that
the jury disagreed in that case.   I don't know,
I don't see why.   But anyway, after all their
work, and all their worry, the jury disagreed.
What effect did that have?

Many have no doubt raised the question

that has been raised over and over since man organized courts--"Can't I get justice?"   Is there a chance to get any? Months passed and this case still was not retried.

They began a campaign such as has been waged against few men and women. Out of the clear air, with nothing on which to rest, strange, slanderous stories were spread over these Islands about Lieutenant Massie and his ravished wife. Stories that she had never been raped, or else that she ravished herself. Stories that her husband, whose faithfulness the doctor has related to you, and it has been plainly evident to every person who sat in this courtroom during these long trying days, broke his wife's jaw. Then they spread the rumor that it was some Navy person who had ravished her. This spread all over the Islands. Everybody heard it. It came to Tommy, it came to Mrs. Massie. And it came to her mother.

Gentlemen, I wonder what Fate has against this family anyhow? And I wonder when it will get through taking its toll and leave them to go in peace, to try and make their own life in comfort for the rest of their days.

Here is the mother. What about her? They wired to her and she came. Poems and rhymes have been written about mothers. I don't want to bring forth further eulogies which are more or less worth while, but I want to call your attention to something more primitive that that. Nature. It is not a case of the greatness of a mother. It is the case of what nature has done. I don't care whether it is a human mother, a mother of beasts or birds of the air, they are all alike.

To them there is one all-important thing and that is a child that they carried in their womb. Without that feeling which is so strong in all life, there would be no life preserved upon this earth. She acted as every mother acts. She felt as your mothers have felt, because the family is the preservation of life.

What did she do?   Immediately she started on a long trip to her daughter.   The daughter was married and a long way off, but she was still her daughter.   I don't care if a mother is seventy-five and her daughter fifty, it is still the mother and the child.

Everything else is forgotten in the emotion that carries her back to the time when this was a little baby in her arms which she bore and loved.   Your mother was that way and my mother, and there can be no other way.   The mother started on a trip of 5,000 miles, over land and sea, to her child.   And here she is now in this courtroom waiting to go to the penitentiary.

Gentlemen: let me say this: If this husband and this mother and these faithful boys go to the penitentiary, it won't be the first time that a penitentiary has been sanctified by its inmates.

When people come to your beautiful Islands, one of the first places that they will wish to see is the prison where the mother and husband are confined because they moved under emotion.   If that does happen, that prison will be the most conspicuous building on this Island, and men will wonder how it happened and will marvel at the injustice and cruelty of men and will pity the inmates and blame Fate for the cruelty, persecution and sorrow that has followed this family.

Gentlemen, you are asked to send these people to the penitentiary.   Do you suppose that if you had been caught in the hands of Fate--would you have done differently?   No, we are not made that way.   Life doesn't come that way.   It comes from a devotion of mothers, of husbands, loves of men and women, that's where life comes from.   Without this love, this devotion, the world will be desolate and cold and will take its lonely course around the sun alone!   Without a human heartbeat, there will be nothing except thin air.   Every instinct

that moves human beings, every feeling that is
with you or any of your kin, every feeling that
moves in the mother of the animal is with us in
this case. You can't fight against it. If you
do you are fighting against nature and life.

Gentlemen of the jury, this campaign a-
gainst Massie and Mrs. Massie began very, very
early. It was very strong when the jury disagreed. Stories have been peddled all over
this town that Massie and his wife were about
to get a divorce. They said that another Navy
officer was out that night with Mrs. Massie.

Stories have been peddled up and down the
streets and broadcast against this woman who
had been raped, and the husband was doing all
he could to help her as any husband would.
What effect could it have on the mind of this
defendant?

Gentlemen of the jury, it was bad enough
that his wife was raped. These vile stories
were circulated and caused great anxiety and
agony. All this is bad enough. But now you
are asked that they must spend the rest of
their lives in prison. All right, gentlemen,
you have the power, but let me say to you--that
if on top of all else that has been heaped upon
the devoted heads of this family, if they
should be sent to prison, it would place a blot
upon the fair name of these Islands that all
the Pacific seas would never wash away.

There is, somewhere deep in the feelings
and instincts of a man, a yearning for justice,
an idea of what is right and wrong, of what is
fair between man and man, that came before the
first law was written and will abide after the
last one is dead. Picture Tommy's and his
wife's minds, when he went up and down investigating these stories. He doubted his friends
and he thought he heard people's footsteps on
the lawn outside in the dead of the night, and
he went out to see and he was harassed and
worried from the time this happened until now.

How much could you, how much could any

human mind stand?   Some men have gone insane by a word, by fear, by fright, others by slow degree, by long trouble, by mishap.

Poor Massie, strong and vigorous, when all of these things were heaped on him.   What did he do?   He began to rid his mind somewhat of his own troubles and of the persecution of the men who performed this deed.   He began to think of vindicating his wife from this slander.   She had been lied about, she had been abused with talk.

Massie was discouraged.   Months of slander since his wife had been dragged into the bushes and raped; months of abuse.   He had ideas and fears and delusions.   The doctor tried to quiet his fears, but they could not be quieted.   He couldn't work--and work has been the first and last aid of many other unfortunates.

He wanted to get a confession.   For what? To get somebody imprisoned?   No--that did not concern him--he was concerned with the girl, whom he had taken in marriage when she was sixteen--sweet sixteen.

Mrs. Fortescue was worrying about the delay of what she thought was justice, and what other people thought was justice.   I fairly well know what law is, but I don't often know what justice is--it is a pattern according to our own personal conceptions.

Mrs. Fortescue, too, believed it necessary to get a confession.   The last thing they wanted to do was to shoot or kill.

What did they do?   They formed a plan to take Kahahawai to their house and get a confession.   They never conceived it to be illegal--it was the ends they thought of--not the means.   Are Jones and Lord, two common seamen, bad?   There are some human virtues that are not common--loyalty, devotion.

Jones had been out there to see that the slanderers didn't kill--but slanderers don't kill that way.   He was faithful as a dog, he was loyal when a shipmate asked for help.   Was he bad?   There are so many ways to measure goodness and badness.

There isn't a single thing that either of these boys did that should bring censure.

I know the state's attorney would rather convict four people instead of two, but I think he would compromise on two--that ought to be enough for one day.

If you needed a friend, would you take one of these gobs, or would you wait outside prayer meetings on Wednesday night--I guess that's the right night?   I say to you I would take one of these, rather than the others.

Tommy had prepared this warrant or subpoena, woven, like Joseph's coat, of many colors.   Jones handed it to the Hawaiian boy and said Major Ress wanted to see him.

They did not want to kill--they made no plan to kill--they didn't know what to do when it happened.   And the house was not a good place to kill--one family thirty feet away, another house twenty-five feet away.   A lovely place to kill someone, isn't it?

Tommy, I say Tommy because he will never be anything else to me.   I have not known him long, but I have learned to love him and respect him.   Tommy was driving the car when it came to the courthouse--this man got in.   Tommy for months had been subject to delusions and fears that bring insanity.

There is nothing in this evidence to indicate that they ever meant to kill--there was never any talk about killing, as far as this evidence is concerned.

I would not want to do anything to add to the sorrow of the mother of the boy (Kahahawai), or the father of the boy, or the cousin, who sit here.   They have human feelings.   I have too.   I want you to have human feelings too.   Any man without human feeling is without life.

The party entered the house.   Tommy had a .45, which is much surer death than a .32, and this unfortunate boy was killed with a .32.

It's no consequence who fired that shot--I am arguing the facts, and the only facts as you get them. Is there any reason in the world why Massie, on top of all these other troubles, should assume the added burden of assuming the responsibility of this killing?

I haven't always had the highest opinion of the average human being; man is none too great at best. He is moved by everything that reaches him, but I have no reason to think there is anybody on this jury who will disregard the truth for some fantastic, imaginary theory. Tommy has told you the fact that there was no intention of killing.

When Kahahawai said, "Yes, I done it," everything was blotted out--here was the man who had ruined his wife.

No man can judge another unless he places himself in the position of the other before he pronounces the verdict.

If you can put yourself in his place, if you can think of his raped wife, of his months of suffering and mental anguish; if you can comfort the unjust, cruel fate that unrolled before him, then you can judge--but you cannot judge any man otherwise.

If you put yourself in Tommy Massie's place, what would you have done? I don't know about you, or you, or you, or you--but at least ten out of twelve men would have done just what poor Tommy Massie did. The thing for which you are asked to send him to prison for the rest of his life.

I shan't detain you much longer. Again I say I cannot understand why the prosecution raises a doubt as to who fired the shot and how.

Massie was there! He rose! The picture came before him! He doubtless shot! One bullet was shot and only one.

Massie saw the picture of his wife pleading, injured, raped--and he shot. There

could have been nobody else.   And then what?
Had any preparations been made to get out this
body? What could they do? What would you have
done with a dead man on your hands? You would
want to protect yourselves.   It might be the
wrong thing to do--but it's only human.

What is the first instinct? Flight.   To
the mountains, to the sea, anywhere but where
they were.   Here was the dead body--they
couldn't leave it--perhaps they could get rid
of it.   There isn't one in ten thousand who
wouldn't get away, no matter how.

That isn't the plan of conduct of someone
who had thought out a definite plan, it is the
hasty,   half-co-ordinated   instinct   of   one
surprised in a situation.   And finally they
were caught. The first few officers found that
these people wouldn't speak.   This is an hour
after the shooting.

Gradually, Lieutenant Massie was coming
back to consciousness and realizing where he
was.   Where is the mystery in a man cracking
after six or eight months of worry?

We are now realizing that many acts have
been punished as crimes that are acts of insanity.   Why? Because lawyers have been too
cruel to look for insanity; because an act is
considered as a crime, not as a consequence of
causes.

He   asked   for   a   cigarette,   a   simple
reaction, something you're used to, something
to do. Does a man think every time he takes a
cigarette? No.   It doesn't mean a thing.   I
have been a cigarette smoker, and I could ask
for a cigarette in my sleep.

Any man in any situation may do it.
Neither   does   turning   away   from   a   camera
indicate anything; it may be just instinct and
means nothing.

As time went on, he, of course, began to
recover.   Two hours later at the city attorney's   office   he   had   recovered   enough   to
refuse to answer questions.

He had had delusions, had lost flesh, had been ill. It's a wonder he didn't go crazy the first night. Many men have gone insane for less, many have gone insane without others realizing it until later.

I believe I've covered this case as far as I care to go. There are little things here and there, but the broad facts are before you.

It was a hard, cruel fateful episode in the lives of these poor people. Is it possible that anyone should think of heaping more sorrows on their heads, to increase their burden and add to their wrongs?

If so, I cannot understand it. There are many things in this world I cannot understand.

Can anyone say that they are of the type on whom prison gates should close to increase their sufferings? Have they ever stolen, assaulted, forged?

They are here because of what has happened to them. Take these poor pursued, suffering people, take them into your care as you would have them take you if you were in their place.

Take them not with anger, but with pity and understanding.

I'd hate to leave here thinking that I had made anyone's life harder, had not sympathized with suffering, had created, not relieved, suffering.

I have looked at this Island, which is a new country to me. I've never had any pre-judice against any race on earth. I didn't learn it, and I defy anyone to find any word of mine to contradict what I say. To me these questions of race must be solved by understanding--not by force.

I have put this case without appeal to the nationality or race of any juror, asking them to pass on it as a human case.

We're all human beings. Take this case with its dire disasters, written all over by the hand of fate, as a case of your own, and I'll be content with your verdict.

What we do is affected by things around us; we're made more than we make.

I want you to help this family, to understand them.   If you understand them, that's all that's necessary.

I'd like to think that I had done my small part to bring peace and justice to an Island wracked and worn by strife.

You have not only the fate but the life of these four people.   What is there for them if you pronounce a sentence of doom on them?   What have they done?

You are a people to heal, not to destroy. I place this in your hands asking you to be kind and considerate both to the living and the dead.

Eulogy of John P. Altgeld

Chicago, 1902

In the great flood of human life that is spawned upon the earth, it is not often that a man is born. The friend and comrade that we mourn to-day was formed of that infinitely rare mixture that now and then at long, long intervals combines to make a man. John P. Altgeld was one of the rarest souls who ever lived and died. His was a humble birth, a fearless life and a dramatic, fitting death. We who knew him, we who loved him, we who rallied to his many hopeless calls, we who dared to praise him while his heart still beat, cannot yet feel that we shall never hear his voice again.

John P. Altgeld was a soldier tried and true; not a soldier clad in uniform, decked with spangles and led by fife and drum in the mad intoxication of the battle-field; such soldiers have not been rare upon the earth in any land or age. John P. Altgeld was a soldier in the everlasting struggle of the human race for liberty and justice on the earth. From the first awakening of his young mind until the last relentless summons came, he was a soldier who had no rest or furlough, who was ever on the field in the forefront of the deadliest and most hopeless fight, whom none but death could muster out. Liberty, the relentless goddess, had turned her fateful smile on John P. Altgeld's face when he was but a child, and to this first, fond love he was faithful unto death.

Liberty is the most jealous and exacting mistress that can beguile the brain and soul of man. She will have nothing from him who will not give her all. She knows that his pretended love serves but to betray. But when once the fierce of her quenchless, lustrous eyes has burned into the victim's heart, he will know no other smile but hers. Liberty will have not but the devoted souls, and by her glorious visions, her lavish promises, her infinitely witching charms, she lures her victims over hard and stony ways, by desolate and dangerous paths, through misery, obloquy and want to a martyr's cruel death. To-day we pay our last sad homage to the most devoted lover, the most abject slave, the fondest, wildest, dreamiest victim that ever gave his life to liberty's immortal cause.

In the history of the country where he lived and died, the life and works of our devoted dead will one day shine in words of everlasting light. When the bitter feelings of the hour have passed away, when the mad and poisonous fever of commercialism shall have run its course, when conscience and honor and justice and liberty shall once more ascend the throne from which the shameless, brazen goddess of power and wealth has driven her away; then this man we knew and loved will find his rightful place in the minds and hearts of the cruel, unwilling world he served. No purer patriot ever lived than the friend we lay at rest to-day. His love of the country was not paraded in the public marts, or bartered in the stalls for gold; his patriotism was that of pure ideal mold that placed the love of man above the love of self.

John P. Altgeld was always and at all times a lover of his fellow man. Those who reviled him have tried to teach the world that he was bitter and relentless, that he hated more than loved. We who knew the man, we who had clasped his hand and heard his voice and looked into his smiling face; we who knew his life of kindness, of charity, of infinite pity to the outcast and the weak; we who knew his human heart, could never be deceived. A truer, greater, gentler, kinder soul has never lived and died; and the fierce bitterness and hatred that sought to destroy this great, grand soul had but one cause--the fact that he really loved his fellow man.

As a youth our dead chieftain risked his life for the cause of the black man, whom he always loved. As a lawyer he was wise and learned; impatient with the forms and machinery which courts and legislators and lawyers have woven to strangle justice through expense and ceremony and delay; as a judge he found a legal way to do what seemed right to him, and if he could not find a legal way, he found a way. As Governor of a great State, he ruled wisely and well. Elected by the greatest personal triumph of any Governor ever chosen by the State, he fearlessly and knowingly bared his devoted head to the fiercest, most vindictive criticism ever heaped upon a public man, because he loved justice and dared to do the right.

In the days now past, John P. Altgeld, our loving chief, in scorn and derision was called John Pardon Altgeld by those who would destroy his power. We who stand to-day around his bier and mourn the brave and loving friend are glad to adopt this name. If, in the infinite economy of nature, there shall be another land where crooked paths shall be made straight, where heaven's justice shall review the judgements of the earth--if there shall be a great, wise, humane judge, before whom the sons of men shall come, we can hope for nothing better for ourselves than to pass into that infinite presence as the comrades and friends of John Pardon Altgeld, who opened the prison doors and set the captives free.

Even admirers have seldom understood the real character of this great human man. These were sometimes wont to feel that the fierce bitterness of the world that assailed him fell on deaf ears and an unresponsive soul. They did not know the man, and they do not feel the subtleties of human life. It was not a callous heart that so often led him to brave the most violent and malicious hate; it was not a callous heart, it was a devoted soul. He so loved justice and truth and liberty and righteousness that all the terrors that the earth could hold were less than the condemnation of his own conscience for an act that was cowardly or mean.

John P. Altgeld, like many of the earth's great souls, was a solitary man. Life to him was serious and earnest--an endless tragedy. The earth was a great hospital of sick, wounded and suffering, and he a devoted surgeon, who had no right to waste one moment's time and whose duty was to cure them all. While he loved his friends, he could work without them, he could live without them, he bid them one by one good-bye, when their courage failed to follow where he led; and he could go alone, out into the silent night, and, looking upward at the changing stars, could find communion there.

My dear, dear friend, long and well known, devoted have we followed you, implicit have we trusted you, fondly have we loved you. Beside your bier we now must say farewell. The heartless call has come, and we must stagger on the best we can alone. In the darkest hours we will look in vain for your loved form, we will listen hopelessly for your devoted, fearless voice. But, though we lay you in the grave and hide you from the sight of man, your brave words will speak for the poor, the oppressed, the captive and the weak; and your devoted life inspire countless souls to do and dare in the holy cause for which you lived and died.

Address to Prisoners in Cook County Jail

Chicago, 1902

If I looked at jails and crimes and prisoners in
the way the ordinary person does, I should not
speak on this subject to you. The reason I talk
to you on the question of crime, its cause and
cure, is because I really do not in the least
believe in crime. There is no such thing as a
crime as the word is generally understood. I do
not believe there is any sort of distinction
between the real moral condition of the people
in and out of jail. One is just as good as the
other. The people here can no more help being
here than the people outside can avoid being
outside. I do not believe that people are in
jail because they deserve to be. They are in
jail simply because they can not avoid it on
account of circumstances which are entirely
beyond their control and for which they are in
no way responsible.

I suppose a great many people on the outside would say I was doing you harm if they
should hear what I say to you this afternoon,
but you can not be hurt a great deal anyway, so
it will not matter. Good people outside would
say that I was really teaching you things that
were calculated to injure society, but it's
worthwhile now and then to hear something different from what you ordinarily get from
preachers and the like. These will tell you
that you should be good and then you get rich
and be happy. Of course we know that people do
not get rich by being good, and that is why so
many of you people try to get rich some other

way, only you do not understand how to do it quite as well as the fellow outside.

There are people who think that everything in this world is an accident. But really there is no such thing as an accident. A great many folks admit that many of the people in jail ought to be there, and many who are outside ought to be in. I think none of them ought to be here. There ought to be no jails, and if it were not for the fact that the people on the outside are so grasping and heartless in their dealings with the people on the inside, there would be no such institutions as jails.

I do not want you to believe that I think all you people here are angels. I do not think that. You are people of all kinds, all of you doing the best you can, and that is evidently not very well--you are people of all kinds and conditions and under all circumstances. In one sense everybody is equally good and equally bad. We all do the best we can under the cir- cumstances. But as to the exact things for which you are sent here, some of you are guilty and did the particular act because you needed the money. Some of you because you are in the habit of doing it, and some of you because you are born to it, and it comes to be as natural as it does, for instance for me to be good.

Most of you probably have nothing against me, and most of you would treat me the same as any other person would; probably better than some of the people on the outside would treat me, because you think I believe in you and they know I do not believe in them. While you would not have the least thing against me in the world you might pick my pockets. I do not think all of you would, but I think some of you would. You would not have anything against me, but that's your profession, a few of you. Some of the rest of you, if my doors were unlocked, might come in if you saw anything you wanted-- not out of any malice to me, but because that is your trade. There is no doubt there are quite a

There may be some of you who would hold up a man on the street, if you did not have something else to do, and needed the money; but when I want to light my house or my office the gas company holds me up. They charge me one dollar for something that is worth twenty-five cents, and still all these people are good people; they are pillars of society and support the churches, and they are respectable.

When I ride on the street cars, I am held up--I pay five cents for a ride that is worth two and a half cents, simply because a body of men have bribed the city council and the legislature, so that all the rest of us have to pay tribute to them.

If I do not want to fall into the clutches of the gas trusts and choose to burn oil instead of gas, then good Mr. Rockefeller holds me up, and he uses a certain portion of his money to build universities and support churches which are engaged in telling us how to be good.

Some of you are here for obtaining property under false pretenses--yet I pick up a great Sunday paper and read the advertisements of a merchant prince--"Shirt waists for 39 cents, marked down from $3.00."

When I read the advertisements in the paper I see they are all lies. When I want to get out and find a place to stand anywhere on the face of the earth, I find that it has all been taken up long ago before I came here, and before you came here, and somebody says, "Get off, swim into the lake, fly into the air; go anywhere, but get off." That is because these people have the police and they have the jails and the judges and the lawyers and the soldiers and all the rest of them to take care of the earth and drive everybody off that comes in their way.

A great many people will tell you that all this is true, but that it does not excuse you. These facts do not excuse some fellow who reaches into my pocket and takes out a five-dollar bill. The fact that the gas company bribes the members of the legislature from year to year, and fixes the law, so that all you people are compelled to be "fleeced" whenever you deal with them; the fact that the streetcar companies and the gas companies have control of the streets; and the fact that the landlords own all the earth--this, they say, has nothing to do with you.

Let us see whether there is any connection between the crimes of the respectable classes and your presence in the jail. Many of you people are in jail because you have stolen something. In the meaning of the law, you have taken some other person's property. Some of you have entered a store and carried off a pair of shoes because you did not have the price. Possibly some of you have committed murder. I cannot tell what all of you did. There are a great many people here who have done some of these things who really do not know themselves why they did them. I think I know why you did them--every one of you; you did these things because you were bound to do them. It looked to you at the time as if you had a chance to do them or not, as you saw fit; but still, after all, you had no choice. There may be people here who had some money in their pockets and who still went out and got some more money in a way society forbids. Now, you may not yourselves see exactly why it was you did this thing, but if you look at the question deeply enough and carefully enough you will see that there were circumstances that drove you to do exactly the thing which you did. You could not help it any more than we outside can help taking the positions that we take. The reformers who tell you to be good and you will be happy, and the people on the outside who have property to protect--they think that the only way to do it is by building jails and locking you up in cells on weekdays and praying for you Sundays.

I think that all of this has nothing what- ever to do with right conduct. I think it is

very easily seen what has to do with right conduct.   Some so-called criminals--and I will use
this word because it is handy, it means nothing
to me--I speak of the criminals who get caught
as distinguished from the criminals who catch
them--some of these so-called criminals are in
jail for their first offenses, but nine tenths
of you are in jail because you did not have a
good lawyer and, of course, you did not have a
good lawyer because you did not have enough
money to pay a good lawyer.   There is no very
great danger of a rich man going to jail.

Some of you may be here for the first time.
If we would open the doors and let you out, and
leave the laws as they are today, some of you
would be back tomorrow.   This is about as good a
place as you can get anyway.   There are many
people here who are so in the habit of coming
that they would not know where else to go.
There are people who are born with the tendency
to break into jail every chance they get, and
they cannot avoid it.   You cannot figure out
your life and see why it was, but still there is
a reason for it; and if we were all wise and
knew all the facts, we could figure it out.

In the first place, there are a good many
more people who go to jail in the wintertime
than in summer.   Why is this?   Is it because
people are more wicked in winter?   No, it is
because the coal trust begins to get in its grip
in the winter.   A few gentlemen take possession
of the coal, and unless the people will pay
seven or eight dollars a ton for something that
is worth three dollars, they will have to
freeze.   Then there is nothing to do but to
break into jail, and so there are many more in
jail in the winter than in summer.   It costs
more for gas in the winter because the nights
are longer, and people go to jail to save gas
bills. The jails are electric-lighted. You may
not know it, but these economic laws are working
all the time, whether we know it or do not know
it.

There are more people who go to jail in hard times than in good times--few people, comparatively, go to jail except when they are hard up. They go to jail because they have no other place to go. They may not know why, but it is true all the same. People are not more wicked in hard times. That is not the reason. The fact is true all over the world that in hard times more people go to jail than in good times, and in winter more people go to jail than in summer. Of course it is pretty hard times for people who go to jail at any time. The people who go to jail are almost always poor people--people who have no other place to live, first and last. When times are hard, then you find large numbers of people who go to jail who would not otherwise be in jail.

Long ago, Mr. Buckle, who was a great philosopher and historian, collected facts, and he showed that the number of people who are arrested increased just as the price of food increased. When they put up the price of gas ten cents a thousand, I do not know who will go to jail, but I do know that a certain number of people will go. When the meat combine raises the price of beef, I do not know who is going to jail, but I know that a large number of people are bound to go. Whenever the Standard Oil Company raises the price of oil, I know that a certain number of girls who are seamstresses, and who will work night after night long hours for somebody else, will be compelled to go out on the streets and ply another trade, and I know that Mr. Rockefeller and his associates are responsible and not the poor girls in the jails.

First and last, people are sent to jail because they are poor. Sometimes, as I say, you may not need money at the particular time, but you wish to have thrifty forehanded habits, and do not always wait until you are in absolute want. Some of you people are perhaps plying the trade, the profession, which is called burglary. No man in his right senses will go into a strange house in the dead of night and prowl around with a dark lantern through unfamiliar rooms and take chances of his life, if he has plenty of the good things of the world in his own home. You would not take any such chances as that. If a man had clothes in his clothes-press and beefsteak in his pantry and money in the bank, he would not navigate around nights in houses where he knows nothing about the premises whatever. It always requires experience and education for this profession, and people who fit themselves for it are no more to blame than I am for being a lawyer. A man would not hold up another man on the street if he had plenty of money in his own pocket. He might do it if he had one dollar or two dollars, but he wouldn't if he had as much money as Mr. Rockefeller has. Mr. Rockefeller has a great deal better hold-up game than that.

The more that is taken from the poor by the rich, who have the chance to take it, the more poor people there are who are compelled to resort to these means for a livelihood. They may not understand it, they may not think so at once, but after all they are driven into that line of employment.

There is a bill before the legislature to punish kidnaping children with death. We have wise members of the legislature. They know the gas trust when they see it and they always see it--they can furnish light enough to be seen; and this legislature thinks it is going to stop kidnaping children by making a law punishing kidnapers of children with death. I don't believe in kidnaping children, but the legis-lature is all wrong. Kidnaping children is not a crime, it is a profession. It has been de-veloped with our modern industrial conditions. There are many ways of making money--many new ways that our ancestors knew nothing about. Our ancestors knew nothing about a billion-dollar trust; and here comes some poor fellow who has no other trade and he discovers the profession of kidnapping children.

This crime is born, not because people are bad; people don't kidnap other people's children because they want the children or because they are devilish, but because they see a chance to get some money out of it. You cannot cure this crime by passing a law punishing by death kidnapers of children. There is one way to cure it. There is one way to cure all these offenses, and that is to give the people a chance to live. There is no other way, and there never was any other way since the world began; and the world is so blind and stupid that it will not see. If every man and woman and child in the world had a chance to make a decent, fair, honest living, there might be no jails and no lawyers and no courts. There might be some persons here or there with some peculiar formation of their brain, like Rockefeller, who would do these things simply to be doing them; but they would be very, very few, and those should be sent to a hospital and treated, and not sent to jail; and they would entirely disappear in the second generation, or at least in the third generation.

I am not talking pure theory. I will just give you two or three illustrations.

The English people once punished criminals by sending them away. They would load them on a ship and export them to Australia. England was owned by lords and nobles and rich people. They owned the whole earth over there, and the other people had to stay in the streets. They could not get a decent living. They used to take their criminals and send them to Australia--I mean the class of criminals who got caught. When these criminals got over there, and nobody else had come, they had the whole continent to run over, and so they could raise sheep and furnish their own meat, which is easier than stealing it. These criminals then became decent, respectable people because they had a chance to live. They did not commit any crimes.

They were just like the English people who sent them there, only better.   And in the second generation the descendants of those criminals were as good and respectable a class of people as there were on the face of the earth, and then they began building churches and jails themselves.

A portion of this country was settled in the same way, landing prisoners down on the southern coast; but when they got here and had a whole continent to run over and plenty of chances to make a living, they became respectable citizens, making their own living just like any other citizen in the world.   But finally the descendants of the English aristocracy who sent the people over to Australia found out they were getting rich, and so they went over to get possession of the earth as they always do, and they organized land syndicates and got control of the land and ores, and then they had just as many criminals in Australia as they did in England.   It was not because the world had grown bad; it was because the earth had been taken away from the people.

Some of you people have lived in the country.   It's prettier than it is here.   And if you have ever lived on a farm you understand that if you put a lot of cattle in a field, when the pasture is short they will jump over the fence; but put them in a good field where there is plenty of pasture, and they will be law-abiding cattle to the end of time.   The human animal is just like the rest of the animals, only a little more so.   The same thing that governs in the one governs in the other.

Everybody makes his living along the lines of least resistance.   A wise man who comes into a country early sees a great undeveloped land. For instance, our rich men twenty-five years ago saw that Chicago was small and knew a lot of people would come here and settle, and they readily saw that if they had all the land around here it would be worth a good deal, so they grabbed the land.   You cannot be a landlord because somebody has got it all. You must find some other calling. In England and Ireland and Scotland less than five per cent own all the land there is, and the people are bound to stay there on any kinds of terms the landlords give. They must live the best they can, so they develop all these various professions--burglary, picking pockets and the like.

Again, people find all sorts of ways of getting rich. These are diseases like everything else. You look at people getting rich, organizing trusts and making a million dollars, and somebody gets the disease and he starts out. He catches it just as a man catches the mumps or the measles; he is not to blame, it is in the air. You will find men speculating beyond their means, because the mania of money-getting is taking possession of them. It is simply a disease--nothing more, nothing less. You cannot avoid catching it; but the fellows who have control of the earth have the advantage of you. See what the law is: when these men get control of things, they make the laws. They do not make the laws to protect anybody; courts are not instruments of justice. When your case gets into court it will make little difference whether you are guilty or innocent, but it's better if you have a smart lawyer. And you cannot have a smart lawyer unless you have money. First and last it's a question of money. Those men who own the earth make the laws to protect what they have. They fix up a sort of fence or pen around what they have, and they fix the law so the fellow on the outside cannot get in. The laws are really organized for the protection of the men who rule the world. They were never organized or enforced to do justice. We have no system for doing justice. We have no system for doing justice, not the slightest in the world.

Let me illustrate: Take the poorest person in this room. If the community had provided a system for doing justice, the poorest person in this room would have as good a lawyer as the richest, would he not? When you went into court you would have just as long a trial and just as fair a trial as the richest person in Chicago. Your case would not be tried in fifteen or twenty minutes, whereas it would take fifteen days to get through with a rich man's case.

Then if you were rich and were beaten, your case would be taken to the Appellate Court. A poor man cannot take his case to the Appellate Court; he has not the price. And then to the Supreme Court. And if he were beaten there he might perhaps go to the United States Supreme Court. And he might die of old age before he got into jail. If you are poor, it's a quick job. You are almost known to be guilty, else you would not be there. Why should anyone be in the criminal court if he were not guilty? He would not be there if he could be anywhere else. The officials have no time to look after all these cases. The people who are on the outside, who are running banks and building churches and making jails, they have no time to examine 600 to 700 prisoners each year to see if they are guilty or innocent. If the courts were organized to promote justice the people would elect somebody to defend all these criminals, somebody as smart as the prosecutor--and give him as many detectives and as many assistants to help, and pay as much money to defend you as to prosecute you. We have a very able man for state's attorney, and he has many assistants, detectives and policemen without end, and judges to hear the cases--everything handy.

Most all of our criminal code consists in offenses against property. People are sent to jail because they have committed a crime against property. It is of very little consequence whether one hundred people more or less go to jail who ought not to go--you must protect property, because in this world property is of more importance than anything else.

How is it done? These people who have property fix it so they can protect what they have. When somebody commits a crime it does not follow that he has done something that is morally wrong. The man on the outside who has committed no crime may have done something. For instance: to take all the coal in the United States and raise the price two dollars or three dollars when there is no need of it, and thus kill thousands of babies and send thousands of perople to the poorhouse and tens of thousands to jail, as is done every year in the United States--this is a greater crime than all the people in our jails ever committed; but the law does not punish it. Why? Because the fellows who control the earth make the laws. If you and I had the making of the laws, the first thing we would do would be to punish the fellow who gets control of the earth. Nature put this coal in the ground for me as well as for them and nature made the prairies up here to raise wheat for me as well as for them, and then the great railroad companies came along and fenced it up.

Most all of the crimes for which we are punished are property crimes. There are a few personal crimes, like murder--but they are very few. The crimes committed are mostly those against property. If this punishment is right the criminals must have a lot of property. How much money is there in this crowd? And yet you are all here for crimes against property. The people up and down the Lake Shore have not committed crime; still they have so much property they don't know what to do with it. It is perfectly plain why these people have not committed crimes against property; they make the laws and therefore do not need to break them. And in order for you to get some property you are obliged to break the rules of the game. I don't know but what some of you may have had a very nice chance to get rich by carrying a hod for one dollar a day, twelve hours. Instead of taking that nice, easy profession, you are a burglar. If you had been given a chance to be a banker you would rather follow that. Some of you may have had a chance to work as a switch-man on a railroad where you know, according to statistics, that you cannot live and keep all your limbs more than seven years, and you can get fifty dollars or seventy-five dollars a month for taking your lives in your hands; and instead of taking that lucrative position you chose to be a sneak thief, or something like that. Some of you made that sort of choice. I don't know which I would take if I was reduced to this choice. I have an easier choice.

I will guarantee to take from this jail, or any jail in the world, five hundred men who have been the worst criminals and lawbreakers who ever got into jail, and I will go down to our lowest streets and take five hundred of the most abandoned prostitutes, and go out somewhere where there is plenty of land, and will give them a chance to make a living, and they will be as good people as the average in the community.

There is a remedy for the sort of con-dition we see here. The world never finds it out, or when it does find it out it does not enforce it. You may pass a law punishing every person with death for burglary, and it will make no difference. Men will commit it just the same. In England there was a time when one hundred different offenses were punishable with death, and it made no difference. The English people strangely found out that so fast as they repealed the severe penalties and so fast as they did away with punishing men by death, crime decreased instead of increased; that the smaller the penalty the fewer the crimes.

Hanging men in our county jails does not prevent murder. It makes murderers.

And this has been the history of the world. It's easy to see how to do away with what we call crime. it is not so easy to do it. I will tell you how to do it. It can be done by giving the people a chance to live--by destroying special privileges.   So long as big criminals can get the coal fields, so long as the big criminals have control of the city council and get the public streets for streetcars and gas rights--this is bound to send thousands of poor people to jail. So long as men are allowed to monopolize all the earth, and compel others to live on such terms as these men see fit to make, then you are bound to get into jail.

The only way in the world to abolish crime and criminals is to abolish the big ones and the little ones together. Make fair conditions of life. Give men a chance to live. Abolish the right of private ownership of land, abolish monopoly, make the world partners in production, partners in the good things of life. Nobody would steal if he could get something of his own some easier way. Nobody will commit burglary when he has a house full. No girl will go out on the streets when she has a comfortable place at home. The man who owns a sweatshop or a department store may not be to blame himself for the condition of his girls, but when he pays them five dollars, three dollars, and two dollars a week, I wonder where he thinks they will get the rest of their money to live. The only way to cure these conditions is by equality. There should be no jails. They do not accomplish what they pretend to accomplish. If you would wipe them out there would be no more criminals than now. They terrorize nobody. They are a blot upon any civilization, and a jail is an evidence of the lack of charity of the people on the outside who make the jails and fill them with the victims of their greed.

Chronology of Speeches

SPEECHES TO THE PUBLIC

"The Workingman and the Tariff," Chicago Herald,
21 February 1889.

"Woman Suffrage," in Sunset Club Yearbook, 1891-
92 (Chicago: Sunset Club, 1893).

"Shall the World's Fair Be Open on Sunday?" in
Sunset Club Yearbook, 1891-92.

"The Eight Hour Day," in Sunset Club Yearbook,
1891-92.

"Free Trade or Protection?" Current Topics
(April 1894).

"Moral Courage Rarer Than Physical Bravery,"
Open Court 8 (17 May 1894).

"The Tyranny of Public Opinion," in Sunset Club
Yearbook, 1893-94 (Chicago: Sunset Club,
1895).

Rights and Wrongs of Ireland: An Address
Delivered at Central Music Hall, Chicago,
Nov. 23, 1895, on the Anniversary of the
Execution of Allen, Larkin, and O'Brien
(Chicago: C. H. Kerr, 1895).

"Strikes and Injunctions," in Sunset Club
Yearbook, 1894-95 (Chicago: Sunset Club,
1896).

"Annexation of Hawaii," in Sunset Club Yearbook,
1898-99 (Chicago: Sunset Club, 1900).

"The Problem of the Negro," International
Socialist Review 2 (1 Nov.1901).

"The Suppression of Vice and Crime in Chicago,"
in Sunset Club Yearbook. 1899-1901
(Chicago: Sunset Club, 1902).

Crime and Criminals; An Address Delivered to the
Prisoners in the Chicago County Jail
(Chicago: C. H. Kerr, 1902).

In Memory of John P. Altgeld; Address at the
Funeral (Chicago: C. H.Kerr, 1902). Also
reprinted in Darrow's autobiography, The
Story of My Life (New York: Grosset &
Dunlop, 1932).

Speech of Hon. Clarence S. Darrow of Chicago at
the Opera House, Youngstown, Ohio, Sunday,
May 2, 1909, n.p, n.d.
Dry vs. Wet. Speech delivered on 2 May 1909;
published in pamphlet form.
Darrow-Lewis Debate. The Theory of Non-
resistance. For: Clarence S. Darrow.
Against: Arthur M. Lewis. Garrick Theatre,
Chicago, Feb. 6, 1910 (Chicago: Workers
University Society, 1910).
Liberty Versus Prohibition; Stenographic Report
of Address at New Bedford, Mass. (New
York: Allied Printing Trades Council,
1910).
Marx vs. Tolstoy; A Debate Between Clarence S.
Darrow and Arthur M. Lewis. (Chicago: C. H.
Kerr, 1911).
Industrial Conspiracies (Portland, Ore.: Turner,
Newman, & Knispel, 1912). Lecture at
Heilig Theatre, Portland, Oregon, 10 Sept.
1912.
"Address on John Brown," Everyman 9 (March
1913). Speech to Radical Club, San
Francisco, December 1912.
"Clarence Darrow on Land and Labor," Everyman 9
(June 1913). Speech to the Single Tax
League, Los Angeles, 27 March 1913.
"Henry George," Everyman 9 (September-October
1913). Speech to the Single Tax
Club, Chicago, 19 Sept. 1913.
"Voltaire," Everyman 9 (January-February 1914).
Speech to the Chicago Society of
Rationalism, 11 Jan. 1914.
"Clarence Darrow on the War," Everyman 10
(October-November 1914). Speech given in
Chicago, 8 Oct. 1914.
"Address to the Prisoners at Joliet," Everyman
11 (Nov. 1915). Address at Joliet,
Illinois, June 1914.
"If Men Had Opportunity," Everyman 10 (January-
February 1915). Labor Day address, San
Francisco, 12 Sept. 1912.
"Address Delivered at the Funeral Service of

John   Howard   Moore,"   <u>Athena</u>   2   (October
  1916).
<u>Is Life Worth Living?   Debate Between George
  Burman Foster and Clarence Darrow</u> (Chicago:
  J. F. Higgins, 1917).
<u>The War, an Address. . .Under the Auspices of
  the National Security League, at Chicago,
  November 1, 1917</u> (New   York: National
  Security League, 1918).
<u>The War in Europe, A Lecture Delivered Before
  the Chicago Society of Rationalism, at
  Germania Theatre, Chicago</u> (Chicago: C. H.
  Kerr, 1918).
<u>Response   of   Clarence   Darrow   to   Birthday
  Greetings, April 18, 1918</u> (Chicago: Walden
  Book Shop, 1918).   Remarks at a dinner
  celebrating his sixty-first birthday.
<u>Are Internationalism and the League of Nations
  Practical and Desirable Schemes for Ending
  War,   Debate   with   Professor   John   C.
  Kennedy, 1918</u>.   Published as a pamphlet.
<u>Voltaire, A Lecture Delivered in the Cort
  Theatre, Sunday Afternoon, February 3,
  1918, Under the Auspices of the Workers
  University   Society,   Arthur   M.   Lewis,
  Permanent   Lecturer,   for   the   Society,
  Presiding</u> (New   York: J.   F.   Higgins,
  Printer, 1918).
<u>Is the Human Race Permanently Progressing
  Toward a Better Civilization?   Debate
  Between John C. Kennedy and Clarence Darrow</u>
  (Chicago: J. F. Higgins, 1919).   A debate
  sponsored   by   the   Workers   University
  Society.   Kennedy was an alderman in
  Chicago's Twenty-Seventh Ward.
<u>War Prisoners: Address at the Garrick Theatre,
  Chicago,   Illinois,   November   9,   1919</u>
  (Chicago: J.   F.   Higgins,   1919).   This
  speech defended entry into World War I and
  pleaded for of conscientious objectors
  jailed during the war.
"George Burman Foster," in <u>Remarks of Clarence
  Darrow at Memorial Services to George</u>

Burman Foster and at the Funeral of John
Peter Altgeld (Chicago: J. F. Higgins,
1919).

Will Socialism Save the World?   Affirmative:
Prof. John C. Kennedy . . . Negative: Mr.
Clarence Darrow . . . at the Garrick
Theatre Chicago, Illinois, January 26, 1919
(Chicago: J. F. Higgins, 1919).   Kennedy
was an alderman in Chicago's Twenty-Seventh
Ward.

Is Civilization a Failure?   Debate: Affirmative,
Clarence   S.   Darrow;   Negative,   Prof.
Frederick   Starr.   Chairman,   Arthur   M.
Lewis. Held at the Garrick Theatre, Sunday
Afternoon, Nov. 8, 1920, Under the Auspices
of the Workers University Society (Chicago:
J. F. Higgins, 1920). Starr was an anthro-
pologist at the University of Chicago.

Darrow-Starr Debate; Is the Human Race Getting
Anywhere?   Frederick Starr, Yes; Clarence
Darrow, No (Chicago: J. F. Higgins, 1920).
Held at the Garrick Theatre, Chicago, 8
February 1920.

Pessimism, A Lecture (Chicago: J. F. Higgins,
1920).   Speech given to the Rationalist
Education   Society   at   Kimball   Hall,
Chicago, 11 January 1920.

Is Life Worth Living?   Negative, Clarence
Darrow;   Affirmative,   Frederick   Starr.
Under   the   Auspices   of   the   Workers
University   Society   (Chicago: J.   F.
Higgins, 1920?).   Debate held at the
Garrick Theatre, March 28, 1920.

Has Religion Ceased to Function? Yes, Clarence
Darrow; No, Shirley Jackson Case. Garrick
Theatre,   January   30,   1921,   under   the
Auspices of the Workers University Society
(Chicago: J.F. Higgins, 1921).   Professor
Case was chair of the department of
religion at the University of Chicago.

Insects and Men: Instinct and Reason, Little
Blue   Book   no.   53   (Girard,   Kans.:
Haldeman-Julius   Co.,   1921?).   Speech

before the Rationalist Society of Chicago.
"How Liberty Is Lost." Speech before third
annual meeting of the American Liberty
League, 1921.
Debate, Resolved: That Capital Punishment Is a
Wise Public Policy . Clarence Darrow,
Negative; Judge Alfred J. Talley,
Affirmative (New York: League for Public
Discussion, 1924). Debate at the Metro-
politan Opera House, 26 October 1924.
Resolved: That the United States Continue the
Policy of Prohibition as Defined in the
Eighteenth Amendment. Clarence Darrow,
Negative, Versus Rev. John Haynes Holmes,
Affirmative (New York: League for Public
Discussion), 1924. Debate at Metropolitan
Opera House, 14 December, 1924.
"Evolution," in Executive Speeches; Selected
Addresses Given Before the Executives
Club of Chicago from September, 1924, to
June, 1928 (Chicago: Executives Club of
Chicago, 1928). Speech on evolution
delivered on 26 February 1926.
"What to Do About Crime," Nebraska Law Bulletin
6 (July 1927). Speech delivered to the
Nebraska Bar Association.
"The Universe," The Daily Northwestern, 26 May
1927. Speech at Northwestern University,
25 May 1927.
"Can the Individual Control His Conduct? A
Debate, Clarence Darrow vs. Dr. Thomas
Smith," Haldeman-Julius Quarterly, 2
(October-November-December 1927).
Is Man a Machine? Clarence Darrow,
Affirmative; Dr. Will Durant, Negative.
(New York: League for Public Discussion,
1927).
Wheeler-Darrow Debate. Carnegie Hall, New
York City, April 23, 1927. Question:
Resolved That Prohibition of the Beverage
Liquor Traffic Is Detrimental to the Public
Welfare (Westerville, Ohio: American
Publishing Co., 1927). Debate with Wayne

B. Wheeler of the Anti-Saloon League of America. "Is Zionism a Progressive Policy for Israel and America?"   Debate with Stephen S. Wise at Sinai Temple, Chicago, 24 October 1927.

Dry Law. Debate with Wayne B. Wheeler, 1927; printed in pamphlet form.

"Crime and Its Treatment," South Dakota Bar Association Annual (1928).

Do Human Beings Have Free Will? A Debate, Affirmative: Professor George Burman Foster, Negative: Clarence Darrow, Little Blue Book no. 1286 (Girard, Kans.: Haldeman-Julius Co., 1928). Foster was a professor of religion at the University of Chicago.

Is Man a Machine? A Debate. Affirmative, C. S. Darrow. Negative, B. B. Brickner (New York: n.p., 1928).

Wishart-Darrow Debate. Resolved, That a Belief in a General Purpose in the Universe Is Rational and Justified by Facts (Grand Rapids, Michigan: Extension Club of Grand Rapids, 1928). Debate at Fountain Street Baptist Church, Grand Rapids, Michigan, 22 February 1928; published from a stenographic report.

"This Is What I Don't Like About the Newspapers." Speech before the American Society of Newspaper Editors, Washington, D.C., 1928.

"Facing Life Fearlessly," American Parade (October-November-December 1928). Lecture at the University of Chicago, 1928.

Is the U.S Immigration Law Beneficial? A Debate. Clarence Darrow vs. Lothrop Stoddard, Little Blue Book no. 1423 (Girard, Kans.: Haldeman-Julius Co., 1929). Dr. Stoddard was an author of books arguing that the white race is superior to all other races.

Facing Life Fearlessly; The Pessimistic Versus the Optimistic View of Life,

Little Blue Book no. 1329 (Girard, Kans.: Haldeman-Julius Co., 1929).

"Why I Am an Agnostic," in <u>Why I Am an Agnostic, Including Expressions of Faith from a Protestant, a Catholic, and a Jew</u>, Little Blue Book no. 1500 (Girard, Kans.: Haldeman-Julius Co.,1929).

<u>Environment vs. Heredity. Debate Between Clarence Darrow and Albert Edward Wiggam</u>, Little Blue Book no. 1581 (Girard, Kans.: Haldeman-Julius Co., 1930?). Text of a debate in Cleveland. Wiggam was a newspaper columnist and popular lecturer.

<u>Is Religion Necessary? Debate, Yes, Rev. Robert MacGowan; No, Clarence Darrow</u> (Girard, Kans.: Haldeman-Julius Co., 1931).

<u>Should the 18th Amendment Be Repealed?</u> Debate with Clarence True Wilson, 1931.

"Why I Am an Agnostic," in <u>Addresses on Why I Am a Catholic...</u>(Chicago: M. M. Cole, 1932). Address at Orchestra Hall, Chicago.

Lecture to Congressional Church, Chicago, 14 January 1932; distributed in mimeographed form.

"Civilization at the Crossroads. Whither Are We Going?" Symposium with Scott Nearing (economics); Dr. Preston Bradley religion); Dr. Louis Mann (the planned society); Darrow (law and government), Sinai Temple, Chicago, 1932. Distributed in mimeographed form.

<u>Why I Am an Agnostic</u>. Symposium with Dr. John A. Lapp (Catholic); Dr. Charles W. Gilkey (Protestant); Rabbi Solomon Goldman (Jewish); Orchestra Hall, Chicago, 1932. Printed in pamphlet form.

"What I Think of Nazi Germany." Symposium with Dr. Preston Bradley and Dr. Louis L. Mann, Washington Boulevard Temple, Chicago, 7 December 1933. Distributed in mimeographed form.

<u>Does Man Live Again? Debate Between M. A.</u>

Musmanno and Clarence Darrow, Reviewers
Library no. 5 (Girard, Kans.: Haldeman-
Julius Co., 1936). Musmanno was a
defense attorney at the Sacco-Vanzetti
trial who later became a judge.
"Can the Church Meet the Needs of Our New
Age?" Debate, Dr. Louis L. Mann and Dr.
Preston Bradley, Affirmative; Darrow and
Harry Elmer Barnes, Negative, n.d.
Distributed in mimeographed form.
"Do the Dead Still Live?" in Beauty for
Ashes: a Discussion of the Laws of
Destiny and Their Application to the
Atomic Era, Together with a Debate with the
Late Clarence Darrow on the Question, Do
the Dead Still Live? (Madison, Wis.:
Democrat Printing Co., 1947). Debate at
Clearwater, Florida, March 1931.

SPEECHES AT TRIALS

Argument for Petitioners, Ex Parte Eugene V.
Debs et al., in the Supreme Court of the
United States, October Term 1894 (n.p.
1894).
"In Re Debs," U. S. Supreme Court Reports, vol.
158 (1895), p. 564.
U. S. Strike Commission, Report of the Chicago
Strike of June-July 1894, with appendices
containing testimony, proceedings, and
recommendations (Washington, D.C.:
Government Printing Office, 1895).
Argument of Clarence S. Darrow in the State of
Wisconsin vs. Thos. I. Kidd, George
Zentner and Michael Troiber for Conspiracy
Arising out of the Strike of Woodworkers at
Oshkosh, Wisconsin (Chicago: Campbell
Printers, 1898). A second edition appeared
in 1900.
John Turner Case Before Supreme Court: Argument
(n.p.: Free Speech League, 1903?).
United States ex. rel. John Turner vs. William
Williams, Commissioner etc. Brief and

Argument of Appellant (Chicago: H. C. Darrow, Law Printer, 1903).

"Closing Speech in Haywood Case," New York Times, 19 July 1907.

"Darrow's Speech in the Haywood Case," Wayland's Monthly (Girard, Kans.) 90 (October 1907).

Argument of Clarence S. Darrow in the Case of Idaho Against Steve Adams at Wallace, Idaho, February, 1907 (Denver: n.p., 1907?).

Darrow's Speech in the Haywood Case (Girard, Kans.: J. A. Wayland, 1908).

The Moyer-Haywood Outrage (New York: Moyer-Haywood Labor Conference, 1908?). Contains an excerpt from Darrow's speech in the Steve Adams trial.

"Darrow Closes in Tears," New York Times, 16 August 1912. Excerpts of Darrow's speech in his own defense.

Plea of Clarence Darrow in His Own Defense to the Jury That Exonerated Him of the Charge of Bribery at Los Angeles, August 1912 (Los Angeles: Golden Press, 1912).

"Second Plea of Clarence Darrow in His Own Defense," Everyman 9 (May 1913).

"An Appeal for the Despoiled," Everyman 11 (January 1916).

Address of Clarence Darrow in the Trial of Arthur Person in Rockford, Illinois, April 24, 1920 (Rockford, Ill.: Communist Labor Party of Illinois, 1920).

Argument of Clarence Darrow in the Case of the Communist Labor Party in the Criminal Court, Chicago (Chicago: C. H. Kerr, 1920).

"Urges Life Terms for Franks Slayers," New York Times, 24 August 1924. Excerpt of speech in Leopold-Loeb trial.

"You May Hang These Boys, But You Will Turn Your Faces to the Past," Chicago Herald-Examiner, August 26, 1924. Text of Darrow summation in Leopold-Loeb case.

Attorney Clarence Darrow's Plea for Mercy and
    Prosecutor Robert E. Crowe's Demand for the
    Death Penalty in the Loeb-Leopold Case, the
    Crime of the Century. (Chicago: Wilson
    Publishing Co., 1924?).
The Plea of Clarence Darrow, August 22, 23, and
    25, 1924, in Defense of Richard Loeb and
    Nathan Leopold, Jr., on Trial for Murder
    (Chicago: R. F. Seymour, 1924).
Argument in People of State of Illinois vs.
    Faherty and Detwiler, Chicago, 1924.
"Argument by Darrow at Dayton Assailing Foes of
    Evolution," New York Times, 14 July 1925.
"Closing Argument for the Defense in the
    Leopold-Loeb Murder Trial, Criminal Court
    of Cook County, Chicago, August 22, 23, 25,
    1925," in Famous American Jury Speeches;
    Addresses Before Juries and Fact-Finding
    Tribunals (St. Paul: West Publishing Co.,
    1925).   Includes complete text of Darrow's
    summation in the Leopold-Loeb case.
The World's Most Famous Court Trial; Tennessee
    Evolution Case; A Complete Stenographic
    Report of the Famous Court Test of the
    Tennessee Anti-Evolution Act, at Dayton,
    July 10 to 21, 1925, Including Speeches and
    Arguments   of   Attorneys   (Cincinnati:
    National Book Co, 1925).
Clarence Darrow's Plea in Defense of Loeb and
    Leopold, the Boy Murderers (August 22, 23,
    25, 1924) (Girard, Kans.: Haldeman-Julius
    Co., 1926).
Argument of Clarence Darrow in the Case of
    Henry   Sweet   (New   York: National
    Association for the Advancement of
    Colored People, 1927).   Speech in second
    Sweet trial.
"Defense of Richard Loeb and Nathan Leopold,
    Jr.," in Classified Speech Models of
    Eighteen Forms of Public Address, ed.
    William N. Brigance (New York: F. S.
    Crofts, 1928).
"A Plea for Mercy," in America Speaks; A

Library of the Best Spoken Thought in
Business and the Professions, ed. Basil G.
Bryon and Frederick R. Coudert (New York:
Modern Eloquence Corp., 1928).
Report to the President by Clarence Darrow,
National Recovery Board. Special and
Supplementary Reports to the President by
Clarence Darrow and William O. Thompson,
members, 1934.

Bibliography

COLLECTIONS OF PAPERS

There are surprisingly few papers available on Darrow. The following list includes the major collections.

James O. Brown Papers, Butler Library, Columbia University, New York City.
Clarence Seward Darrow Papers, Library of Congress, Washington, D.C. Includes materials used by Irving Stone for Clarence Darrow for the Defense and letters by Darrow's wife, Ruby Darrow.
Darrow Collection, Michigan Historical Society, University of Michigan, Ann Arbor, Michigan.
Darrow Collection, Special Collections, University of Chicago.
Darrow Collection, Newberry Library, Chicago, Illinois.
Elmer Gertz Papers, Northwestern University, Evanston, Illinois.
Papers of the National Association of Colored People (NAACP), Library of Congress, Washington, D.C.
Bancroft Library, University of California, Berkeley, California.

REPRINTS OF DARROW SPEECHES

"Funeral Speech." Congressional Record, 76th Cong., 3d sess., 18 April 1940, p. 2225. Reprint of Darrow's eulogy of John P. Altgeld on the second anniversary of Darrow's death.
"Plea for Mercy." In World's Great Speeches, edited by Lewis Copeland, 423-16. Garden City, N.Y.: Garden City Publishing Co., 1942. Excerpt of Darrow's closing speech at the Leopold-Loeb trial.

<u>How to Abolish Unfair Taxation; An Address
Before a Los Angeles Audience, Delivered
March 1913</u>. San Francisco: San Francisco
Pacific News, 1945. Reprint of a pamphlet
published in 1913 under the title "Clarence
Darrow on Land and Labor."

Phillips, Edgar J., "Do the Dead Still Live?" in
<u>Beauty for Ashes; A Discussion of the Laws
of Destiny and Their Application to the
Atomic Era, Together with a Debate with the
Late Clarence Darrow on the Question, Do
the Dead Still Live?</u> pp. 55-82. Madison,
Wis.: Democrat Printing Co., 1947.
Transcript of a debate between Darrow and
Edgar J. Phillips in Clearwater, Florida,
in March of 1931.

"Clarence Darrow Pleads for Justice for the
Negro, 'I Do Not Believe in the Law of
Hate,'" in <u>Treasury of the World's Great
Speeches</u>, edited by Houston Peterson,
737-40. New York: Simon & Schuster, 1954.

<u>The Darrow Bribery Trial, with Background Facts
of McNamara Case, and Including Darrow's
Address to the Jury</u>, edited by Patrick H.
Ford. Whittier, Calif.: Western Printing
Co, 1956.

"Plea to the Jury in the Sweet Trial."
<u>Congressional Record</u>, 85th Cong., 1st
sess., 13 June 1957, p. 9024. Excerpts
from the <u>Sweet</u> trial inserted in honor of
the 100th anniversary of Darrow's birth.

<u>Attorney for the Damned</u>, edited by Arthur
Weinberg. New York: Simon & Schuster,
1957. This book is a collection of
Darrow's speeches and writings.
Transcripts of speeches at the <u>Leopold and
Loeb</u> trial, the Communist trial in 1920,
the <u>Adams</u> and <u>Haywood</u> trials, the <u>Kidd</u>
trial, the Miners' Arbitration case,
Darrow's speech of self-defense, the Massie
trial, the <u>Sweet</u> trial, and the <u>Scopes</u>
trial; speeches to the prisoners at the
Cook County Jail (1902) and in honor of

John Brown; his eulogy of John Peter
Altgeld; and excerpts from a debate on
capital punishment with Judge Talley in
1924.

"I Am Pleading That We Overcome Cruelty with
Kindness and Hatred with Love."   In A
Treasury of Great American Speeches,
edited by   Charles Hurd, 159-62. New
York: Hawthorne Books, 1959.

"Epilogue--'John Peter Altgeld, 1847-1902.'" In
The Mind and Spirit of John Peter Altgeld;
Selected Writings and Addresses, edited by
Henry   Christman,   180-83.   Urbana:
University of Illinois Press, 1960. Eulogy
at Altgeld's funeral.

"Summation in the Sweet Case." In The World of
Law; A Treasury of Great Writing About and
in the Law--Short Stories, Plays, Essays,
Accounts,   Letters,   Opinions,   Pleas,
Transcripts of Testimony--From Biblical
Times to the Present. Vol. 2, edited by
Ephraim London, 346-75. New York: Simon &
Schuster, 1960.

"Crime   and   Criminals."   In   The Speaker's
Resource Book: An Anthology, Handbook, and
Glossary, edited by   Carroll C. Arnold,
Douglas Ehninger, and John C. Gerber, 136-
42.   Chicago: Scott, Foresman, & Co.,
1961.   Speech to the prisoners at the Cook
County Jail (1902).

Verdicts Out of Court, edited by Arthur
Weinberg and Lila Weinberg. Chicago:
Quadrangle Books, 1963.   This book
contains the   following   thirty-three
essays, articles, speeches, and debates: an
article on Darrow's methods of choosing a
jury; "The Breaker Boy", a short story;
"Brief for the War", an article justifying
his support of World War I; "Childhood
Surroundings," an excerpt from Farmington;
"Conduct and Profession," an essay on his
philosophy of life; "Consolations of
Pessimism," a reprint of a lecture given in

1920; "The Divorce Problem," a reprint of a 1927 article; "Facing Life Fearlessly: Omar Khayyam and A. E. Housman," transcript of a lecture given in 1929; "Foreign Debt and America," a 1927 article; "Free Trade or Protection," an article written in 1894; "The Futility of the Death Penalty," a 1928 article; "The Holdup Man," a 1909 article; "Ideal of a Labor Union," a 1922 speech; "If Man Had Opportunity," a 1915 article; "The Immigration Law," excerpts from a 1929 debate; "Is Man Fundamentally Dishonest?"; "Little Louis Epstein," a short story published in 1903; "The Myth of the Soul," a 1928 article; "The NRA and 'Fair Competition,'" a 1934 article; "The Open Shop," a 1904 article; "The Problem of the Negro," a 1901 article; "Prohibition," excerpts from a 1924 debate; "Realism in Literature," an essay; "Response to Birthday Greetings, Sixty-First Birthday Anniversary"; "Right of Revolution," an 1895 speech; "Robert Burns," an essay; "The Skeleton in the Closet," an essay; "The Theory of Non-Resistance," excerpt of a 1910 debate; "This Is What I Don't Like About Newspapers," a speech in 1928; "Walt Whitman," an essay; "Who Knows Justice?" an essay; "Why I Am an Agnostic," a speech in 1929.

"A Plea for Mercy." In <u>Great Speeches from Pericles to Kennedy</u>, edited by William D. Boutwell, Wesley P. Calendar, Jr., and Robert E. Gerber, 178-92. New York: Scholastic Book Services, 1965. Excerpt from speech in <u>Leopold-Loeb</u> trial.

"A Plea from Mercy for Leopold and Loeb." In <u>Dolphin Book of Speeches</u>, edited by George W. Hibbitt, 88-93. New York: Dolphin Books, Doubleday, 1965.

"Race Prejudice and Self-Defense; Argument in the Sweet Case." In <u>Classic Speeches: Words That Shook the World</u>, edited by

Richard   Crosscup,   129-52.   New   York:
Philosophical Library, 1965. Excerpt from
speech at <u>Sweet</u> trial.

"Marx vs. Tolstoi." in <u>Nonviolence in America:
A Documentary History</u>, edited by Staughton
Lynd, 150-60. Indianapolis: Bobbs-Merrill,
1966. Excerpt from 1911 debate.

"Against   Capital   Punishment."   In   <u>Famous
American   Speeches</u>,   ed.   Stewart   H.
Benedict, 149-157. New York: Dell, 1967.

"To   the   Jury: Self-Defense,   August   14-15,
1912." in <u>Great American Speeches, 1898-
1963, Texts and Studies</u>, edited by John
Graham, 31-35. New York: Appleton-Century-
Crofts, 1970.   Excerpts of summary in his
first self-defense trial.

<u>The World's Most Famous Court Trial: Tennessee
Evolution Case; A Complete Stenographic
Report of the Famous Court Test of the
Tennessee Anti-Evolution Act, at Dayton,
July 10 to 21, 1925, Including Speeches and
Arguments of Attorneys</u>.   New York: DeCapo
Press, 1971.

<u>Marx versus Tolstoy; A Debate Between Clarence
Darrow and Arthur M.Lewis</u>. New York: J. S.
Ozer, 1972. A 1911 debate.

Sayer,   James   E,   "Clarence   Darrow--Public
Debater: A   Rhetorical   Analysis."   Ph.D.
diss.,   Bowling   Green   State   University,
1974.   The dissertation contains texts of
several debates: "Debate on Prohibition,"
1927; "Debate on Life," 1927; "Debate on
Immigration,"   1929,   "Debate   on
Prohibition," 1924; and "Debate on Capital
Punishment," 1924.

"In Re Debs." In <u>Landmark Briefs and Arguments
of the Supreme Court of the United States:
Constitutional   Law</u>,   edited   by   Philip
B.Kurland and Gerhard Caspar. Washington,
D.C.: University Publications of America,
1975.   Brief and argument in the <u>Pullman</u>
case.

<u>Crime and Criminals; An Address Delivered to the</u>

Prisoners   in   the   Cook   County   Jail.
Chicago: C. H. Kerr, 1975.
"It Is Too Horrible a Thing for a State to
Undertake."   In Voices Against Death;
American Opposition to Capital Punishment,
1787-1975, edited by Philip E. Mackey,
167-79. New York: Burt Franklin, 1976.
Excerpts from a 1924 debate.

WRITINGS BY DARROW

Drones and Parasites. Chicago: C. H. Kerr, 1890.
"Realism in Literature and Art." Arena (December
     1893): 98-113.
"The Revenue Law as It Should Be." The Public 2
     (4 November 1899): 14-15.
A Persian Pearl and Other Essays. East Aurora,
     N.Y.: Roycroft Shop 1899.
"Tolstoi." Rubric 1 (January 1902): 21-38.
"Latest Literary Sensation, 'Mary MacLane Is
     Little Short of Miracle' Says Clarence
     Darrow." Chicago American, 4 May 1902, sec.
     2, p. 2.   Review of an autobiography
     entitled The Story of Mary MacLane.
"Easy Lessons in Law," a series of short stories
     showing how the wealthy and powerful are
     treated better than workingmen by the law.
     The stories which appeared each Sunday in
     the Chicago American, include "Easy Lessons
     in Law; Doctrine of Assumed Risk" (6 July
     1902); "Easy Lessons in Law; Doctrine of
     Assumed Risk" (13 July 1902); "Easy Lessons
     in Law; Doctrine of Assumed Risk" (20 July
     1902); "Easy Lessons in Law; Doctrine of
     Assumed Risk" (27 July 1902); "Easy Lessons
     in Law; Doctrine of Fellow Servant" (3
     August 1902); "Easy Lessons in Law;
     Doctrine of Fellow Servant" (10 August
     1902); "Easy Lessons in Law; Influences
     That Make the Law" (17 August 1902); "Easy
     Lessons in Law; A Story with a Pleasant
     Ending" (24 August 1902); "Easy Lessons in
     Law; Results of the Law's Delay" (31 August

1902); "Easy Lessons in Law; Results of the Law's Delay" (7 September 1902); "Easy Lessons in Law; For the Public Good" (14 September 1902); "Easy Lessons in Law; Triumph of Justice" (21 September 1902); "Easy Lessons in Law" (28 September 1902). "Conduct and Profession." Rubric 2 (August 1902): 37-49.

"The Breaker Boy." Chicago American, December 1902.   Considered   Darrow's   most effective short story.

Resist Not Evil. Chicago: C. H. Kerr, 1902.

"Little Louis Epstein." Pilgrim 9 (December 1903): 9-10.

Farmington. Chicago: A. C. McClurg, 1904.   An autobiographical novel about his childhood years.

The Open Shop. Social Economic Series. Chicago: Hammersmark   Publishing   Co.,   1904.

"Literary Style." Tomorrow 1 (January 1905): 25-29.

"The Chicago Traction Question." International Quarterly 12 (October 1905): 13-22.

An Eye for an Eye. New York: Fox, Duffield, 1905.   A novel about a murder.   Darrow shows how poverty and society led to the murder.

"Acquittal of Haywood." Mirror 17 (1 August 1907): 3.

"Russian's Message." Arena 40 (December 1908): 584-91.

"The Hold-up Man." International Socialist Review 9 (February 1909): 594-597.

"The U. S. Prosperity Bulletin." Mirror 19 (29 October 1909): 7.

"The Late Elections." Mirror 20 (17 November 1910): 1-2.

"Patriotism." International Socialist Review 11 (1910-1911): 159-60.

"Our American Yeomanry." Mirror 20 (16 February 1911): 7.

"Why Men Fight for the Closed Shop." American Magazine 71 (September 1911): 544-51.

Industrial Conspiracies. Portland, Ore.: Turner,
     Newman, & Knispel, 1912.
"Clarence Darrow on the Single Tax." Everyman 10
     (October-November 1914).
"The Cost of War." International Socialist
     Review 15 (1914-1915): 361-62.
"Straight Talk to the Rails." International
     Socialist Review 16 (1915-1916) 718-20.
"Robert Burns." Everyman 11 (February 1916): 9-
     13.
"Nietzsche." Athena 1 (June-July 1916): 6-16.
"The Land Belongs to the People." Everyman 11
     (September 1916): 9-10.
"Crime and Economic Conditions." International
     Socialist Review 17 (1916): 219-22.
"Schopenhauer." Liberal Review 2 (March
     1917): 9-23.
"Brief for the War." Liberal Review 2 (July
     1917).
"Woodrow Wilson." Reedy's Mirror 24 (15 April
     1920): 311-13.
"Rules of Conduct." Reconstruction 2 (April
     1920): 181-83.
Defense of Free Speech. Chicago: C. H. Kerr,
     1920.
How Voltaire Fooled Priest and King. People's
     Pocket Series, no. 188. Girard, Kans.:
     Appeal to Reason, 1921.
Crime; Its Cause and Treatment. New York: Thomas
     Y. Crowell, 1922.
Introduction to John Reed Under the Kremlin by
     Lincoln Steffens. Chicago: W. Ransom, 1922.
"Darrow Asks W. J. Bryan to Answer These."
     Chicago Tribune, 4 July 1923, pp. 1, 12.
"The Ordeal of Prohibition." American Mercury 2
     (August 1924): 419-27.
Bridges, Horace J., and Clarence Darrow. "Crime
     and Punishment," Century 109 (March 1925):
     606-25.
"Salesmanship." American Mercury 5 (August
     1925): 385-92.
"The Edwardses and the Jukeses." American
     Mercury 6 (October 1925): 147-57.

"George Burman Foster." In <u>Realism in Literature</u>
    <u>and Art</u> 47-54. Little Blue Book no. 634.
Girard, Kans.: Haldeman-Julius Co., 1925.
    Introduction to <u>The Autobiography of Mother</u>
    <u>Jones</u> by Mary Harris Jones. Chicago: C. H.
    Kerr, 1925.
"Eugenics Cult." <u>American Mercury</u> 7 (June 1926):
    129-37.
"Crime and the Alarmists." <u>Harper's Magazine</u> 158
    (October 1926): 535-44.
"John Brown." <u>Crisis</u> 32 (May 1926): 12-16.
"Liberty, Equality, Fraternity." <u>Vanity Fair</u>: 27
    (December 1926): 74, 110.
"Foreign Debt and America." <u>Vanity Fair</u> 27
    (February 1927): 39-40.
"Tyranny and the Volstead Act." <u>Vanity Fair</u> 28
    (March 1927): 45-46,116.
"What Is the Matter with the Farmer." <u>Vanity</u>
    <u>Fair</u> 28 (April 1927): 50, 110.
"The War on Modern Science." <u>Modern World</u> 1
    (July 1927): 301-03.
"The Divorce Problem." <u>Vanity Fair</u> 28 (August
    1927): 31-32.
"Should Capital Punishment Be Retained?"
    <u>Congressional Digest</u> 6 (August-September
    1927): 230-31.
"Is Man Fundamentally Dishonest?" <u>Forum</u> 78
    (December 1927): 884-89.
"Name Your Poison." <u>Plain Talk</u> 1 (October 1927):
    3-8.
"Capital Punishment." <u>New York Herald Tribune</u>
    <u>Magazine</u> 1 (January 1928): 4-5.
"Our Growing Tyranny." <u>Vanity Fair</u> 29 (February
    1928): 39, 104.
"The Lord's Day Alliance." <u>Plain Talk</u> 2
    (March 1928): 257-70.
"Why I Have Found Life Worth Living." <u>Christian</u>
    <u>Century</u> 40 (19 April 1928): 504-05.
"Frank Lowden, the Farmer's Friend." <u>Scribner's</u>
    <u>Magazine</u> 83 (April 1928): 395-403.
"Futility of the Death Penalty." <u>Forum</u> 80
    (September 1928): 327-32.
"Prohibition Cowardice." <u>Vanity Fair</u> 31

(September 1928): 53, 100.

"Why Was God So Hard on Women and Snakes?" Haldeman-Julius Monthly 8 (September 1928): 122-24.

"The Myth of the Soul." Forum 80 (October 1928): 524-33.

"The Black Sheep." Liberty 5 (3 November 1928): 17-18, 20.   A short story that may be about his own father.

"Personal Liberty." In Freedom in the Modern World; Lectures Delivered at the New School for Social Research, edited by Horace M. Kallen, 114-37. New York: Coward-McCann, 1928.

Absurdities of the Bible. Little Blue Book no. 1637.   Girard, Kans.:   Haldeman-Julius Company, 1928.

"Anti-Prohibition Law Case Stated by a Wet." New York Times, 27 January 1929, sec. 10, p. 4.

"Review of Bryan by Morris R. Werner." New Republic 58 (15 May 1929): 363-64.

"Power of Congress Re Volstead Act." Lawyer and Banker 22 (May-June 1929): 167-68.

"Emperor or President." Nation 128 (5 June 1929): 672-73.

"At Seventy-Two." Saturday Evening Post 202 (6 July 1929): 23, 109, 114.

"Who Is the Farmer's Friend?" Plain Talk 5 (November 1929): 513-19.

"Combatting Crime." Forum 82 (November 1929): 271-275.

Foreword to Fifty Years of Free Thought; Being the Story of the "Truth Seeker" with the Natural History of Its Third Editor by George E. MacDonald. New York: Truth Seeker Co., 1929-31.

"The Human Being's World." in Man and His World. Vol 1. edited by Baker Brownell, 67-99. New York: D. Van Nostrand, 1929.

Darrow, Clarence, and Wallace Rice. Infidels and Heretics; An Agnostic's Anthology. Boston: Stratford Co., 1929.

Introduction to Best of All Possible Worlds;

Romances and Tales by Francois Voltaire.
    New York: Vanguard Press, 1929.
"Letter to the Editor." *New York Times*, 26 April
    1930, p. 18.
Wilson, Clarence T., and Clarence Darrow.
    "Lawful Liquor." *Colliers* 86 (27 September
    1930): 7-9.
"Let No Man Therefore Judge You in Meat, or in
    Drink." *Colliers* 86 (11 October 1930): 10-
    11, 44, 47.
"John Brown--He Who Struck the First Blow."
    Abbott's Monthly 1 (November 1930): 16-19,
    21, 23.
"The Religion of the American Negro." *Crisis* 38
    (June 1931): 190.
"Why the 18th Amendment Cannot Be Repealed."
    Vanity Fair 37 (November 1931): 62, 84.
Foreword, to *Ill-Starred Prohibition Cases; A
    Study in Judicial Pathology* by Forrest R.
    Black.   Boston: R. G. Badger, 1931.
"Who Knows Justice?" *Scribner's Magazine* 91
    (February 1932): 73-77.
"Scottsboro." *Crisis* 39 (March 1932): 81.
"The Massie Trial." *Scribner's Magazine* 92
    (October 1932): 213-18.
The Story of My Life. New York: Grosset &
    Dunlap, 1932.
"Capital Punishment? No, It Fails to Get at
    Crime's Causes." *Rotarian* 43 (November
    1933): 14-15.
"Review of *Trial by Prejudice* by Arthur G.
    Hays," *Columbia Law Review* 33 (December
    1933): 1467-68.
"Review of *Insanity as a Defense in Criminal Law*
    by Henry Weihofen. London: Oxford Univer-
    sity Press, 1933 in *New York University Law
    Quarterly Review* II (March 1934): 491-92.
"Report of Clarence Darrow of National Recovery
    Review Board." *Women's Wear Daily*, 21 May
    1934, p. 1.
"Text of Second Darrow Report, Assailing Retail
    Code."   *Women's Wear Daily*, 12 June
    1934, p. 1.

"NRA and Fair Competition." Rotarian 45 (November 1934): 12-13.

First Report to the President of the United States. U.S. National Recovery Review Board. Washington, D.C.: Earle Building, Jesse L. Ward, 1934.

Second Report to the President of the United States. U.S. National Recovery Review Board. Washington, D.C.: Earle Building, Jesse L. Ward, 1934.

Third Report to the President of the United States. U.S. National Recovery Review Board. Washington, D.C.: Earle Building, Jesse L. Ward, 1934.

"Many Faults in NRA." Commercial Bulletin and Apparel Merchant 57 (February 1935): 38-42.

"The Lord's Soldier Joshua and the Sun and the Moon." Truth Seeker 62 (September 1935): 97-98.

"Attorney for the Defense." Esquire 5 (May 1936): 36-37. An article detailing Darrow's strategy in selecting a jury.

WRITINGS ABOUT DARROW

Ade, George. "My Own All-American Team." Hearst's International--Cosmopolitan 82 (May 1927): 74-75, 221.

Aldeman, Abram E. "Clarence Darrow--Take Him for All in All." Age of Reason (October 1955): 1-4. Anderson, Paul Y. "Clarence Darrow, Humanitarian." St. Louis Post-Dispatch, 3 July 1927, pp. 1C, 3C.

Anderson, Paul Y. "The Darrow Report." Nation 138 (30 May 1934): 611.

Anderson, Paul Y. "Interview with Darrow." St. Louis Post-Dispatch, 10 May 1925, pp. 1b, 4b.

"Another Debate on Prohibition." Outlook 117 (2 November 1927): 263-64.

Arado, Charles C. "Darrow at the Defense Table." Chicago Bar Record 22 (November 1940): 83.

Barnes, Harry Elmer. "Clarence Darrow--the Man
    and the Philosopher." Unity 121 (16 May
    1938): 93-94.
Bell, Stephen. "The Darrow Report." Commerce
    and Finance 23 (23 May 1934): 447.
Bennema, J. G. "Clarence Darrow's Birthday
    Party." International Engineer 51 (May
    1927): 391-392.
Brainin, Joseph. "The Case Against Anti-
    Semitism." Jewish Times, 24 April 1931,
    pp. 3, 8.
Bridges, Horace J. "Mr. Clarence Darrow on
    Mechanism and Irresponsibility." In The
    God of Fundamentalism and Other Studies,
    edited by Horace J. Bridges, 117-68.
    Chicago: P. Covici, 1925.
Bryan and Darrow at Dayton: The Record and
    Documents of the Bible--Evolution Trial,
    edited by Leslie H. Allen. New York: A.
    Lee, 1925.
"Bryan Brushes Darrow Bible Queries Aside."
    Chicago Tribune, 5 July 1923, p. 15.
Christeson, Richard D. "An Analysis of Darrow's
    Plea to the Jury in the Massie-Fortescue
    Case." Master's thesis, St. Cloud State
    College, 1961.
"Clarence Darrow: Ace Jury-Picker." Literary
    Digest 121 (16 May 1936): 35.
"Clarence Darrow Is Dead in Chicago." New York
    Times, 14 March 1938, p. 15.
"Clarence Darrow: Partisan of the Unpopular."
    Senior Scholastic 96 (18 April 1969): 13.
"Clarence Darrow Said." Truth Seeker 66 (April
    1939): 63.
Connolly, Christopher P.,   "The Saving of
    Clarence Darrow: Dramatic Close of the
    McNamara Case." Colliers 43 (23 December
    1911): 9-10.
Conway, James P. "Invention in Clarence
    Darrow's Defense of John T. Scopes."
    Master's thesis, State University of Iowa,
    1960.
Cotton, Edward H. "Clarence Darrow." Christian

Register 106 (19 May 1927): 401-02. Text of an interview with Darrow.

Crandall, Allen. _The Man from Kinsman_. Sterling, Colo.: n.p., 1933.

"Darrow Asks W. J. Bryan to Answer These." _Chicago Tribune_, 4 July 1923, pp. 1, 12.

"Darrow Chicago's Counsel." _New York Times_, 13 April 1905, p. 1.

"Darrow Likes Plan for Crime Hospital." _New York Times_, 22 September 1924, p. 21.

"Darrow Enlisted to Help Save Grant." _New York Times_, 23 September 1924, p. 13.

"Darrow and Talley on Death Penalty." _New York Times_, 27 October 1924, p. 40. Report of a debate on the death penalty in which Darrow participated.

"Darrow Fights Death Penalty." _New York Times_, 2 July 1928, p. 5.

"Darrow Addresses Bronx Bar." _New York Times_, 27 April 1934, p. 8.

"Darrow Again." _National Hotel and Travel Gazette_ (Washington, D.C.) 27 (15 May 1934): 3.

"Darrow and Wheeler Debate Prohibition." _New York Times_, 28 March 1926, p. 22.

"Darrow on Prohibition." _Central Law Journal_ 100 (25 February 1927): 135.

"Darrow Opposes Prisons for Crime." _New York Times_, 16 March 1927, p. 11.

"Darrow on the Talesman." _New York Times_, 10 May 1907, p. 2.

"Darrow Pokes Fun at Book Censorship." _New York Times_, 17 April 1929, pp. 1-2.

"The Darrow Rocket." _Business Week_, 26 May 1934, p. 9.

"Darrow Talks of the Day." _New York Times_, 14 May 1907, p. 2.

"Darrow: Tender-Hearted Cynic and Feature of American Law." _Newsweek_ 3 (19 May 1934): 14.

"Darrow Can Find No Goal in Life." _New York Times_, 1 December 1924, p. 7. Report of a debate in which Darrow participated.

Davis Kenneth S.   "Darrow: Man of a Thousand Battles."   New York Times Magazine, 28 April 1957, pp. 12, 64, 66-67.

Douglas, Melvyn.   "Discovering Darrow."   New Republic 136 (27 May 1957):14-16.

Duffus, R. L.   "Darrow Stirs Up New Controversy."   New York Times, 27 May 1934, sec. 9, p. 2.

Duncan-Clark, S. J.   "Clarence Darrow's Fight Against the Death Penalty."   Success (December 1924): 28-31, 123.

Eaton, Walter P.   "Clarence Darrow: Crusader for Social Justice."   Current History 35 (March 1932): 786-91.

Edgar, M. L.,   "Clarence S. Darrow."   Mirror 17 (16 May 1907): 13-14.

Editorial on Darrow and his socialist ideas, Denver Post, 7 May 1907, p. 16.

Ellet, Marion.   "Mr. Darrow and His Expressive Shoulders."   Kansas Teacher 35 (April 1932): 22-23.

"Errands of Mercy That Failed."   Literary Digest 46 (8 March 1913), 547-50.

Essell, Nathan.   "The Study Table."   Unity 111 (6 February 1933): 332-34.

"An Evening with Clarence Darrow."   Etcetera 1 (September 1930): 8-11, 30.

"The Exploitation of Tolerance."   Christian Century 48 (9 December 1931): 1550-52.

Faber, Doris.   Clarence Darrow: Defender of the People.   Englewood Cliffs, N.J.: Prentice-Hall, 1965.

Feinberg, Matilda.   "Clarence Darrow."   Chicago Bar Record 39 (1958): 165-68.

Feinberg, Matilda.   "Clarence Darrow at His Best."   Chicago Bar Record 41 (1960): 460-66.

Feinberg, Matilda.   "I Remember Clarence Darrow."   Chicago History 2 (Fall-Winter, 1973): 216-23.

Feinberg, Matilda.   "The Most Unforgettable Character I've Met."   Reader's Digest 74 (April 1959): 83-88.

"Fight Opens to End Death Penalty in State; Darrow and Malone Declare It Is Stupid." New York Times, 1 February 1926, p. 1.

"For the Defense." Coronet 25 (December 1948): 24-25.

"Four Debate Socialism." New York Times, 31 January 1931, p. 10.

"French Medal for Clarence Darrow." Chicago Evening American, 27 December 1902, p. 8.

"Free Speech, Free Press--Darrow on Boycotts and Injunctions." Union Labor Advocate 10 (March 1909): 10-14.

Fulkerson, Raymond G. "A Study of Clarence Darrow's Summation Speech in the 1926 Henry Sweet Trial." Master's thesis, University of Illinois, 1966.

Ginger, Ray. Altgeld's America: The Lincoln Ideal Versus Changing Reality. New York: Funk & Wagnalls, 1958.

Ginger, Ray. "The Idea of Process in American Social Thought." American Quarterly 4 (Fall 1952): 253-65.

Ginger, Ray. "Clarence Seward Darrow, 1857-1938." Antioch Review 1 (March 1953): 13, 52-66.

Giovannitti, Arturo. "Communism on Trial." Liberator 3 (March 1920): 5-8.

"Glorifying an Atheist." Presbyterian of the South 105 (November 20, 1935): 4.

Golden, W. E. "Magic in the Courtroom." Coronet 33 (December 1952): 78.

Greene, Harry W. "The Debates and Religious Forums of Clarence Darrow." Master's thesis, Northern Illinois University, 1970.

Grossbach, Barry L. "The Scopes Trial: A Turning Point in American Thought?" Ph.D. diss., Indiana University, 1964.

Grover, David H. Debaters and Dynamiters; The Story of the Haywood Trial. Corvallis: Oregon State University Press, 1964.

Grover, David H. "Debaters and Dynamiters: The Rhetoric of the Haywood Trial." Ph.D. diss., University of Oregon, 1962.

Gunn, John W.   "A Day with Clarence Darrow."
     Haldeman-Julius Monthly 2 (July 1925).

Gurke, Miriam.   Clarence Darrow.   New York:
     Thomas Y. Crowell, 1965.

"Had Darrow Been a Journalist." Nation 125 (10
     August 1927): 131-32.

Hagopian, John K.   "Clarence Darrow for the
     Defense." Journal of the State Bar of
     California 16 (March-April 1942): 90-94.

Haldeman-Julius, Marcet.   Clarence Darrow's Two
     Great Trials: Reports of the Scopes Anti-
     evolution Case and the Dr. Sweet Negro
     Trial. Girard, Kans.: Haldeman-Julius Co.,
     1927.

Harrison, George Y. Clarence Darrow. New York:
     William Morrow, 1931.

Hays, Arthur G. Trial by Prejudice. New York:
     Covici, Friede, 1933.

"Haywood Defense Laid Out." New York Times, 25
     June 1907, p. 3.

"Haywood Defense to Show a Plot."   New York
     Times, 28 June 1907, p. 3.

Hazlitt, Henry.   "Debate (G. Chesterton and C.
     Darrow on 'Will the World Return to
     Religion?')."   Nation 132 (4 February
     1931): 130.

"He Was a Friend of Labor." Railroad Trainman
     55 (April 1938): 152.

"Here Is a Lawyer Whose Long Record Is the Best
     Proof of His Strong Love for the People."
     Chicago Evening American, 25 October 1902,
     p. 3.

Hill, Edwin C. "Darrow, Colossal Court Rebel."
     New York Sun, 23 December 1927, p. 15.

"Hot One from Darrow." Chicago Tribune, 9 July
     1904, p. 2.

House, Walter. "Darrow on Divorce." Liberty 2
     (16 January 1926): 9-10, 13.

Hynd, Alan. "Clarence Darrow." In Defenders of
     the Damned, 65-122. New York: A.S. Barnes,
     1960.

"Inside Story of Darrow Forums." Christian
     Century 48 (2 December 1931): 1539.

Jackson, James H.   "Clarence Darrow's Plea in
     Defense of Himself."   Western Speech 20
     (Fall 1956): 185-95.
Johnson, Frank W. C.   "Rhetorical Criticism of
     the Speaking of William Jennings Bryan and
     Clarence Seward Darrow at the Scopes
     Trial."   Ph.D. diss., Case Western Reserve
     University, 1961.
Jones, Llewellyn.   "Save City Schools From
     Wreckers or Build More Jails, Says Darrow."
     American Teacher 18 (December 1933): 22.
Kahn, Karl M.   "Clarence Darrow Looks at
     America." Real America 1 (April 1933): 10-
     15, 93, 96.
Karsner, David.   "Clarence Darrow." In Sixteen
     Authors to One; Intimate Sketches of
     Leading American Story-tellers, 177-97.
     New York: Lewis Copeland, 1928.
Katz, Arthur W.   "A Study and Analysis of the
     Speech of Clarence S. Darrow."   Master's
     thesis, University of Michigan, 1942.
Kelley, Richard D.   "The Rhetorical and Legal
     Strategies of Clarence Darrow."   Master's
     thesis, Indiana University, 1978.
Kinney, Charlotte.   "Clarence Darrow As He Is,
     Not As the Newspapers Say He Is."
     Psychology 19 (August 1932): 15-17, 46-47.
Kunstler, William M.   "Clarence Seward Darrow,"
     in The Case for Courage, 201-36. New York:
     William Morrow, 1962.
Kurland, Gerald. Clarence Darrow: Attorney for
     the Damned. Charlottesville, N.Y.: Sam Har
     Press, 1972.
Lardner, Rex. "Clarence Darrow, Lawyer." In 10
     Heroes of the Twenties. New York: Putnam,
     1966.
Leisure, George S.   "Reflections on Clarence
     Darrow." Virginia Law Review 45 (1959):
     414-18.
"Let Us Take Stock."   Business Week, 26 May
     1934, p. 40.
Lewis, Arthur M.   "A Darrow Lecture."   Truth
     Seeker 65 (15 May 1938): 156.

Lilienthal, David E. "Clarence Darrow." Nation
    126 (20 April 1927): 416-19.
Livingston, John C.   "Clarence Darrow: Senti-
    mental Rebel." Ph.D. diss., University of
    Washington, 1965.
Mackey, Philip E. "Clarence Darrow." In Voices
    Against Death; American Opposition to
    Capital Punishment, 1787-1975, edited by
    Philip E. Mackey. New York: Burt Franklin,
    1976.
Majors, Randall E.   "Clarence Darrow in Defense
    of Leopold and Loeb.   A Case Study in
    Forensic Argumentation."   Ph.D. diss.,
    Indiana University, 1978.
Maloney, Martin J.   "Clarence Darrow."   In A
    History and Criticism of American Public
    Address.   Vol 3,   edited by Marie
    Hochmuth, 262-313.   New York: Longmans,
    Green, 1955.
Maloney, Martin J.   "The Forensic Speaking of
    Clarence Darrow."   Ph.D. diss., North-
    western University, 1942.
Maloney, Martin J.   "Forensic Speaking of
    Clarence Darrow."   Speech Monographs 14
    (1947): 111-26.
Mason, Lowell. "Darrow vs. Johnson." North
    American Review 238 (1934): 524-32.
"McConnell and Darrow Debate Life's Origins."
    Christian Century 42 (5 November 1925):
    1386.
Meissel, Richard A.   "The Rhetoric of Legal
    Self-Defense: The   Socrates-More-Darrow
    Analog." Master's thesis, Queens College,
    1971.
Mencken, Henry L. "The Great Defender--Clarence
    Darrow." Vanity Fair 28 (March 1927): 44.
Michelson, Charles. "Darrow vs. Bryan." In The
    Best in the World; A Selection of News and
    Feature Stories, Editorials, Humor, Poems,
    and Reviews from 1921 to 1928, edited by
    John K. Hutchens and George Oppenheimer,
    204-13. New York: Viking Press, 1973.
"Milestones." Time 31 (21 March 1938): 34.

Mordell, Albert.   Clarence Darrow, Eugene V.
    Debs, and Haldeman--Julius; Incidents in
    the Career of an Author, Editor and
    Publisher. Girard, Kans.: Haldeman-Julius
    Co., 1950.
Myers, Raymond H.   "Persuasive Methods of
    Clarence Darrow."   Master's thesis,
    University of Wisconsin, 1935.
Nathan, George Jean.   "Clarence Darrow."   In
    Intimate Notebooks of George Jean Nathan,
    80-94. New York: Alfred A. Knopf, 1932.
Noble, Iris. Clarence Darrow, Defense Attorney.
    New York: Julius Messner, 1958.
North, Luke, "A Man of the People." Golden Elk
    6 (May 1907): 18-24.
O'Day, F.   "Varied Types--Clarence Darrow."
    Town Talk 20 (1 June 1912): 11.   An
    interview with Darrow during his self-
    defense trial.
"The Outlook for Coal." Harper's Weekly 47 (7
    March 1903): 372.
Owen, Russell. "Darrow, A Pessimist with Hope--
    Is Eighty." New York Times Magazine, 18
    April 1937, pp. 5, 31.
Owen, Russell. "Darrow Likes to Fight for Lost
    Causes." New York Times Magazine, 26 July
    1925, p. 2.
Payne, Alma J. "Clarence S. Darrow, Literary
Realist: Theory   and   Practice."   In
    MidAmerica: Yearbook of the Society for the
    Study of Midwestern Literature, 36-45.
    East Lansing: Michigan State University,
    1974.
"People Talked About." Leslie's Weekly 91 (1
    January 1903): 3.
"Pleads Hands of Fate in Illinois Murder Case."
    Newsweek 1 (17 February 1933): 29-30.
Rashkopf, Horace G.   "The Speaking of Clarence
    Darrow," in American Public Address;
    Studies in Honor of Albert Craig Baird,
    edited by Loren Reid, 201-36.   Columbia:
    University of Missouri Press, 1961.
Ravitz, Abe C. Clarence Darrow and the American

Literary Tradition. Cleveland: Western Reserve University Press, 1962.

Reilly, George. "A Rhetorical Analysis of Clarence Darrow's Invention and Disposition in Two Courtroom Summation Pleas." Master's thesis, South Dakota State College, 1958.

"Report of Clarence Darrow of National Recovery Board." _Commercial and Financial Chronicle_ 138 (26 May 1934): 9.

Rintels, David W. _Clarence Darrow: A One-Man Play_. Garden City, N.Y.: Doubleday, 1975.

Roberts, John B. "The Speech Philosophy of Clarence Darrow" Master's thesis, State University of Iowa, 1941.

Roussel, Herbert. "Ace of Doubters; That Darrow. . . ." _Houston Gargoyle_, 4 (15 March 1931): 13-14.

Rusterholtz, Wallace. "Clarence Darrow: Champion of the Prosecuted and Persecuted." In _American Heretics and Saints_, 251-72. Boston: Manthorne & Burack, 1938.

Sanbonmatsu, Akira. "Adaptation and Debate Strategies in the Speaking of Clarence Darrow and Alexander Rorke in New York vs. Gitlow." Ph.D. diss., Pennsylvania State University, 1968.

Sanbonmatsu, Akira. "Darrow and Rorke's Use of Burkeian Identification Strategies in 'New York vs. Gitlow,'" _Speech Monographs_ 38 (March 1971): 36-48.

Sayer, James E. _Clarence Darrow: Public Advocate_. Dayton, Ohio: Wright State University, 1978.

Sayer, James E. "Clarence Darrow--Public Debater: A Rhetorical Analysis." Ph.D. diss., Bowling Green State University, 1974.

"Says Death Penalty Does Not Stop Crime." _New York Times_, 2 February 1926, p. 18.

Shaw, Charles G. "Clarence Darrow." In _The Low-Down_, 1-13. New York: Henry Holt, 1928.

Shaw, Charles G. "Clarence Darrow." In _Vanity Fair, Selections From America's Most_

Memorable Magazine, edited by Cleveland Amory and Frederick Bradlee, 142-43. New York: Viking Press, 1960.

Shine, Howard L. "A Critical Analysis of the Persuasive Techniques of Clarence Darrow in the Trial of John T. Scopes." Master's thesis, Bowling Green State University, 1958.

Shuman, R. Baird. "Clarence Darrow on Education." _School and Society_ 90 (3 November 1962): 377-79.

Simons, H. Austin. "Guilty: the General Strike." _Liberator_ 3 (September 1920): 12.

Speeches and Proceedings at a Banquet in Honor of Clarence Darrow. Chicago: Barnard & Miller, 1913.

"Spoils a Hopkins Joke." _Chicago Tribune_, 9 July 1904, p. 2. Report of Darrow's speech seconding the nomination of William Randolph Hearst for president.

Starr, James H. "The Methods of Proof Used By Clarence Darrow in the Loeb-Leopold Murder Trial." Master's thesis, University of Washington, 1943.

Stone, Irving. _Clarence Darrow for the Defense, A Biography_. Garden City, N.Y.: Doubleday, 1941.

"Tariff Reform Convention." _Chicago Tribune_, 22 February 1889, p. 2. Darrow mentioned in coverage of convention.

"Texts of Statements by Darrow and Johnson on the NRA." _New York Times_, 22 May 1934, p. 9.

"Thinks Haywood Jury Hard to Get." _New York Times_, 7 May 1907, p. 2.

Tierney, Kevin. _Darrow: A Biography_. New York: Thomas Y. Crowell, 1979.

"Transition." _Newsweek_ 11 (21 March 1938): 32, 34.

Ward, William. "That Man Darrow." _Hearst's International_ 47 (January 1925): 56-57, 112-13.

Weinberg, Arthur. "Clarence S. Darrow." _New_

<u>Republic</u> 126 (14 April 1952): 2.

Weinberg, Arthur. "Clarence Darrow's Son Says: 'I Remember Father.'"   <u>Chicago Tribune Magazine</u>, 6 May 1956, p. 19.

Weingerg, Arthur, and Lila Weinberg. "Clarence Seward Darrow: Lawyer and Humanist."   In <u>Some Dissenting Voices: The Story of Six American Dissenters</u>, pp. 87-117. New York: World Publishing Co., 1970.

Weinberg, Arthur and Lila Weinberg. <u>Clarence Darrow; A Sentimental Rebel</u>. New York: G. P. Putnam, 1980.

Weinberg, Arthur and Lila Weinberg. "The Spirit of Darrow Speaks to Us Still."   <u>Chicago Tribune</u>, 28 January 1974, sec. 2, pp. 7-8.

"Wheeler Clashes with Darrow Here in Dry Law Debate."   <u>New York Times</u>, 24 April 1927, pp. 1, 28.

"Where Are the Pre-War Radicals? A Symposium." <u>Survey Graphic</u> 8 (February 1926): 566.

Whitehead, George S. <u>Clarence Darrow--The Big Minority Man</u>.   Girard, Kans.: Haldeman-Julius Co., 1929.

Whitehead, George G.   <u>Clarence Darrow: Evangelist of Sane Thinking</u>.   Girard, Kans.: Haldeman-Julius Company, 1931.

"Who Is This Man Darrow?" <u>Current Literature</u> 43 (August 1907): 157-59.

Willingham, Mary J.   "An Analysis of the Leopold-Loeb Murder Trial in Light of Clarence Darrow's Ethos as a Persuader." Master's thesis, Ohio University, 1967.

Wolfe, Don M.   "On the Ways of Man: Darrow, Steffens, and Broun." In <u>The Image of Man in America</u>, pp. 265-86. 2nd ed. New York: Thomas Y. Crowell, 1970.

Yarros, Victor S. <u>My 11 Years with Clarence Darrow.</u> Girard, Kans.: Haldeman-Julius Co., 1950.

A SELECTED BIBLIOGRAPHY OF ARTICLES ON THE SPEECHES COVERED IN THE TEXT

Pullman Strike, 1894

White, Horace. "Pullman Boycott." Nation 59 (5
    July 1894): 305-06.
Clark, Edward D.   "Gov. Altgeld and the
    President." Nation 59 (12 July 1894): 22.
Sherman, John D.   "Situation in Chicago."
    Harper's Weekly 38 (14 July 1894): 665-67.
Lane, M. A. "Strike." Harper's Weekly 38 (21
    July 1894): 687.
Grant, Thomas B.   "Pullman and Its Lessons."
    American Journal of Politics 5 (August
    1894): 190-204.
Means, David M. "The Debs Case." Nation 59 (13
    September 1894): 190-91.
Burna, W. F.   The Pullman Boycott; A Complete
    History of the Great Railroad Strike.   St.
    Paul, Minn.: McGill Printing Co., 1894.
Carwardine, William H.   The Pullman Strike.
    Chicago: C. H. Kerr, 1894.
"In re Debs et al."   Supreme Court Register 15
    (1895): 900-12.
Day, Stephen A.   "A Celebrated Illinois Case
    That Made History."   Illinois Historical
    Society Transactions (1917): 99-108.

William D. Haywood, 1907

Grant, Luke. "Idaho Murder Trial." Outlook 85
    (6 April 1907): 805-11.
"Moyer-Haywood Trial." Outlook 86 (4 May 1907):
    1-2.
"Idaho Murder Trial."   Independent 62 (16 May
    1907): 1117-19.
"Haywood Trial."   Outlook 86 (22 June 1907):
    350-51.
"History of the Case." Current Literature 42
    (June 1907): 587-95.
Langdon, Emma F. Labor's Greatest Conflicts; A
    History of the Moyer, Haywood and Petti-
    bone Kidnapping Cases.   Denver: Press of
    Great Western Publishing Co., 1908.
Connolly, Christopher P. "Protest by Dynamite;

Similarities and Contrasts Between the
McNamara Affair and the Moyer-Haywood-
Pettibone Trial." Collier's 48 (13 January
1912): 9-10.

Haywood, William D. Bill Haywood's Book: The
Autobiography of William D. Haywood. New
York: International Publishing Co., 1929.

Ravitz, Abe C. and James N. Primm. The Haywood
Case: Materials for Analysis.   San
Francisco: Chandler Publishing Co., 1960.

McNamara Case, 1911

Connolly, Christopher P. "Trial at Los Angeles."
Collier's 48 (14 October 1911): 17.

"McNamara Trial,"   Current Literature 51
(November 1911): 467.

Connolly, Christopher P.   "The Saving of
Clarence Darrow: Dramatic Close of the
McNamara Case." Collier's 48 (23 December
1911): 9-10.

Gompers, Samuel. The McNamara Case. Washington,
D.C.: American Federation of Labor, 1911.

Robinson, William W.   Bombs and Bribery: The
Story of the McNamara and Darrow Trials
Following the Dynamiting in 1910 of the Los
Angeles Times Building.   Los Angeles:
Dawson's Book Shop, 1969.

Shapiro, Herbert. "The McNamara Case: A Crisis
of the Progressive Era."   Southern
California Quarterly 59 (Fall 1977): 271-
87.

Darrow's Self-Defense, 1912

"The Darrow Acquittal." Literary Digest 45 (31
August 1912): 323.

"Darrow's Triumph."   Organized Labor 12 (31
August 1912): 70.

Jackson, James H.   "Clarence Darrow's Plea in
Defense of Himself." Western Speech 20
(Fall 1956): 185-95.

"Trial of Clarence Darrow." New York University

Intramural Law Review 14 (May 1959): 206.
Giesler, Jerry. "Defending Darrow."   In The
     Jerry Geisler Story. New York: Simon &
     Schuster, 1960.

Leopold-Loeb Case, 1924

"'Intellectual' Murder in Chicago."   Literary
     Digest 82 (5 July 1924).
"Leopold-Loeb Decision." New Republic 40 (24
     September 1924): 88-89.
"Murder   Most   Foul."   Outlook   138   (24
     September 1924): 115-16.
"Rich and Poor Murderers." Literary Digest 82
     (27 September 1924): 10-11.
Levin, Meyer. Compulsion, New York: Simon &
     Schuster, 1956.   A novel based on the
     murder trial.
McKernan, Maureen, ed. The Amazing Crime and
     Trial of Leopold and Loeb. New York: New
     American Library, 1957.
Leopold, Nathan F. Life Plus Ninety-Nine Years.
     Garden City, N.Y.: Doubleday, 1958.
Wolfe, Don M. "The Leopold-Loeb Case." In The
     Image of Man in America, 287-94. 2d ed.
     New York: Thomas Y. Crowell, 1970.
Higdon, Hal. The Crime of the Century; The
     Leopold-Loeb Case. New York: Putnam, 1975.

Scopes Trial, 1925

"No Monkeying with Evolution in Tennessee."
     Literary Digest 85 (18 April 1925): 258-60.
"Freedom in the Mountains; Tennessee's Anti-
     Evolution Law." Outlook 115 (27 May 1925):
     131-32.
"Battle of Tennessee." Nation 120 (27 May 1925),
     589-90.
Mencken, Henry L. "In Tennessee." Nation 121 (1
     July 1925): 21-22.
Hollister, Howard K. "In Dayton, Tennessee."
     Nation 121 (8 July 1925): 61-62.
Krutch, Joseph W. "Tennessee: Where the Cowards

Rule." Nation 121 (15 July 1925): 88-89.
Shepherd, William G. "Monkey Business in
    Tennessee." Collier's 76 (18 July 1925):
    8-9.
Williams, Michael. "At Dayton, Tennessee."
    Commonweal 2 (22 July 1925): 262-65.
"Dayton's Amazing Trial." Literary Digest 86 (25
    July 1925): 5-7.
"The Great Trial." Time 2 (27 July 1925): 15.
Krutch, Joseph W. "Darrow vs. Bryan." Nation 121
    (29 July 1925): 136-137.
Hays, Arthur G. "Strategy of the Scopes
    Defense." Nation 121 (5 August 1925): 157-
    58.
Keebler, Robert S. The Tennessee Evolution Case.
    Memphis: Davis Printing Co., 1925.
Bailey, Kenneth K. "Enactment of Tennessee's
    Antievolution Law." Journal of Southern
    History 16 (November 1950): 472-90.
Weaver, Richard M. "Dialectic and Rhetoric at
    Dayton, Tennessee." In Ethics of Rhetoric,
    27-54. Chicago: Henry Regnery, 1953: 27-54.
Ginger, Ray. Six Days or Forever? Tennessee v.
    John Thomas Scopes. Boston: Beacon Press,
    1958.
Monkey Trial: The State of Tennessee vs. John
    Thomas Scopes. Boston: Houghton Mifflin,
    1960.
Scopes, John T. "The Trial That Rocked the
    Nation." Reader's Digest 128 (March 1961):
    136-144.
Dickler, Gerald. "The Scopes Trial, 1925." In
    Man on Trial; History--Making Trials from
    Socrates to Oppenheimer, 173-200. Garden
    City, N.Y.: Doubleday, 1962.
Smith, Sherwin D. "The Great 'Monkey Trial.'"
    New York Times Magazine, 4 July 1965, pp.
    8, 14.
Tompkins, Jerry R., ed. D-Days at Dayton;
    Reflections on the Scopes Trial. Baton
    Rouge: Louisiana State University Press,
    1965.
Scopes, John T. and James Presley. Center of the

<u>Storm: Memoirs of John T. Scopes</u>. New York:
Holt, Rinehart, 1967.
De Camp, L. Sprague. <u>The Great Monkey Trial</u>.
Garden City, N.Y.: Doubleday, 1968.
Kaplan, Morris B. "The Trial of John T. Scopes."
In <u>Six Trials</u>, edited by Robert S.
Brumbaugh, 107-19. New York: Thomas Y.
Crowell, 1969.

Sweet Trials, 1926

White, Walter. "The Sweet Trial." <u>Crisis</u> 31
(January 1926): 125-29.
Feinberg, Matilda, "Clarence Darrow at His
Best." <u>Chicago Law Record</u> 41 (1960): 460-
66.
Fleming, Thomas J. "Take the Hatred Away and You
Have Nothing Left." <u>American Heritage</u> 20
(December 1968): 74-80.
Weinberg, Kenneth G. <u>A Man's Home, a Man's
Castle</u>. New York: McCall Publishing Co.,
1971.

Massie Trial, 1932

"Violence in Hawaii." <u>Outlook</u> 115 (20 January
1932): 734.
"Honolulu Uproar." <u>Literary Digest</u> 112 (30
January 1932): 10.
"Massie Case; Issues of Fundamental Im-
portance." <u>Commonweal</u> 16 (18 May 1932): 60.
"Murder." <u>Nation</u> 134 (29 June 1932): 727.
Brown, Ernest F. "Massie Trial." <u>Current History</u>
36 (June 1932): 334.

Index

About the Author

RICHARD J. JENSEN is a Professor of Rhetoric in the Greenspun School of Communication at the University of Nevada, Las Vegas. He has previously taught at Humboldt State University and the University of New Mexico. He is the author of *A War of Words* (with John C. Hammerback and José Angel Gutierrez), *In Search of Justice* (with John C. Hammerback), and has edited *Great Speeches in American History* (with William H. Lyon and Philip Reed Rulon). He is currently working on a book about Cesar Chavez.

Great American Orators

Defender of the Union: The Oratory of Daniel Webster
Craig R. Smith

Harry Emerson Fosdick: Persuasive Preacher
Halford R. Ryan

Eugene Talmadge: Rhetoric and Response
Calvin McLeod Logue

The Search of Self-Sovereignty: The Oratory of Elizabeth Cady Stanton
Beth M. Waggenspack

Richard Nixon: Rhetorical Strategist
Hal W. Bochin

Henry Ward Beecher: Peripatetic Preacher
Halford R. Ryan

Edward Everett: Unionist Orator
Ronald F. Reid

Theodore Roosevelt and the Rhetoric of Militant Decency
Robert V. Friedenberg

Patrick Henry, The Orator
David A. McCants

Anna Howard Shaw: Suffrage Orator and Social Reformer
Wil A. Linkugel and Martha Solomon

William Jennings Bryan: Orator of Small-Town America
Donald K. Springen

Robert M. La Follette, Sr.: The Voice of Conscience
Carl R. Burgchardt

Ronald Reagan: The Great Communicator
Kurt Ritter and David Henry